TURNING POINTS
Making Decisions in American History

TURNING POINTS
Making Decisions in American History

Volume II

Edited by

David Burner

and

Anthony Marcus

BRANDYWINE PRESS • St. James, New York

ISBN: 1-881089-54-1

Copyright © 1999 by Brandywine Press

1st Printing 1999

Telephone Orders: 1-800-345-1776

Printed in the United States of America

TABLE OF CONTENTS

INTRODUCTION

Decisions are the drama of history that textbooks only occasionally explicate. For what actually happened—the historical facts that students learn—thrusts the past into an apparently inevitable direction that obsures the crossroads, the detours, the faint and vine-clogged paths that could have created a different present. Unless students journey down some of these roads less traveled or not traveled at all, they will miss the past as an adventure in which contingency and human agency matter. Inevitability is not the stuff of history.

Turning Points: Making Decisions in American History reintroduces students to the uncertainty, the adventure that Americans have continuously experienced. The decisions examined here all had complex historical roots, multiple causes that could have led to quite differing outcomes. They were not simply made in one intense moment by some single important individual. Even when an identifiable leader acted with the authority of Woodrow Wilson in declaring war or Harry S Truman in ordering the use of nuclear weapons, the action was in response to the previous decisions of many, sometimes countless people. And in other instances—when women went to work in factories during World War II, for example, or families moved to the suburbs afterward—major changes in American life resulted from the private decisions of millions of Americans.

In *Turning Points* students will encounter what happened in the past in the light of what might have happened. They will see the points where human will and judgment produced one result rather than another. This they will learn in the history of Reconstruction and race relations after the Civil War, in conflicts between Indians and whites during the great Sioux War, in the development of American immigration policy as a result of anti-Chinese sentiment, in making use of the American environment in damming the Hetch Hetchy Valley. They will recognize the contingencies bearing upon narcotic legislation early in the twentieth century, the nation's entry into World War I, the battle over birth control, the labor wars of the 1930s, the entrance of women into previously male occupations during World War II, the use of atomic weapons against both civilian and military targets in Japan. Events, issues, and individual acts closer to their own time they will understand to have been not inevitable but the product of human will: the movement of Americans to the suburbs after the war, the civil rights movement, resisting the Vietnam War, confronting the unresolved question of the future of Social Security.

We would like to thank the many people who helped us with this book, especially Robert Marcus, who assisted throughout the project, Jill Gussow, who designed the cover, Tom West, who edited the manuscript, and Charles A. Peach, who produced the books.

David Burner
Anthony Marcus

Chapter 1

"FORTY ACRES AND A MULE": LAND FOR THE EX-SLAVES?

Defeat in the Civil War devastated the South. Cities and railroads were destroyed, farms and buildings burned or abandoned, bridges and roadways impassable, men by the tens of thousands missing legs or arms, Confederate money worthless, bank capital dissipated. Slavery, the basis of the southern economy, was gone, and no one knew what would replace it. The former slaves were free: many roamed the countryside or moved to the cities. Soon black men would possess for a time the opportunity to vote. But the freed blacks lacked one essential basis of independence and equality: they had no property. Both races in the postwar South recognized the importance of property in land. "The way we can best take care of ourselves is to have land and turn it and till it by our labor," asserted a delegation of freed people in 1865. This was exactly what former slaveholders feared most, and they determined early to prevent blacks from owning land. "They who own the real estate of a country control its vote," warned one observer. Nor were many influential northerners willing to extend the precedent of emancipation, the taking from the owner of private property in slaves, to the further step of confiscating land and giving it to black southerners.

Many—perhaps most—freed blacks expected the federal government to seize ex-slaveholders' land and give it to them. "When is de land goin' fur to be dewided?" one field hand asked a visiting journalist. Many, hoping to receive land that they had worked, refused either to leave their old plantations or to sign contracts to do field work for the next planting season: "De home-house might come to me . . . in de dewision." A black preacher in Florida summed up these common hopes: "It's de white man's turn ter labor now. He ain't got nuthin' lef' but his lan', and de lan' won't be his'n long, fur de Guverment is gwine ter gie ter ev'ry Nigger forty acres of lan' an' a mule." A black soldier told his white officer: "Every colored man will be a slave and feel himself a slave until he could raise his own bale of cotton and put his own mark upon it and say, 'Dis is mine!' "

Observers dismissed these aspirations as the product of provincialism and ignorance: "That so absurd ideas as these could exist I would not believe till I found them myself," wrote a northern journalist whose descriptions of his travels in the

1

South in 1865 were widely read. Believing in private property, whites were more inclined to protect its existing owners than to give property to people who had been excluded from it. Yet these hopes were more than ignorant fancies: the former slaves had been given reasons to nourish such dreams.

LAND FOR THE FREEDMEN?

As he marched through Georgia and the Carolinas in the last phase of the war, General William T. Sherman found his army slowed by thousands of homeless and hungry freed slave families. With Secretary of War Henry B. Stanton, on January 12, 1865, Sherman met with twenty black leaders in Savannah to discuss this immediate problem. The blacks, however, talked about longer term issues; one asserted that "We want to be placed on land until we are able to buy it, and make it our own." A few days later Sherman issued his Special Field Order No. 15. This electrifying pronouncement gave legitimacy to recent acts in parts of the South where slaves had seized plantations abandoned by fleeing owners. Several months later Andrew Johnson, who had become President after Lincoln's assassination, in his Proclamation of Amnesty countermanded Sherman's order. But expectations had already been formed.

GENERAL WILLIAM T. SHERMAN, SPECIAL FIELD ORDER NO. 15

I. The islands from Charleston south, the abandoned rice fields along the rivers for thirty miles back from the sea, and the country bordering the St. John's river, Florida, are reserved and set apart for the settlement of the negroes now made free by the acts of war and the proclamation of the President of the United States.

II. At Beaufort, Hilton Head, Savannah, Fernandina, St. Augustine, and Jacksonville, the blacks may remain in their chosen or accustomed vocations, but on the islands, and in the settlements hereafter to be established, no white person whatever, unless military officers and soldiers, detailed for duty, will be permitted to reside; and the sole and exclusive management of affairs will be left to the freed people themselves, subject only to the United States military authority and the acts of Congress. By the laws of war and orders of the President of the United States the negro is free, and must be dealt with as such. He cannot be subjected to conscription or forced military service, save by the written orders of the highest military authority of the department, under such regulations as the President or Congress may prescribe. Domestic servants, blacksmiths, carpenters, and other mechanics, will be free to select their own work and residence, but the young and able-bodied negroes must be encouraged to enlist as soldiers in the service of the United States, to contribute their share towards maintaining their own freedom, and securing their rights as citizens of the United States. . . .

III. Whenever three respectable negroes, heads of families, shall desire to settle on lands, and shall have selected for that purpose an island or a locality clearly defined, within the limits above designated, the inspector of settlements and plantations will himself, or by such subordinate officer as he may appoint, give them a license to settle such island or district, and afford them such assistance as he can to enable them to establish a peaceable agricultural settlement. The three parties named will subdivide the land, under the supervision of the inspector, among themselves and such others as may choose to settle near them, so that each family shall have a plot of not more than forty (40) acres of tillable ground, and when it borders on some water channel, with not more than 800 feet water front, in the possession of which land the military authorities will afford them protection until such time as they can protect themselves, or until Congress shall regulate their title. The quartermaster may, on the requisition of the inspector of settlements and plantations, place at the disposal of the inspector one or more of the captured steamers, to ply between the settlements and one or more of the commercial points heretofore named in orders, to afford the settlers the opportunity to supply their necessary wants, and to sell the products of their land and labor.

IV. Whenever a negro has enlisted in the military service of the United States he may locate his family in any one of the settlements at pleasure, and acquire a homestead and all other rights and privileges of a settler, as though present in person. In like manner negroes may settle their families and engage on board the gunboats, or in fishing, or in the navigation of the inland waters, without losing any claim to land or other advantage derived from this system. But no one, unless an actual settler as above defined, or unless absent on government service, will be entitled to claim any right to land or property in any settlement by virtue of these orders.

V. In order to carry out this system of settlement, a general officer will be detailed as inspector of settlements and plantations, whose duty it shall be to visit the settlements, to regulate their police and general management, and who will furnish personally to each head of a family, subject to the approval of the President of the United States, a possessory title in writing, giving as near as possible the description of boundaries, and who shall adjust all claims or conflicts that may arise under the same, subject to the like approval, treating such titles altogether as possessory. The same general officer will also be charged with the enlistment and organization of the negro recruits, and protecting their interests while absent from their settlements, and will be governed by the rules and regulations prescribed by the War Department for such purposes.

Source: War Department Archives, Special Field Order No. 15, Military Division of the Mississippi.

PRESIDENT ANDREW JOHNSON, PROCLAMATION OF AMNESTY, MAY 29, 1865

Whereas the President of the United States, on the 8th day of December, A. D., 1863, and on the 26th day of March, 1864, did, with the object to suppress the existing rebellion, to induce all persons to return to their loyalty, and to restore the authority of the United States, issue proclamations offering amnesty and pardon to certain persons who had directly, or by implication, participated in the said rebellion; and

Whereas many persons who had so engaged in said rebellion have, since the issuance of said proclamations, failed or neglected to take the benefits offered thereby; and

Whereas many persons who have been justly deprived of all claim to amnesty and pardon thereunder by reason of their participation, directly or by implication, in said rebellion, and continued hostility to the Government of the United States since the date of said proclamations, now desire to apply for and obtain amnesty and pardon.

To the end, therefore, that the authority of the Government of the United States may be restored, and that peace, order, and freedom may be established, I, Andrew Johnson, President of the United States, do proclaim and declare that I hereby grant to all persons who have, directly or indirectly, participated in the existing rebellion, except as hereinafter excepted, amnesty and pardon, with restoration of all rights of property, except as to slaves and except in cases where legal proceedings, under the laws of the United States providing for the confiscation of property of persons engaged in rebellion, have been instituted; but upon the condition, nevertheless, that every such person shall take and subscribe the following oath (or affirmation), and thence forward keep and maintain said oath inviolate; and which oath shall be registered for permanent preservation, and shall be of the tenor and effect following, to wit:

"I, —— ——, do solemnly swear (or affirm), in presence of Almighty God, that I will henceforth faithfully support, protect, and defend the Constitution of the United States, and the Union of the States thereunder; and that I will, in like manner, abide by and faithfully support all laws and proclamations which have been made during the existing rebellion, with reference to the emancipation of slaves. So help me God."

Source: James D. Richardson, *A Compilation of the Messages and Papers of the Presidents, 1789–1897* (Washington, 1896–1899), VI: 310.

SOUTHERN BLACKS RESPOND

The Freedmen's Bureau, though containing officers like Rufus Saxton and Oliver O. Howard who were highly sympathetic to the ex-slave's hopes, was forced to carry out President Johnson's policies. The sense of betrayal among blacks sometimes escalated into threats of violence or in at least one instance into confiscation of land, but state authorities soon returned it to white owners. In trying to understand General O. O. Howard's comments, it is important to remember that they were expressed in memoirs four decades later and opinions had changed in the intervening years.

GENERAL RUFUS SAXTON, REPORT, DECEMBER 6, 1865

The impression is universal among the freedmen that they are to have the abandoned and confiscated lands, in homesteads of forty acres, in January next. It is understood that previous to the termination of the late war the negroes heard from those in rebellion that it was the purpose of our government to divide up the southern plantations among them. . . . Our own acts of Congress, and particularly the act creating this bureau, which was extensively circulated among them, still further strengthened them in the belief that they were to possess homesteads, and has caused a great unwillingness upon the part of the freedmen to make any contracts whatever. . . . All the officers and agents of this bureau have been instructed to do everything in their power to correct these impressions among the freedmen, and to urge them in every possible way to make contracts with their former owners; but so deep-seated a conviction has been found difficult to eradicate. . .

The question of next importance has been the status of the sea islands. By General Sherman's order . . . some forty thousand destitute freedmen, who followed in the wake of and came in with his army, were promised homes on the sea islands, and urged by myself and others to emigrate there and select them. Public meetings were called, and every exertion used by those whose duty it was to carry out the order to encourage emigration to the sea islands. The greatest success attended our efforts. . . . Thousands of acres were cleared up and planted, and provisions enough were raised to provide for those who were located in season to plant, besides large quantities of sea island cotton. . . .

On some of the islands the freedmen have established civil government, with constitutions and laws for the regulation of their internal affairs, with all the different departments for schools, churches, building roads, and other improvements. . . . The former owners have recently been using every exertion to have these lands restored to their possession, and to secure this end promised to make such arrangements with the freedmen as to absorb their labor, and give them homes and employment on their estates. The officer detailed by yourself to restore these lands has been unable thus far to make any arrangement, nor do I believe it will be possible for him to make any satisfactory arrangement. The freedmen have their hearts set upon the possession of these islands, and nothing but that or its equivalent will satisfy them. They refuse to contract, and express a determination to leave the islands rather than do so. The efforts made by the former owners to obtain the possession of the lands have caused a great excitement among the settlers. Inasmuch as the faith of the government has been pledged to these freedmen to maintain them in the possession of their homes, and as to break its promise in the hour of its triumph is not becoming a just government . . . I would respectfully suggest that a practical solution of the whole question of lands . . . may be had by the appropriation of money by Congress to purchase the whole tract set apart by this order [of Sherman]. . . .

Source: Senate Executive Documents, No. 27, 39th Congress, 1st Session, 140.

Major General Oliver O. Howard,
The Abandoned Lands

Perhaps nothing excited higher hopes in the minds of those who had for years suffered and labored for emancipation, than the provision of law that was to open up the abandoned estates and certain public lands for prompt settlement by the newly emancipated.

Much in vogue at the end of the war was that plan of allotting abandoned lands to freedmen. This course the Government during the latter part of the war, as we have seen, for those lands along the Atlantic coast and in the Mississippi Valley had constantly followed first in legislative and then in executive action. Only about one five-hundredth, however, of the entire amount of land in the States seceding was available; it was all that had ever been held by the United States as abandoned. Had this project been carried out and the negroes generally been so settled on farms, either more land must have been added or the [Freedmen's] Bureau would only have been able to furnish about an acre to a family.

The law existing at the inauguration of the Bureau, though imperfect in many respects, could hardly have contemplated such extensive action for the drifting hordes of negroes. There was, however, some public wild land in the South, which might have answered; but undoubtedly the land intended by the law makers was that of those Confederates who had been in arms against the National Government.

Such use, however, of even the small amount which was turned over to the Freedmen's Bureau, was nullified by the President's pardon, granted to those who had abandoned the lands in order to engage in the war; orders of restoration to all such immediately followed the presentation of the executive pardon; this was very soon after I had obtained the control of Bureau matters. . . .

I soon saw that very little, if any, [land] had been confiscated by formal court decision; so that wholesale pardons in a brief time completed the restoration of the remainder of our lands; all done for the advantage of the late Confederates and for the disadvantage and displacement of the freedmen. Very many had in good faith occupied and cultivated the farms guaranteed to them by the provision and promise of the United States.

My heart was sad enough when by constraint I sent out that circular letter; it was chagrined when not a month later I received the following orders issued by President Johnson:

"Whereas certain tracts of land, situated on the coast of South Carolina, Georgia, and Florida, at the time for the most part vacant, were set apart by Major General W. T. Sherman's special field order No. 15 for the benefit of refugees and freedmen that had been congregated by the operations of the war, or had been left to take care of themselves by their former owners; and whereas an expectation was thereby created that they would be able to retain possession of said lands; and whereas a large number of the former owners are earnestly soliciting the restoration of the same, and promising to absorb the labor and care for the freedmen:

"It is ordered: That Major General Howard, Commissioner of the Bureau of Refugees, Freedmen and Abandoned Lands, *proceed* to the several above-named States and endeavor to effect an agreement mutually satisfactory to the freedmen and the land owners, and make report. And in case a mutual satisfactory arrangement can be effected, he is duly empowered and directed to issue such orders as may become necessary, after a full and careful investigation of the interests of the parties concerned." Why did I not resign? Because I even yet strongly hoped in some way to befriend the freed people.

Obeying my instructions I reached Charleston, S.C., October 17, 1865. General Saxton's headquarters were then in that city. I had a conference with him and with many of the land owners concerned. The truth was soon evident to me that nothing effective could be done without consulting the freedmen themselves who were equally interested. Therefore, accompanied by several officers and by Mr. William Whaley, who represented the planters, I went to Edisto Island, and met the freedmen of that vicinity who came together in a large meeting house. The auditorium and the galleries were filled. The rumor preceding my coming had reached the people that I was obliged by the President's orders to restore the lands to the old planters, so that strong evidence of dissatisfaction and sorrow were manifested from every part of the assembly. In the noise and confusion no progress was had till a sweet-voiced negro woman began the hymn "Nobody knows the trouble I feel—Nobody knows but Jesus," which, joined in by all, had a quieting effect on the audience. Then I endeavored as clearly and gently as I could to explain to them the wishes of the President, as they were made known to me in an interview I had with him just before leaving Washington. Those wishes were also substantially embodied in my instructions. My address, however kind in manner I rendered it, met with no apparent favor. They did not hiss, but their eyes flashed unpleasantly, and with one voice they cried, *"No, no!"* Speeches full of feeling and rough eloquence came back in response. One very black man, thick set and strong, cried out from the gallery: "Why, General Howard, why do you take away our lands? You take them from us who are true, always true to the Government! You give them to our all-time enemies! That is not right!"

At my request, the assembly chose three of their number, and to them I submitted with explanations the propositions to which the land owners were willing to subscribe. . . . But their committee after considering all the matters submitted to them said that on no condition would the freedmen work for their late owners as formerly they did under overseers; but if they could rent lands from them, they would consent to all the other arrangements proposed. Some without overseers would work for wages; but the general desire was to rent lands and work them. . . .

After the work under the President's instructions extending as far as Mobile had been finished, I returned to Washington November 18th, and submitted an account of the journey to Mr. Stanton. These were my closing words:

"It is exceedingly difficult to reconcile the conflicting interests now arising with regard to lands that have been so long in possession of the Government as those along the coast of South Carolina, Georgia, and Florida. I would recommend that the attention of Congress be called to the subject of this report at as early a day as possible, and that these lands or a part of them be purchased by the United States with a view to the rental and subsequent sale to the freedmen."

Congress soon had the situation clearly stated, but pursued its own plan of reconstruction, as did the President his own, regardless of such minor justice as making good to thousands of freedmen that promise of land which was at that time so essential to their maintenance and their independence. . . .

The positive adverse action of President Johnson and the non-action of Congress caused a complete reversal of the Government's generous provision for the late slaves. Thus early officers and agents were constrained to undertake to make bricks without straw.

Source: Oliver O. Howard, *Autobiography of Oliver Otis Howard* (New York, 1907), II: 229–230, 236–239, 241, 244.

Here is what happened at one southern farm.

REBELLION AT TAYLOR'S FARM

The Norfolk *Virginian* gives the following account of the difficulty with the negroes in regard to the Taylor Farm property, near that city:

"We give below the facts in regard to the proceedings of the blacks on TAYLOR's farm. It seems that they have determined to hold high carnival and fight it out on that line in defiance of Mr. JOHNSON, the Freedmen's Bureau, or any other man. It appears that a party of gentlemen visited TAYLOR's farm, on Sunday, the 6th inst., among whom were officials authorized to offer each negro family a house and employment, or sell them cleared lands at a low price, and give them three and five years to pay for them. The negroes called a meeting, and organized by electing ANTHONY BUTLER President, and ETHAN ROCKET Secretary.

Propositions were made to the negro people for their consideration by Capt. JOHN DE PASS, who in a very brief manner explained to them that they were occupying the Taylor Farm without warrant of law; that the Government had turned the property over to Mr. TAYLOR, and he was the only person now who could give them a legal right to occupy it; that the Government would provide places for them, and desired them to vacate the farm; he besought them to act sensibly, and if they thought there was any desire to take any advantage of them, to appoint a committee of five, and let that committee proceed to examine the property and locality (Wise's farm) and if the change would be to their interest they could then determine what would be best for them.

After this advice was given, a negro named ANTHONY BUTLER gained the stand and harangued the people in the following strain:

"That persons were continually telling them that they had no right to occupy the farm, as President JOHNSON had pardoned Mr. TAYLOR and restored his property, but he did not care if the President did pardon him, the reconstruction acts of Congress did not recognize the President's pardon, and the property was their own and they would hold it in defiance of all opposition."

RICHARD PARKER, negro, better known as "Uncle Dick," next addressed the crowd. He informed the people that the Indians were the original owners of the land, and were driven off by force; that the white man took the land from the Indians by force, and we (the blacks) will take it from the whites by force. They have no right to it and shall not have it. We fought for it, and we are going to keep it. We don't care for the President nor Freedmen's Bureau. We have suffered long enough; let the white man suffer now. The time was when the white man could say, "Come here, John, and black my boots," and the poor black man had to go; but, my friends, the times have changed, and I hope I will live to see the day when I can say to the white man, "Come here, John, and black my boots," and he must come. I will never be satisfied until the white man is forced to serve the black man, as the black was formerly compelled to serve the white. Now, my friends, we must drive them away. If they want to stay they must be our servants. If they are not satisfied with that, let them go somewhere else. We do not intend to allow Secesh or Yankee to drive us off this property, because it is ours. We fought for it, and we will fight now to defend it if necessary.

The negroes became excited to such an extend that it was unsafe to remain longer, consequently the delegation retired and left the revered "Uncle Dick" in possession of the field.

Source: New York Times, October 13, 1865.

A NEW LABOR AND
CREDIT SYSTEM EMERGES

In many areas immediately after the war, wage labor structured by contracts for the planting season replaced slavery. But blacks insisted on more independence than that: working under the direct supervision of white people seemed too much like a new version of slavery. When the hope for land ownership faded, sharecropping emerged as the dominant system. In this form of tenancy the worker—and there were many white as well as black sharecroppers in the South during the next seventy years—labored largely under day-to-day self-direction on a landlord's property and split the proceeds of the crop with him at the end of the year. At first sharecropping seemed a promising arrangement and some proportion of croppers did, in fact, eventually earn enough to own their land. Despite huge obstacles, about a fifth of black agricultural workers purchased land by 1880. But for most, the system proved a poor substitute for land ownership. The documents here suggest some of its problems, particularly the ills of the credit system that accompanied it.

D. AUGUSTUS STRAKER, THE CREDIT SYSTEM

At the close of the war, added to the renting of small farms to the colored man by whites, to be paid in certain proportions of the crop, was the system of making advances to this class of farmers of such necessary farming utensils and necessities for food and clothing. . . . This system in its incipiency had nothing in its intent discommendable, but it afterwards grew into the strongest engine of power, political and civil, as turned against the colored laborer and the poor white. The profit to be delivered from such an occupation, in which total ignorance had to compete with panoplied intelligence, soon caused numerous small merchants . . . to set up small stores on every plantation cultivated. In most instances the merchant was also landlord, and in this combination commenced a system of usury, unrivalled by the Jews of Lombardy in ancient times. The poor, ignorant colored and white man, renting small farms and relying on the merchant for advances to make his crop, were and still are compelled to pay the exorbitant interest, frequently of fifty per cent and not unusually of seventy or ninety per cent. A coat which cost the merchant one dollar, was frequently sold for two; a pound of meat that cost six cents was sold for twelve; a hat which cost fifty cents was sold for $1.50; so likewise with shoes and other things. . . . I have seen colored men who, having a large family, rent a small farm and take advances for a year to make a crop, and at the end of said year, after paying such debts to the merchant as were incurred in making said crop, [do] not have money enough to buy a suit of clothing for any one of the family. I have also seen the taking of all the crop by the merchant, and also, the horse or mule and other chattels which were given as collateral security for the debt in making a crop in one year.

Source: D. Augustus Straker, *The New South Investigated* (Detroit, 1888), 87.

A SHARECROPPING CONTRACT

To every one applying to rent land upon shares, the following conditions must be read, and *agreed to*.

To every 30 or 35 acres, I agree to furnish the team, plow, and farming implements, except cotton planters, and I *do not* agree to furnish a cart to every cropper. The croppers are to have half of the cotton, corn and fodder (and peas and pumpkins and potatoes if any are planted) if the following conditions are complied with, but—if not—they are to have only two fifths (2\5). Croppers are to have no part or interest in the cotton seed raised from the crop planted and worked by them. No vine crops of any description, that is, no watermelons, muskmelons, . . . squashes or anything of that kind, except peas and pumpkins, and potatoes, are to be planted in the cotton or corn. All must work under my direction. All plantation work to be done by the croppers. My part of the crop to be *housed* by them, and the fodder and oats to be hauled and put in the house. All the cotton must be topped about 1st August. If any cropper fails from any cause to save all the fodder from his crop, I am to have enough fodder to make it equal to one half of the whole if the whole amount of fodder had been saved.

For every mule or horse furnished by me there must be 1000 good sized rails . . . hauled, and the fence repaired as far as they will go, the fence to be torn down and put up from the bottom if I so direct. All croppers to haul rails and work on fence whenever I may order. Rails to be split when I may say. Each cropper to clean out every ditch in his crop, and where a ditch runs between two croppers, the cleaning out of that ditch is to be divided equally between them. Every ditch bank in the crop must be shrubbed down and cleaned off before the crop is planted and must be cut down every time the land is worked with his hoe and when the crop is "laid by," the ditch banks must be left clean of bushes, weeds, and seeds. The cleaning out of all ditches must be done by the first of October. The rails must be split and the fence repaired before corn is planted.

Each cropper must keep in good repair all bridges in his crop or over ditches that he has to clean out and when a bridge needs repairing that is outside of all their crops, then any one that I call on must repair it.

Fence jams to be done as ditch banks. If any cotton is planted on the land outside of the plantation fence, I am to have *three fourths* of all the cotton made in those patches, that is to say, no cotton must be planted by croppers in their home patches.

All croppers must clean out stables and fill them with straw, and haul straw in front of stables whenever I direct. All the cotton must be manured, and enough fertilizer must be brought to manure each crop highly, the croppers to pay for one half of all manure bought, the quantity to be purchased for each crop must be left to me.

No cropper to work off the plantation when there is any work to be done on the land he has rented, or when his work is needed by me or other croppers. Trees to be cut down on Orchard, House field & Evanson fences, leaving such as I may designate.

Road field to be planted from the *very edge of the ditch to the fence,* and all the land to be planted close up to the ditches and fences. *No stock of any kind* belonging to croppers to run in the plantation after crops are gathered.

If the fence should be blown down, or if trees should fall on the fence outside of the land planted by any of the croppers, any one or all that I may call upon must put it up and repair it. Every cropper must feed, or have fed, the team he works, Saturday nights, Sundays, and every morning before going to work, beginning to feed his team (morning, noon, and night *every day* in the week) on the day he rents and feeding it to and including the 31st day of December. If any cropper shall from any cause fail to repair his fence as far as 1000 rails will go, or shall fail to clean out any part of his ditches, or shall fail to leave his ditch banks, any part of them, well shrubbed and clean when his crop is laid by, or shall fail to clean out stables, fill them up and haul straw in front of them whenever he is told, he shall have only two-fifths (2/5) of the cotton, corn, fodder, peas and pumpkins made on the land he cultivates.

If any cropper shall fail to feed his team Saturday nights, all day Sunday and all the rest of the week, morning, noon, and night, for every time he so fails he must pay me five cents.

No corn nor cotton stalks must be burned, but must be cut down, cut up and plowed in. Nothing must be burned off the land except when it is *impossible* to plow it in.

Every cropper must be responsible for all gear and farming implements placed in his hands, and if not returned must be paid for unless it is worn out by use.

Croppers must sow & plow in oats and haul them to the crib, but *must have no part of them.* Nothing to be sold from their crops, nor fodder nor corn to be carried out of the fields until my rent is all paid, and all amounts they owe me and for which I am responsible are paid in full.

I am to gin & pack all the cotton and charge every cropper an eighteenth of his part, the cropper to furnish his part of the bagging, ties, & twine.

The sale of every cropper's part of the cotton to be made by me when and where I choose to sell, and after deducting all they owe me and all sums that I may be responsible for on their accounts, to pay them their half of the net proceeds. Work of every description, particularly the work on fences and ditches, to be done to my satisfaction, and must be done over until I am satisfied that it is done as it should be.

No wood to burn, nor light wood, nor poles, nor timber for boards, nor wood for any purpose whatever must be gotten above the house occupied by Henry Beasley—nor must any trees be cut down nor any wood used for any purpose, except for firewood, without my permission.

———————————

Source: Grimes Family Papers.

Chapter 2

GEORGE CUSTER, SITTING BULL, AND THE SIOUX WAR

In the eighteenth century and the early nineteenth century, the Sioux, bedecked in European beads, on horses descended from steeds imported by the Spanish, and carrying English rifles, swept eastward across the Great Plains. They conquered many local Indians and combined their rituals and cultures into the amalgam that most Americans still identify as the quintessential American Indian: in the historian William Brandon's description, the "feather-streaming, buffalo-chasing, wild-riding, recklessly fighting Indian of the Plain." Then the tide of empire shifted. Westward across the plains came whites, and African Americans as well as eastern Indians pushed relentlessly west. In the two decades after 1850, the new population of the plains swelled fivefold. Hundreds of thousands made the journey on foot or on mules and horses, in ox-drawn wagons, or by railroad. And with them came the military power of the United States government, symbolized for many by George A. Custer, whose swagger and recklessness appeared a match for any Sioux warrior.

The Civil War deeply affected the Plains Indians, initiating a generation of warfare throughout much of the region. The army, battling against the Santee Sioux during the war, ran afoul of the Lakota tribe by pursuing fugitives into their territory along the upper Missouri River. The Lakota won the ensuing Powder River War of 1866 and 1867. The 1868 Treaty of Fort Laramie concluding the war established a reservation for Indians agreeing to adopt some white ways and provided a vast "unceded Indian territory" for traditional Sioux in which white settlers were forbidden. Some of the Sioux agreed to the reservation, but a number of bands led by Sitting Bull chose the old ways in the Big Horn Mountains of present-day Wyoming and Montana. The treaty provided only a brief and uneasy peace. In 1872 after the government allowed the Northern Pacific Railroad to begin laying track across Sioux lands, skirmishing began. Two years later in response to rumors of gold in the Black Hills, Custer was ordered to lead an exploring party into Sioux lands. His enthusiastic report of gold and good grazing land stimulated a rush of prospectors and would-be settlers. What came to be called the Great Sioux War had begun.

CAUSES OF THE WAR

Sitting Bull, a Hunkpapa medicine man, became leader of the Sioux who rejected the reservation. Here he gives his version of what caused the war.

SITTING BULL, SPEECH, 1875

Behold, my brothers, the spring has come; the earth has received the embraces of the sun and we shall soon see the results of that love!

Every seed is awakened and so has all animal life. It is through this mysterious power that we too have our being and we therefore yield to our neighbors, even our animal neighbors, the same right as ourselves, to inhabit this land.

Yet, hear me, people, we have now to deal with another race—small and feeble when our fathers first met them but now great and overbearing. Strangely enough they have a mind to till the soil and the love of possession is a disease with them. These people have made many rules that the rich may break but the poor may not. They take tithes from the poor and weak to support the rich who rule. They claim this mother of ours, the earth, for their own and fence their neighbors away; they deface her with their buildings and their refuse. That nation is like a spring freshet that overruns its banks and destroys all who are in its path.

We cannot dwell side by side. Only seven years ago we made a treaty by which we were assured that the buffalo country should be left to us forever. Now they threaten to take that away from us. My brothers, shall we submit or shall we say to them: "First kill me before you take possession of my Fatherland. . . ."

Source: Frederick W. Turner III, *The Portable North American Indian Reader* (New York: Viking Press, 1974), 255.

Frederick Whittaker, an officer who had served under Custer during the Civil War, published in December 1876 the first lengthy biography of Custer. This heroic, often fanciful portrait that began the Custer legend tries to present Custer's view of Indian warfare.

LIEUTENANT COLONEL GEORGE ARMSTRONG CUSTER

In March 1873, the Seventh Cavalry was once more ordered to the Plains, this time up in Dakota.

This order perfectly delighted Custer. He was getting heartily sick of the useless life he had been leading, and he knew that work was coming, real work. When the whole Seventh Cavalry was ordered out in a body, it meant business. Once before they had been ordered out, and had ended in conquering the southwest. Now it was necessary to overrun the northwest. When Custer pacified the Kiowas, Arapahoes, and Cheyennes by force, physical and moral, the Sioux of the northwest had fared very differently. They had frightened the Government into a treaty, the treaty of 1868, by which the United States had promised to give up to them forever a large expanse of country, and not to trespass thereon.

Now that the danger was over, and the Pacific Railroad safely completed to the south, thanks to Custer, the treaty with the Northern Indians became irksome. It was all well enough to *promise* a lot of half-naked savages to give them so much land, but it could not be expected that such a promise should be *kept* a moment longer than was necessary to secure a quiet building of the railroad. It was now time to break the treaty. A northern Pacific road had become necessary, and its route was to lie right through the very midst of the territory solemnly promised the Indians by the treaty of 1868. As a practical measure to provoke an Indian war, there is nothing so certain as the commencement of a railroad. With the power to run it through, however, a different state of things ensues, as Custer himself forcibly illustrates, in narrating the events of the Yellowstone expedition, the last in which we are able to follow his words.

"The experience of the past," says Custer, "particularly that of recent years, has shown too that no one measure so quickly and effectually frees a country from the horrors and devastations of Indian wars and Indian depredations generally as *the building and successful operation of a railroad* through the region overrun."

Nothing can be truer than this, when once the railroad is completed, but the trouble is that while it is being built, the war has to be paid for at the same time, for the Indians, recognizing that the railroad will be their ruin, do all they can to hinder it.

Source: Frederick Whittaker, *A Complete Life of Gen. George A. Custer* (New York, 1876), 478–479.

CUSTER'S BLACK HILLS EXPEDITION

The army was obligated by the Treaty of Fort Laramie to keep prospectors and settlers out of the Black Hills. While Custer acknowledges this, he makes clear his own view.

INTERVIEW WITH CUSTER, BISMARCK *TRIBUNE* (DAKOTA TERRITORY), SEPTEMBER 2, 1874

A Tribune reporter was dispatched yesterday to interview Gen. Custer relating to the Black Hills Gold Discoveries, the probable policy of the military authorities in relations to exploring parties seeking to enter the Black Hills prior to the extinguishment of the Indian title, the best route to reach the Eldorado, &c., &c., with the following result: . . .

Reporter—I see you endorse fully the reports of the explorers and correspondents concerning the Gold Discoveries and therefore presume there can be no doubt as to the richness of the discoveries.

Custer—The reports are not exaggerated in the least; the prospects are even better than represented. I am familiar with and to somewhat extent interested in Colorado mines, and I saw localities in the Black Hills similar, as to formation, to the richest regions in Colorado, where the Geologists insisted the precious metals must be found, that were not explored by the miners at all. These localities were met with in my rambles along the valleys when the explorers were not within reach.

Reporter—What was the best prospect reported to you?

Custer—The product of one pan of earth was laid on my table which was worth not less than two dollars. It contained some fifty particles of gold . . . averaging about the size of a pin head.

Reporter—Was gold found in localities other than in Custer's Park?

Custer—Yes at various points, though the explorers report the richest prospects there; but as I said before, the scientific gentlemen are satisfied that far richer discoveries will be made on further exploration. The miners also agree with this view of the case. . . .

Reporter—What is the best route to reach the Black Hills Mines from the Missouri River?

Custer—Unquestionably a direct route from Bismarck in the direction of Bear Butte.

Reporter—What is the distance from Bismarck to the Gold region, and the nature of the country?

Custer—The distance from Bismarck to Bear Butte is about one hundred and ninety-eight miles. Harney's Peak is 35 miles southwest of Bear Butte. Custer's Gulch can be reached by a march of two hundred and forty miles over an excellent country, affording good grazing, a fair amount of timber, and abundance of water and everything essential to building up prosperous villages along the route. A route which offers absolutely no engineering difficulties should occasion demand the construction of a railroad from Bismarck to the hills. . . .

Reporter—What is the probable policy of the military toward persons seeking to enter the Black Hills this fall?

Custer—The government has entered into a solemn treaty with the Indians whereby they agree to keep off all tresspassers [sic]. This is a law of the land, and should be respected, and Gen. Sheridan has already issued instruction to the military to prevent expeditions entering upon the reservation and parties contemplating going have been warned to keep off.

Reporter—But, General, you are aware that you have a long line to guard and small parties may slip across the line and enter the reservation while the military is powerless to prevent it.

Custer—That is true to some extent but until Congress authorizes the settlement of the country the military will do its duty. When the Indian title is extinguished the military will aid the settlers in every way possible. I shall recommend the extinguishment of the Indian title at the earliest moment practicable for military reasons.

Reporter—What are those reasons General?

Custer—The Black Hills region is not occupied by the Indians and is seldom visited by them. It is used as sort of a back-room to which they may escape after committing depredations, remaining in safety until quiet is again restored. It is available in keeping up communication between the agency Indians and the hostile tribes located in the buffalo region northwest of the Hills, and if the Black Hills region is wrested from them this communication will be broken up and a fruitful source of trouble will be removed. The extinguishment of the Indian title to the Black Hills, and the establishment of a military post in the vicinity of Harney's Peak and another at some point on the Little Missouri will settle the Indian question so far as the Northwest is concerned. . . .

Source: Herbert Krause and Gary D. Olson, *Prelude to Glory: A Newspaper Accounting of Custer's 1874 Expedition to the Black Hills* (Sioux Falls, SD: Brevet Press, 1974), 231–233.

THE BATTLE OF THE LITTLE BIG HORN

On June 25, 1876, while Alexander Graham Bell was demonstrating his new telephone at the Centennial Exposition in Philadelphia, Custer along with his men of the Seventh United States Cavalry were slaughtered by the Sioux at the battle of the Little Big Horn. The news reached the East on July 5, the day after the nation's official centennial observance. Custer's disaster has been a subject of intense debate for over a century. His orders enable the reader to examine the role of his superiors; the official report of the battle presents the army's account of what happened.

CUSTER'S ORDERS

Lieut. Col. Custer, Seventh Cavalry:

COLONEL:—The Brigadier-General Commanding directs that as soon as your regiment can be made ready for the march you proceed up the Rosebud in pursuit of the Indians whose trail was discovered by Major Reno a few days since. It is, of course, impossible to give any definite instructions in regard to this movement, and, were it not impossible to do so, the Department Commander places too much confidence in your zeal, energy and ability to wish to impose upon you precise orders which might hamper your action when nearly in contact with the enemy. He will, however, indicate to you his own views of what your action should be, and he desires that you should conform to them unless you shall see sufficient reason for departing from them. He thinks that you should proceed up the Rosebud until you ascertain definitely the direction in which the trail above spoken of leads. Should it be found, as it appears to be almost certain that it will be found, to turn toward the Little Big Horn, he thinks that you should still proceed southward, perhaps, as far as the head-waters of the Tongue, and then turn toward the Little Big Horn, feeling constantly, however, to your left so as to preclude the possibility of the escape of the Indians to the south or south-east by passing around your left flank. The column of Col. Gibbon is now in motion for the mouth of the Big Horn. As soon as it reaches that point it will cross the Yellowstone and move up at least as far as the [valleys] of the Big and Little Big Horn. Of course its future movements must be controlled by circumstances as they arise; but it is hoped that the Indians, if upon the Little Big Horn, may be so nearly inclosed by two columns that their escape will be impossible. The Department Commander desires that on your way up the Rosebud you should thoroughly examine the upper part of Tulloch's Creek, and that you should endeavor to send a scout through to Col. Gibbon's column with information of the result of your examination. The lower part of this creek will be examined by a detachment from Col. Gibbon's command. The supply steamer will be pushed up the Big Horn as far as the forks of the river are found to be navigable for that space, and the Department Commander, who will accompany the column of Col. Gibbon, desires you to report to him there not later than the expiration of the time for which your troops are rationed, unless in the meantime you receive further orders.

> Respectfully, etc.,
> E. W. SMITH, Captain 18th Infantry.
> Acting Assistant Adjutant-General.

Source: Whittaker, *Complete Life*, 574–575.

GENERAL ALFRED H. TERRY, OFFICIAL REPORT OF THE BATTLE

> Headquarters Department of Dakota,
> Camp on Little Big Horn River.
> June 27, 1876.

It is my painful duty to report that, day before yesterday, the 25th inst., a great disaster overtook Gen. Custer and the troops under his command. At 12 o'clock on the 22d he started, with his whole regiment and a strong detachment of scouts and guards, from the mouth of the Rosebud. Proceeding up that river about twenty miles he struck a very heavy Indian trail, which had previously been discovered, and pursuing it, found a village of almost unexampled extent, and at once attacked it with that portion of his force which was immediately at hand. Major Reno with three companies, A, G, and M, of the regiment was sent into the valley of the stream at the point where the trail struck it. Gen. Custer, with five companies, C, E, F, I, and L, attempted to enter it about three miles lower down. Reno forded the river, charged down its left bank, dismounted and fought on foot, until finally completely overwhelmed by numbers he was compelled to mount, recross the river, and seek refuge on the high bluffs which overlooked its right bank. Just as he recrossed, Capt. Benteen, who with three companies, D, H, and K, was some two miles to the left of Reno when the action commenced, but who had been ordered by Gen. Custer to return, came to the river, and rightly concluding that it would be useless for his force to attempt to renew the fight in the valley, he joined Reno on the bluffs. Capt. McDougall with Company B was at first at some distance in the rear with a train of pack-mules. He also came to Reno soon. This united force was nearly surrounded by Indians, many of whom, armed with rifles, occupied positions which commanded the ground held by the cavalry, ground from which there was no escape. Rifle-pits were dug and the fight was maintained with heavy loss, from about 2:30 o'clock of the 25th till 6 o'clock of the 26th, when the Indians withdrew from the valley, taking with them their village.

Of the movements of Gen. Custer and the five companies under his immediate command scarcely anything is known from those who witnessed them, for no soldier or officer who accompanied him has yet been found alive. His trail from the point where Reno crossed the stream passes along and in the rear of the crest of the bluffs on the right bank for nearly or quite three miles, then it comes down to the bank of the river, but at once diverges from it as if he had unsuccessfully attempted to cross; then turns upon itself, almost completes a circle and closes. It is marked by the remains of his officers and men, the bodies of his horses, some of them dropped along the path, others heaped where halts appear to have been made. There is abundant evidence that a gallant resistance was offered by the troops, but they were beset on all sides by overpowering numbers. . . .

At the mouth of the Rosebud I [had] informed Gen. Custer that I should take the supply steamer Far West up the Yellowstone to ferry Gen. Gibbon's column over the river; that I should personally accompany that column, and that I would in all probability reach the mouth of the Little Big Horn on the 26th inst. The steamer reached Gen. Gibbon's troops, near the mouth of the Big Horn, early in the morning of the 24th, and at 4 o'clock in the afternoon all his men and animals were across the Yellowstone. At 5 o'clock the column, consisting of five companies of the Seventh Infantry, four companies of the Second Cavalry, and a battery of Gatling guns, marched out to and across Tullock's Creek, starting soon after 5 o'clock in the morning of the 25th. The infantry made a march of twenty-two miles over the most difficult country which I have ever seen, in order that scouts might be sent into the Valley of the Little Big Horn. The cavalry, with the battery, was then pushed on thirteen or fourteen miles further, reaching camp at midnight. The scouts were sent out at 4:30 on the morning of the 26th. The scouts discovered the Indians, who were at first supposed to be Sioux, but when overtaken they proved to be Crows, who had been with Gen. Custer. They brought the first intelligence of the battle. Their story was not credited. It was supposed that some fighting, perhaps severe fighting, had taken place, but it was not believed that disaster could have overtaken so large a force as twelve companies of cavalry. The infantry, which had broken camp very early soon came up, and the whole column entered and moved up the Valley of the Little Big Horn. During the afternoon, efforts were made to send scouts through to what was supposed to be Gen. Custer's position, and to obtain information of the condition of affairs; but those who were sent out were driven back by parties of Indians, who, in increasing numbers, were seen hovering in Gen. Gibbon's front.

At 8:40 o'clock in the evening the infantry had marched between twenty-nine and thirty miles. The men were very weary, and daylight was fading. The column was therefore halted for the night, at a point about eleven miles in a straight line above the stream. This morning the movement was resumed, and after a march of nine miles, Major Reno's entrenched position was reached. The withdrawal of the Indians from around Reno's command and from the valley was undoubtedly caused by the appearance of Gen. Gibbon's troops.

Major Reno and Capt. Benteen, both of whom are officers of great experience, accustomed to see large masses of mounted men, estimated the number of Indians engaged as not less than 2,500. Other officers think that the number was greater than this. The village in the valley was about three miles in length, and about a mile in width. . . . It is believed that the loss of the Indians was large. I have yet received no official reports in regard to the battle but what is here stated is gathered from the officers who were on the grounds then, and from those who have been over it since.

Source: New York Times, July 9, 1876.

The historian Stanley Vestal's reconstruction of Sitting Bull's role is based on pioneering research into tribal traditions and the personal accounts of Sioux and other participants.

RECONSTRUCTION OF THE BATTLE
FROM SITTING BULL'S PERSPECTIVE

Sitting Bull sprang up and, throwing aside the door flap of the council lodge, limped as fast as he could toward his own tipi, not far off. It was nearest to the soldiers. While he was hurrying, there was a yell of alarm. A man was pointing, yelling, and everyone turned to look where he pointed—south—upriver. There in the bottoms they saw a tower of dust coming, and in it, as it came, the blue shirts of soldiers, the heads of horses! While they stared, the column of soldiers widened into a line, smoke bloomed from its front, and they heard the snarl of the carbines.

Sitting Bull hurried into his tipi to get his arms. He had a revolver, calibre .45, and an 1873 model carbine Winchester, .44, center fire, with one band. Both weapons were gifts from his nephew, White Bull. In the tent he found One Bull bent on the same errand. One Bull had a muzzle-loader, but he knew it would be useless in hand-to-hand fighting. He caught up his stone-headed war club, and offered the gun to Sitting Bull. Already the bullets were whining overhead, and one of the tent poles was splintered above them.

One Bull was just twenty-three. "Uncle," he said, "I am going to fight."

"Good," said Sitting Bull. "Go ahead. Fear nothing. Go right straight in."

Taking his own shield from its buckskin case, he flung the carrying-strap over One Bull's head, so that it protected his chest. Together they ran out of the lodge. Sitting Bull was buckling on his cartridge belt. Already someone had caught up his war horse—the famous black with white face and stockings given him by Makes-Room. Sitting Bull leaped upon its bare back.

All around him was confusion. Old men were yelling advice, young men dashing away to catch their horses, women and children rushing off afoot and on horseback to the north end of that three-mile camp, fleeing from the soldiers. They left their tents standing, grabbed their babies, called their older children, and hurried away, frightened girls shrinking under their shawls, matrons puffing for breath, hobbling old women, wrinkled and peering, with their sticks, making off as best they could, crying children, lost children, dogs getting in everybody's way and being kicked for their pains, nervous horses resisting the tug of the reins, and over all the sound of the shooting. First of all, Sitting Bull saw that his old mother was safely mounted and on her way.

Four Horns was there, old as he was, on a mixed roan-and-bay horse, armed with a bow and arrows. No newfangled firearms for that old-timer! And now White Bull, out with his horses to the north of the Sans Arc camp, had seen the soldiers coming, mounted his war horse, and, carrying his Winchester, came dashing down to his uncle's camp. Every man able to fight was mounted and ready by that time, and White Bull could hear Sitting Bull's resonant bellow: "Be brave, boys. It will be a hard time. Be brave!"

The Hunkpapa stood their ground bravely, covering the retreat of their women and children down the flat. Veterans of that fight say, "It was sure hard luck for Major Reno that he struck the Hunkpapa camp first."

White-Hair-on-Face had had to run and catch his pony. Now he came galloping back to take part in the fighting. He could see Sitting Bull out in front of all the warriors, shouting to them. Everybody was yelling and giving orders; nobody was listening. White-Hair-on-Face met his mother-in-law running to safety; she was dragging one child by the hand. He gave her his horse. She put the little fellow behind her, the big girl in front, and away they all went—three of them on one horse.

As fast as the Sioux were mounted, they rode out to meet the soldiers on the flat. Those who had guns fired occasionally, falling back slowly, trying to cover the retreat of the women streaming to the north. Every moment reinforcements came up, and the firing grew constantly heavier, until there were enough Indians to stop the soldiers in their tracks. . . .

And now the soldiers stopped sure enough, got off their horses and began to shoot and fight on foot. The Sioux took courage. The women and children were safe. They charged on the soldiers from the west side, as well as from the north, and the soldiers began to give way and drop back eastward into the timber. Pretty soon their line was behind a cutbank among the trees, where the river bed used to be, and they were facing southwest. The Sioux were all around them then. . . .

Sitting Bull was puzzled by Reno's behavior. He had come against that huge camp with a handful, and then—instead of charging, the only way he could hope to fight his way through—he had dismounted his men and was fighting them afoot. Sitting Bull thought Reno was acting like a fool. But Sitting Bull was much too intelligent to underestimate his enemy. He wondered what was up. Therefore he remained with the warriors to the north of the troops, between the camp and the enemy. "Look out!" he yelled, "there must be some trick about this." . . .

By that time the soldiers in the timber had mounted their horses, dashed from the trees, and were galloping up the west bank of the river as hard as they could go, all strung out, looking for a place to cross. The moment Sitting Bull saw them running like that, without order, every man for himself, he knew that Reno's attack on the village had not been inspired by unusual bravery. He guessed the answer to his puzzle then: those soldiers had been *waiting* for somebody to come and help them; that was why they fought on foot and took cover in the trees. Right away Sitting Bull surmised that there was another war party of enemies somewhere around. After that he did not urge the young men to rush the soldiers.

But they needed no urging. They were all over those fleeing troopers, killing them with war clubs and the butts of their guns, shooting arrows into them, riding them down. "We killed the soldiers easy; it was just like running buffalo. One blow killed them," said the old men. "They were shot in the back; they offered no resistance." Away they went, plunging through the river, and up the steep, sprawling ridges of that high bluff, to find a breathing space on top. Thirty of them lay dead and a few had been left in the timber. It was an utter rout, due to bad leadership. Reno had never fought Indians before.

In this part of the fighting, Dog-with-Horns was killed and Chased-by-Owls mortally wounded. The Indians chased the soldiers right to the bank of the river, and some of them rode their ponies over. Sitting Bull could not stop them.

"In this fight there was no leader; all were brave," they told me. "There was no need to give orders; everybody knew what to do—stop the soldiers, save the ponies, protect the women and children." And so every man did as he thought best. Everybody shouted suggestions and encouragement; nobody paid much attention. No one was in command. "I was not standing around looking on; I was shooting." That is what they told me. There must have been a thousand warriors against Reno's three troops. Benteen, who saw them chasing Reno, estimated nine hundred.

Just then One Bull came up with others and reached the bank of the river. Some of the warriors had crossed, and the last of the soldiers were scrambling up the steep bluffs. Last of all went four horse holders who had been left behind. One Bull and his comrades, hot with victory, started to plunge into the stream, ford it, and kill these. But Sitting Bull objected. "Let them go!" he yelled. "Let them go! Let them live to tell the truth about this battle." He wanted the white men to know that this fight had been begun by the soldiers, not the Sioux. They came shooting and fired the first shot. He was sick and tired of being blamed for the sins of others. Everything that went wrong in the Sioux country was laid at his door. . . .

Sitting Bull rode north through the abandoned camps, one after the other. The tents stood empty and forlorn, their gaping doors open to the hungry, prowling dogs which sneaked in looking for meat, hardly able to believe that their good luck was real, and running off guiltily when they heard the hoofbeats of the black war horse. Here and there lay a dead horse where some stray bullet had found it. Sitting Bull hurried on up the flat to the north and west. He could see the women and children gathered there, boys and old men trying to keep them together. By this time they had learned that the soldiers had been routed upriver and were streaming back to their tents again.

But just then another war party of enemies was seen upon the bluffs across the river to the east, Custer's five companies trotting along the ridge, apparently looking for a place to cross. Sitting Bull's hunch was justified: there *was* a second war party! . . .

The white soldiers were trotting along the hilltop in a cloud of dust, making toward the ford. Four Cheyennes rode out to face them, only four at first. But those four—Bob-Tail-Horses was one—seemed to daunt them. At any rate, the soldiers stopped. Shooting began. The smoke rolled down the hill in a dense cloud. The Indians were all around, more and more of them. What with the dust and the smoke there was not much to see.

One Bull was eager to go and join the fighting. He urged his uncle to go with him. But Sitting Bull replied: "No. Stay here and help protect the women. Perhaps there is another war party of enemies coming. There are plenty of Indians yonder to take care of those." By "those," of course, he meant Custer's immediate command. Once Sitting Bull's suspicions were aroused, they did not readily sleep again. Having been greatly puzzled by Reno's strange behavior, he was even more puzzled by Custer's. Why, *why,* had he halted just when he should have charged? Unless he was waiting for someone. Once more, Sitting Bull's hunch was right. If Benteen had not been delayed, he might have struck the village from the west side.

Such skill in forecasting the enemy's movements, such canny sizing-up of a situation, were what made Sitting Bull peerless as a leader of the warlike Sioux. Brave men were plenty in their camps: but a man who combined intelligence and skill and courage as Sitting Bull did was hardly to be found. He knew, as Napoleon knew—and said—that "battles are won by the power of the mind."

Sitting Bull was too seasoned a warrior to become excited when there was no need. He knew what would happen. Over beyond the river, up on the tumbled ridges, under that haze of smoke and dust, it was happening very swiftly. Cheyennes and Sioux were making quick work of Custer's tired troopers.

Some of the cavalry units were still mounted and moving when the horde of mounted Indians caught up with them, and the warriors at their backs had them at a great disadvantage.

Among others, Sitting Bull's nephew, White Bull, side by side with Crazy Horse, Iron Lightning, Owl's-Horn, and others were jerking soldiers off their horses, counting *coups,* capturing guns and horses and dashing between and around the troops in bravado.

But once all the soldiers had dismounted and let their horses go, it was quite the other way around. Then the soldiers' fire power quickly blasted the Indians out of their saddles.

Then for a time it was all shooting, and after the Indians captured the soldiers' horses and found pistols and ammunition in their saddlebags, the firing increased in volume. Then some of the soldiers were killed, or retreated, and the Indians obtained carbines and cartridge belts, advanced up the coulees and ravines and the firing grew hotter and hotter. But as the number of Indians' guns increased, the number of troopers diminished, and the Indians rushed in to fight hand to hand. . . .

When the fighting was over, Sitting Bull rode across the river and asked, "Are they all killed?" Someone answered, "Yes."

Sitting Bull said, "Let's go back to camp.". . .

Sitting Bull returned to camp. The soldiers on the hill imagined they heard scalp dances going on down in the bottoms; but by all accounts they were in a very anxious and excited condition. There were no scalp dances that night; old Sioux are indignant at such an indecent suggestion. Too many Sioux warriors had fallen; there were too many mourners in the camps. That was no time for rejoicing. It was never the custom to hold a victory dance, under such circumstances, until after four days had elapsed and the mourners had given permission. Sitting Bull mourned with the others. Said he, "My heart is full of sorrow that so many were killed on each side, but when they compel us to fight, we must fight." And he commanded, "Tonight we shall mourn for our dead, and for those brave white men lying up yonder on the hillside." So it was done.

***

Source: Stanley Vestal, *Sitting Bull, Champion of the Sioux* (Norman, OK: University of Oklahoma Press, 1957), 160–168, 173–174.

CONCLUSION

The Sioux won the battle but lost the war. In response to the defeat at the Little Big Horn, Lieutenant General Philip Sheridan, commander of the western army, waged a campaign as ruthless as the warfare he had conducted in the Shenandoah Valley near the close of the Civil War, and with the same result. While Sitting Bull and a small band moved over the Canadian border and avoided the army for several years afterward, the Sioux war was quickly over. Prospectors rushed into the Black Hills; the Northern Pacific Railroad pushed through to the Pacific; and the Lakota Sioux and their allies entered the reservations and ceased roaming the Great Plains.

FREDERICK WHITTAKER ON CUSTER AND THE SIOUX WAR

As long as the Black Hills were regarded as worthless, the Indians were allowed to retain them. As soon as it was discovered that gold was there, all restraints of treaties were thrown aside, and Custer was ordered on the Black Hills expedition. That was the first wrong act, and from it flowed all the rest. Afterwards, when the miners began to crowd in, the government tried to keep its word by putting them out, but the first interlopers, the men who made the first trouble, were the troopers of Custer's column who started from Fort Lincoln July 1, 1874, in obedience to the orders of the United States Government.

It is a sad and humiliating confession to be made, but the irresistible logic of truth compels it, that all the subsequent trouble of the Sioux war really sprang from the deliberate violation by the United States Government of its own freely plighted faith, when Custer was ordered to lead his column from Fort Lincoln to the Black Hills. The avowed purpose of the journey was to find out whether gold existed there, a matter which concerned no one but the owners. All the subsequent efforts of the government were mere palliations of its own first fault, and perfectly useless. Strange, but an illustration of poetic justice, that the very man, who, in obeying his orders, became the instrument of injustice towards the Indians, should fall a victim in the contest which ensued.

Strange but true! Yet we cannot blame Custer, as we approach the tragic close of so bright and hopeful a career. He was a soldier, bound to obey orders, and a mere instrument in the hand of power. He was ordered to explore the Black Hills, and he went there. He was ordered on the trail of the Sioux, and he went. None the less, the pleasant-seeming and roseate hues of that long picnic party called the Black Hills Expedition close the brightness of his career. From thenceforth clouds began to gather, and the time was swiftly coming when his sun should set in death.

Source: Whittaker, *Complete Life*, 512–513.

CROW CHIEF PLENTY COUPS: ADDRESS AT THE LITTLE BIG HORN COUNCIL GROUNDS, MONTANA, 1909

The Ground on which we stand is sacred ground. It is the dust and blood of our ancestors. On these plains the Great White Father at Washington sent his soldiers armed with long knives and rifles to slay the Indian. Many of them sleep on yonder hill where Pahaska—White Chief of the Long Hair [General Custer]—so bravely fought and fell. A few more passing suns will see us here no more, and our dust and bones will mingle with these same prairies. I see as in a vision the dying spark of our council fires, the ashes cold and white. I see no longer the curling smoke rising from our lodge poles. I hear no longer the songs of the women as they prepare the meal. The antelope have gone; the buffalo wallows are empty. Only the wail of the coyote is heard. The white man's medicine is stronger than ours; his iron horse rushes over the buffalo trail. He talks to us through his "whispering spirit" [the telephone]. We are like birds with a broken wing. My heart is cold within me. My eyes are growing dim—I am old. . . .

Source: Turner, *Portable North American Indian Reader*, 256.

Chapter 3

SELECTIVE IMMIGRATION: THE CHINESE CASE

By the terms of the Immigration Act of 1965, every year the Immigration and Naturalization Service (INS) holds a lottery for residency papers; every year it decides which countries will be entitled to slots. Yet prior to the Civil War and for some years after it, the United States had no significant restrictions on settlement by immigrants, most of whom were European. A predominantly rural country with huge amounts of uncultivated land, the nation in the nineteenth century was plagued by labor shortages. Some states and companies advertised in Europe for immigrants. Though many, particularly the Irish, were mistreated when they arrived, no one was excluded. All this changed when the Chinese arrived on the West Coast.

Like many in the other groups traveling to California in the 1840s and 1850s, the Chinese came for gold. They had a particularly difficult journey. Until 1860, leaving China was a violation of imperial law punishable by death. The first Chinese Forty-Niners bribed soldiers to look the other way and paid ship captains huge sums to defy Chinese law and take them to the United States seven thousand miles away. Once there they panned for gold in the rivers of northern California. In 1850 the state imposed the Foreign Miners License Law. Though it was written to include all foreign miners, the Chinese as the most visible foreigners paid nearly eighty-five percent of all miners' taxes.

As the initial fury of gold fever dissipated with the exhaustion of surface gold and prospecting taxes cut into Chinese miners' incomes, those who stayed in California drifted into San Francisco and elsewhere in search of other work. Some tried farming, but most started small businesses or took jobs in mines or small factories or on the waterfront. Though never fully accepted in California, they were tolerated as long as there was work for all.

In 1864 the building of the transcontinental railroad began. The Central Pacific Railroad began hiring Chinese for its construction crews. Though the job was dangerous, the pay was adequate and Chinese flocked to the railroad sites. At one time Central Pacific had as many as ten thousand Chinese in its employ. But difficult times were coming.

On July 28, 1868, the United States and the emperor of China concluded the Burlingame Treaty, which accorded Chinese and Americans each the right to visit or reside in the country of the other while asserting that the arrangement did not affect citizenship. This clause probably reflected American xenophobia as well as the interest of the Chinese emperor, whose country had been greatly weakened by external conflict and civil war. Easy naturalization in the vastly more prosperous and politically democratic United States might drain China of desperately needed labor.

On May 10, 1869, when the final spike was hammered into the final tie of the transcontinental railroad, twenty-five thousand people on the West Coast were suddenly out of work. The Chinese found themselves trapped in an unruly frontier state surrendering to economic panic. Without basic rights and government protection, they became easy scapegoats. Demagogues like Dennis Kearney, a bankrupted gold speculator, gave streetcorner speeches against the Chinese, whom he blamed for the hard times. Publicized by the San Francisco newspapers, which are reported to have helped him write his speeches, Kearney founded the Workingman's Party. Taking as its slogan "the Chinese must go," this party sparked riots and organized paramilitary groups. During the fifteen years after the completion of the railroad, hundreds of anti-Chinese pogroms burned people's homes, while thousands were injured and some killed. Because Chinese received no police protection and were not allowed to testify in courts, few perpetrators were brought to justice.

The Chinese Exclusion Act, finally passed in May 1882, reinforced what the mobs and California courts had already done. It led to regional laws banning Chinese from working in most professions, marrying whites, or serving in the army. The Geary Bill of 1892 absolutely excluded immigration to the United States of members of "the Chinese race," whatever their country of origin. These laws, extended several times, stood until 1943, when President Franklin D. Roosevelt, seeking to cement an alliance with China against the Japanese, persuaded Congress to repeal them. "Nations," he wrote, "like individuals make mistakes. We must be big enough to acknowledge our mistakes of the past and to correct them." The policy of Chinese exclusion ended after six decades, but the precedent had been set for highly selective immigration.

ANTI-CHINESE SENTIMENT ON THE WEST COAST

By 1855 a Chinese merchants' association had already organized to resist prejudice against the Chinese. The document here was submitted to the governor and printed as a pamphlet.

REMARKS OF CHINESE MERCHANTS OF SAN FRANCISCO UPON GOVERNOR BIGLER'S MESSAGE, 1855

We have read the message of the Governor.

Firstly—it is stated that "too large a number of the men of the Flowery Kingdom have emigrated to this country, and that they have come here alone, without their families." They are unused to winds and waves; and it is exceedingly difficult to bring families upon distant journeys over great oceans. Yet a few have come; nor are they all. And further, there have been several injunctions warning the people of the Flowery land not to come here, which have fostered doubts; nor have our hearts found peace in regard to bringing families. Suppose you say, "we will restrain only those who work in the mines; we would not forbid merchants," it is replied, that the merchandize imported by Chinese merchants chiefly depends upon Chinese consumption. If there be no Chinese miners allowed, what business can we have to do? The occupations are mutually dependent, like tooth and lip; neither can spare the other.

It is, we are assured, the principle of your honorable country to protect the people; and it has benevolence to mankind at heart. Now, the natives of China, or of any strange country, have one nature. All consider that good and evil cannot be in unison. All nations are really the same. Confucius says: "Though a city had but ten houses, there must be some in it honest and true." Suppose then we see it declared that "the people of the Flowery land are altogether without good," we can not but fear that the rulers do not exercise a liberal public spirit, and that they defer their own knowledge of right to an undue desire to please men. . . .

If it be observed that the "number of our merchants in your honorable State is not great," we reply, that nevertheless the amount of merchandize arriving here is not small, embracing imports by men of all other nations, as well as the business of our own traders. And this mutual general traffic fills the coffers of thousands, and involves the interests of myriads of people. But the miner in the mountain, and the workman in the shop, do no less than the merchant, pay respect to your customs. . . .

Some have remarked that "emigrants from other countries bring their families; that their homes are distributed over the State; that some engage in manual employments, and amass wealth; that thus mutual interests are created, mutual civilities extended, and common sympathies excited; that while in every respect they adopt your customs, on the contrary the Chinese do not." To this we rejoin, that the manners and customs of China and of foreign countries are not alike. This is an ancient principle, and is prevalent now. What if other countries do differ somewhat from your honorable nation in hats, and clothes, and letters, and other things, while there is much that is common? In China itself, the people differ. In China, there are some distinctions in the inhabitants of various provinces, or departments, or counties, or townships, or even villages. Their dialects, their manners, their sentiments, do not wholly accord. Their articles of use are not all made by one rule. Their common customs all differ. One line cannot be drawn for all. And just so it must be in all parts of the world. It would certainly appear unreasonable, when the officers and the merchants of your honorable country come to our Middle Kingdom, were they rebuked for not knowing our language, or for not being acquainted with our affairs. . . .

Finally. It is said that "henceforth you would prevent the emigration of people of the Flowery land." Hitherto our people have been imbued with your sacred doctrines; we have tried to exercise modesty and reason. If we can henceforth be treated with mutual courtesy, then we shall be glad to dwell within your honorable boundaries. But if the rabble are to harass us, we wish to return to our former homes. We will speedily send and arrest the embarkation of any that have not yet come. And now we, who are here, do earnestly request that a definite time be fixed, by which we may be governed, within which we can return our merchandize, and make any necessary arrangements. We trust that in that case the friendly intercourse of previous days will not be interrupted; and that your honorable nation may maintain its principles in tenderly cherishing the strangers from afar. If there be no definite regulation upon this subject, but only these incessant rumors about forbidding the Chinese emigration, we fear the result will be that the class who know nothing, of every nation, will be seeking occasions to make trouble; that our Chinese people in the mines will be subjected to much concealed violence, to robbery of their property, and quarrels about their claims. Thus there will be unlimited trouble; and where will be the end of it?

Source: "Remarks of the Chinese Merchants of San Francisco Upon Governor Bigler's Message and Some Common Questions; With Some Explanations of the Character of the Chinese Companies and the Laboring Class in California," pamphlet (San Francisco: Whitton, Towne and Co., 1855), 3–6.

THE BURLINGAME TREATY, 1868

The Burlingame Treaty, though not extending citizenship, allowed Chinese to come as visitors or residents, but prevented them from ever becoming citizens. The writer Samuel L. Clemens (Mark Twain) welcomed the treaty for giving Chinese the right to be in the United States. Two years after the treaty was signed, the great abolitionist Republican senator from Massachusetts Charles Sumner, who had fought legal battles over basic rights for African Americans, opposed any effort to put racial limits on access to citizenship.

THE BURLINGAME TREATY, JULY 28, 1868

Article V

The United States of America and the Emperor of China cordially recognize the inherent and inalienable right of man to change his home and allegiance, and also the mutual advantage of the free migration and emigration of their citizens and subjects, respectively, from the one country to the other, for purposes of curiosity, of trade, or as permanent residents. The high contracting parties, therefore, join in reprobating any other than an entirely voluntary emigration for these purposes. They consequently agree to pass laws making it a penal offense for a citizen of the United States or Chinese subjects to take Chinese subjects either to the United States or to any other foreign country, or for a Chinese subject or citizen of the United States to take citizens of the United States to China or to any other foreign country, without their free and voluntary consent respectively.

Article VI

Citizens of the United States visiting or residing in China shall enjoy the same privileges, immunities, or exemptions in respect to travel or residence as may there be enjoyed by the citizens or subjects of the most favored nation. And, reciprocally, Chinese subjects visiting or residing in the United States, shall enjoy the same privileges, immunities, and exemptions in respect to travel or residence as may there be enjoyed by the citizens or subjects of the most favored nation. But nothing herein contained shall be held to confer naturalization upon citizens of the United States in China, nor upon the subjects of China in the United States.

Source: Report of the Joint Special Committee to Investigate Chinese Immigration, 44th Congress, 2nd Session (Washington, 1877), 1182–1183.

SAMUEL L. CLEMENS, "THE TREATY WITH CHINA"

They can never beat and bang and set the dogs on the Chinamen any more. These pastimes are lost to them forever. In San Francisco, a large part of the most interesting local news in the daily papers consists of gorgeous compliments to the 'able and efficient' Officer This and That for arresting Ah Foo, or Ching Wang, or Song Hi for stealing a chicken; but when some white brute breaks an unoffending Chinaman's head with a brick, the paper does not compliment any officer for arresting the assaulter, for the simple reason that the officer does not make the arrest; the shedding of Chinese blood only makes him laugh; he considers it fun of the most entertaining description. I have seen dogs almost tear helpless Chinamen to pieces in broad daylight in San Francisco, and I have seen hod-carriers who help to make Presidents stand around and enjoy the sport. I have seen troops of boys assault a Chinaman with stones when he was walking quietly along about his business, and send him bruised and bleeding home. I have seen Chinamen abused and maltreated in all the mean, cowardly ways possible to the invention of a degraded nature, but I never saw a Chinaman righted in a court of justice for wrongs thus done him. The California laws do not allow Chinamen to testify against white men. California is one of the most liberal and progressive States in the Union, and the best and worthiest of her citizens will be glad to know that the days of persecuting Chinamen are over, in California.

Source: New York Tribune, August 9, 1868.

SENATOR CHARLES SUMNER
"NO DISTINCTION OF RACE OR COLOR," JULY 2, 1870

Mr. SUMNER. I offer a new section, which has already been reported upon favorably by the Judiciary Committee:

> And be it further enacted, That all acts of Congress relating to naturalization be, and the same are hereby, amended by striking out the word "white" wherever it occurs, so that in naturalization there shall be no distinction of race or color. . . .

Never till this moment has it been in my power to have a vote on a question which I deem of vital importance. I have here on my table at this moment letters from different States—from California, from Florida, from Virginia—all showing a considerable number of colored persons—shall I say of African blood?—aliens under our laws, who cannot be naturalized on account of that word "white."

Now, sir, there is a practical grievance which needs a remedy. This is the first time that I have been able to vote upon it, and I should be unworthy of my seat here if, because Senators rise and say they will vote it down on the ground that it is out [of] place, I should hesitate to persevere. Senators will vote as they please; I shall vote for it. . . . You are now revising the naturalization system, and I propose to strike out from that system a requirement disgraceful to this country and to this age. I propose to bring our system in harmony with the Declaration of Independence and the Constitution of the United States. The word "white" cannot be found in either of these two great title-deeds of this Republic. How can you place it in your statutes?

Source: Congressional Globe, 41st Congress, 2nd Session, pt. 6: 5121–5123.

RIOTS AGAINST THE CHINESE

The Chinese on the Pacific Coast were repeatedly attacked in the 1870s and 1880s. The pogrom in Los Angeles in 1871 described here was one of many in the West. Among the more infamous were occurrences in Truckee, California in 1876, Denver, Colorado in 1880, Rock Springs, Wyoming in 1885, and Log Cabin, Oregon in 1886.

RIOTING IN LOS ANGELES, 1871

One of the most horrible tragedies that ever disgraced any civilized community. . . . The denizens of Nigger Valley are cosmopolitan, consist of the dregs of society, some of the greatest desperadoes on the Pacific Coast. Murderers, horse-thieves, highwaymen, burglars . . . make this their rendezvous. In this place also the Chinese Congregate, monopolizing about two-thirds of an entire block . . .

The streets rattled with a deafening din. . . . The entire block was surrounded by an unbroken link of human devils, thirsting for revenge. Curses and loud denunciations of the whole "heathen" crew arose on all sides. . . . The yelling and cursing were frightful to hear. . . . Trembling, moaning, wounded Chinese were hauled from their hiding places; ropes quickly enriched their necks; they were dragged to the nearest improvised gallows. Three thus suffered in a cluster, to the end of a water spout. A large wagon close by had four victims hanging from its sides . . . Three others dangled from an awning . . . Five more were taken to the gateway and lynched . . . Hellish proceedings. . . . A little urchin, not over ten years old, was as active as anyone in doing the hanging. His childish voice sounded strange at that place, as he called aloud for more victims; a stranger and sadder sight still to see him lay his hands to the rope and help to haul them up. In the background a woman was looking on. . . . She loudly congratulated the lynchers on their diabolical work, and encouraged them to continue . . . Every nook, corner, chest, trunk, and drawer in Chinatown was carefully ransacked. Even the victims executed were robbed. The Chinese Doctor had his garments stripped from off his person while hanging; others had their pockets cut out with knives, which entered into and fearfully lacerated the flesh, the lynchers having neither time nor patience to rifle them in the usual way! . . . $6000 was extracted from a box in the Chinese store.

Source: New York Times, October 27, 1871.

THE CHINESE EXCLUSION ACT, 1882

Responding to sentiment against the Chinese, Congress held hearings on excluding them. Public opinion largely supported exclusion. Among opponents were Chinese themselves and abolitionists like William Lloyd Garrison, who believed that the denial of basic citizenship rights to long-settled American Chinese was suggestive of the racist injustice that had expressed itself in slavery. In 1882, the act passed. Its remarkably simple and straightforward language indicates perhaps that few felt any shame at treating the Chinese differently.

CONGRESSIONAL HEARINGS ON CHINESE IMMIGRATION: TESTIMONY IN FAVOR OF EXCLUDING THE CHINESE

Henry George, California State Inspector of Gas Meters, 1877

Question. I understand that the theory is advanced by those who are in favor of Chinese immigration that they are a great benefit to the State, and that our industries are carried on by them? . . . —Answer. I understand that theory is that if you get type set so much less a thousand, you produce a cheaper newspaper; if you get boots made at so much less, you produce cheaper boots; and if you raise and harvest wheat so much cheaper, you produce cheaper flour; so that Chinese labor is really a benefit to all classes in giving cheaper commodities. . . .

Q. What is your response to that argument?—A. I do not think that will hold water a minute. . . . Between a Chinaman working here cheaply and a Chinaman working cheaply in China, there is a very great difference. He can work as cheaply as he pleases in China, and, in my opinion, only benefit us if we exchange freely with him. Here he only injures us. If their race there works cheaply and exchanges with us, it really adds to our production. Here he affects the distribution of the product between the various classes by reducing the share which the laborer gets, and increasing the share of the capitalist.

Q. As this is a sort of political discussion, allow me to ask you if you do not get your theory mixed? Are you now proposing to protect American labor by excluding Chinese cheap labor?—A. That certainly would be my proposition.

Q. If you propose to protect American labor by excluding cheap Chinese labor, what is the difference in theory between excluding a cheap product in China that comes in contact with our own products?—A. The Chinaman by laboring in China cheaply does not affect the rate of wages here, that is, he does not affect the distribution of our production. If we ship a cargo of flour to China and get back a cargo of tea, the more tea we can get for our flour the better we are off—the greater is the aggregate sum that we have to divide among all classes; but when the Chinaman comes here and works for low wages the effect is to make a great many other men also work for low wages and to lessen the rate of wages that is given to the working classes. . . .

Q. You are acquainted with the working and mechanical population of San Francisco?—A. Yes, sir.

Q. How do our mechanics and laboring men, our operatives, live generally?—A. They do not live as well as they ought to live.

Q. Do not a great many of them live in their own houses?—A. A good many of them do. The number who do of course in proportion is gradually becoming less and less.

Q. They send their children to school, I presume?—A. O, yes; they all send their children to school.

Q. Has this influx of Chinese tended to degrade the dignity of labor?—A. Undoubtedly.

Q. Has it had a tendency to bring white labor into the same repute that slavery did in the Southern States?—A. I think its ultimate effects are precisely the same upon the white race as slavery. . . .

Q. Is there not a general distrust and perturbation among the mechanical portion of this community in relation to Chinese labor? Is it not held in terrorem over them by their employers that if they do not submit to their exactions as to price of labor, they will employ Chinese?—A. Yes, sir.

Q. That is a fact?—A. Yes, sir; I think that is one reason why some of the employers really favor Chinese immigration; it gives them a rod.

Q. So that they may subjugate the American or white laborers to their prices and demands?—A. Yes, sir; the effect is to break the power of trades unions and workingmen's combinations.

Source: Report of the Joint Special Committee to Investigate Chinese Immigration, 44th Congress, 2nd Session (Washington, 1877), 280–283.

Edward L. Cortage, Workingman, 1877

Question. What is your occupation?—Answer. My occupation is a working-man in a broom factory. . . .

Q. How many Chinese do you think there are employed on the coast in broom-making?—A. Somewhere between ninety and one hundred. I cannot exactly tell to a "t," but there is pretty nearly that amount, exclusively of Oregon. There are a few small factories. I do not know that they have one, two, or three, but they all have some Chinese.

Q. What is your opinion as to whether that industry can be carried on without the use of Chinese labor on this coast?—A. It can be carried on just as well without Chinese, because it has been carried on without [their labor] to the same full extent to what it is carried on now.

Q. Can we compete with the eastern manufacturers by white labor?—A. We have driven them out of this market by white labor.

Q. State anything else in connection with broom-manufacturing, so far as it is affected by Chinese labor, that occurs to you.—A. Gentlemen, I had no notion to come up here until yesterday at dinner-time I was invited to come. My object is not to run against the Chinamen. I am in favor of anybody making a living that possibly can, but I am a married man and have a family of four little children suffering here, and I would like to see them do something in the world. Years ago I could average $20 and $21 a week. . . . My average wages for the last week is $14.89. I put in about fourteen hours a day, including traveling backward and forward from Oakland. If the Chinaman has a mind to work for my firm he gets employment and I have to compete with him. He offers to work for about one-third less the price I am working for now. That would reduce my wages to a little above $9, not quite $10, and I think it is impossible to live on $10 a week in this country. . . . $10 a week for a family, a wife and four children, is hardly sufficient to live on. Rents in our days for white men are seldom less than $15 a month. If a man wants to live anywhere decently with three little rooms he has to pay that, and if he has a trifle of elbow-room to give his children he cannot live for less, unless he moves in the fourth story of a tenement, and then it will cost him $12 a month, where they all live together.

Q. So, the competition is in living? You could not afford to live like a Chinaman?—A. No, we could not, because a Chinaman is single and can live on 19 cents a day, at the same rate as our prisoners live in jail.

Q. You do not like a bare struggle for existence? You want some comforts for your family?—A. I do not talk particularly for comforts. I like to clothe them decently and give them an education. I have a tolerably good schooling, because I was instructed in the German language; but I want to learn my children something a little better than merely to be in competition with Chinamen, if they are capable.

Source: Ibid., 359–361.

Albert Winn, Bay Area Union Leader, 1877

Chinese immigration and cheap labor presents to our consideration a complicated question of political economy. It has two sides, each possessing the elements of discussion for every class of people. Most of the rich want cheap labor to carry on their shops and farms to the best advantage for an increase of profits; the poor cannot afford to compete with labor so far below the American standard of industry. This creates a conflict of opinion between the rich and the poor. . . .

Comparisons are often made as between the Chinese and other foreigners without taking into consideration that Chinese can never assimilate with our people, and will always be Chinamen; while from every other country the people delight in becoming American citizens, and their children are native Americans as much as those who descend from the revolutionary fathers. The free schools form their mind, while our contact with them in everyday life establishes their republican principles.

China can send her millions of men to this country who may become a Trojan horse in time of war with any power opposed to a republican form of government. I do not believe in underrating the skill and power of an enemy. With a few brave, energetic white men they would be a formidable army, when their prejudices are ripened into revenge. The cornered coward often exhibits astonishing courage; and it might be so with them.

Source: Ibid., 321–322.

CONGRESSIONAL HEARINGS ON CHINESE IMMIGRATION: TESTIMONY AGAINST EXCLUDING THE CHINESE

Frederick Bee, Congressman, 1876

The Chinese immigrant has been brought to our shores, opened up the riches of China to our merchant marine, dotted the ocean with our merchant ships, and maintained a line of steamships which is a pride to every American citizen. All these advantages we are willing to forego, and why? Because this great empire of boundless extent, whose shores are washed by two oceans, three thousand miles apart is invaded by 150,000 honest toilers. The great State of California, sufficient to support 10,000,000 people, is threatened with destruction because during a period of 24 years, 150,000 Chinese have come here and by willing industry have contributed largely to her present standing and wealth.

Let us see under what circumstances he comes and how he is received in this free and enlightened republic—the land of the free and oppressed. I regret exceedingly, Mr. Chairman and gentlemen, to bring to your attention scenes and acts which have transpired upon the streets of this city [San Francisco], which are a disgrace to any and all civilization. No country, no government, I undertake to say, on the face of God's footstool, has ever permitted indignities to be cast upon any race of people that the government and municipality of San Francisco and the State of California have permitted upon this class of people. I have seen, myself, one of the Pacific Mail steamships hauled into the docks here in this city, loaded, probably, with a thousand or fifteen hundred of these people. I have seen them loaded into express wagons to be taken to the Chinese quarter. What I say has been seen by thousands of our citizens. I have seen them stoned from the time they passed out of the ship, rocks thrown at them, until they reached Kearny street. I have seen them leaning over the sides of the wagons with their scalps cut open. I have seen them stoned when going afoot from the steamships. No arrests were made, no police interfered. I do not recollect, within my knowledge, (I may be wrong in an instance or two), of ever an arrest being made when these street hoodlums and Arabs attacked these people on their landing here. It does not stop there. There are portions of this city, and I say it with shame, where none of these people dare frequent. There are portions of the city of San Francisco where these Chinamen dare not visit. If they do so, they go in large numbers, and they must have large numbers; because one of these hoodlums will drive fifty of them. That is not an exaggeration. I am speaking of those who first landed here.

I say, and I say it with shame, that these people have no privileges. They do not seem to have extended to them the protection of the law in any particular. When a Chinaman lands upon this coast he seeks for work. He comes here a laborer. He comes here for the purpose of bettering his condition. He comes here a law-abiding citizen. We shall show upon investigation that the Chinese residents of this city and of the State of California compare favorably, and I think are the peer of any foreign population which comes here, in their appreciation of the laws and usage of the country.

Source: "Opening Argument of F. A. Bee before the Joint Committee of the Two Houses of Congress on Chinese Immigration," pamphlet (San Francisco, 1876).

Solomon Heydenfeldt, California Justice, 1877

Question. I should like to have you detail your information as to the facts, if any, since the Chinese advent to California.—Answer. I think California owes its prosperity to the industry of the Chinese who have come to this country. I think without them we would not have had our harbor filled with ships; we would not have had railroads crossing our mountains, and we would have been behind, probably, a great number of years. I think we would not have had as many white people here if the Chinese had not come.

Q. You think, then, that the Chinese who are among us have conduced to bring white people here and give white people homes and employment?—A. I do.

Q. As to the construction of this new railroad, the Southern Pacific, which is some 400 hundred miles in length, would that have been built but for the Chinese, in your opinion?—A. I think not; and I have been assured so by those who are interested in completing it.

Q. It has opened a vast new territory of farming land to the immigration of this State?—A. It has.

Q. Do you think that the benefits of the Chinese among us have been widespread?—A. I do.

Q. How do you look upon the Chinese, as a class, for honesty, integrity, &c.?—A. I think they are the best laboring class we have among us. . . .

Q. Do you think we have a surplus of labor in this State, either white or yellow?—A. No, sir; I think there is employment enough for everybody. . . .

Q. What is your opinion of the unrestricted immigration of the Chinese?—A. I will answer the question by stating in the first place that I am not in favor of the immigration of anybody to the United States. I think we have people enough for production and for progress. I am very much in favor of leaving some room for the descendants of the people we have; but if people will come we cannot help it; and if people will come I think it is as much to our advantage to have Chinese as any other people. . . .

Q. If immigration is to come, do you think there is no choice in the character of the immigration; in other words, are European families not better than the people who come from China?—A. Not a particle better.

Q. Do they assimilate with us soon?—A. Hardly. Give the Chinese a chance and I think they will assimilate with us.

Q. That chance would embrace the elective franchise.—A. Certainly.

Q. Would you be in favor of giving the franchise to the Chinese the same as to European immigrants?—A. Unquestionably. If the one is entitled to it I would give it to the other; and if the negro is entitled to it, I do not see why it should not be given to the Chinese.

Q. Then you regard the Chinaman as equal in all respects to the European immigrants?—A. I see no reason why he is not equal.

Q. Is the Chinaman equal in his civilization and morals?—A. In every respect. . . .

Q. The cry used to be "Would you have your daughter marry a negro?" I was going to ask you, in the same sense, would you have your daughter marry a Chinaman?—A. I do not see why the Chinese should not intermarry. I think if you will look at the question practically, as a question of providing for family by industry and frugality, and in regard to that kindness and consideration which is due a woman, that the Chinamen would make better husbands than usually fall to the lot of our poor girls.

Source: Report of the Joint Special Committee to Investigate Chinese Immigration, 44th Congress, 2nd Session (Washington, 1877), 504–506, 508.

Charles Peck, Teamster, 1877

Question. How long have you been in this country?—Answer. A little over 18 years.

Q. What is your occupation?—A. Drayman or teamster, whichever you please to call it; drayman, I suppose.

Q. What class of people do you do business for principally?—A. With the Chinese almost exclusively. We, however, do other work if we are called upon. . . .

Q. How have you found them as to their honesty and integrity in dealing with them?—A. We have found them very honest; indeed I may say strictly honest. I do not know that we ever lost anything by them. . . .

Q. Have you an extensive acquaintance among the draymen and laboring classes, the white people you are brought in contact with?—A. I have.

Q. What is their opinion in reference to Chinese immigration?—A. The general opinion seems to be that the Chinese have been beneficial to the State, and that what is here is well enough; but they think there should be some measures taken perhaps to limit the immigration in the future; some think so and some do not. Some think that the immigration will be according to supply and demand. . . . If more came, that is if the Chinese population should increase in a certain ratio with the white population, it would be beneficial to the State and country.

Q. Suppose they did not increase with the ratio of white people, then how would it be?—A. I do not know that I am capable of judging.

Q. From your experience of what we have had here, with a population of seven hundred or eight hundred thousand white people at the present time, which is about the population of the State, suppose that we had a population of 1,200,000 people, could we endure another 50,000 Chinese?—A. I think we could. . . .

Q. Do you think there is a very large element here opposed to Chinese immigration?—A. There is a certain class; I do not think it is a very large element.

Q. From your observation, who are that class; what are they composed of?—A. The laboring classes. . . .

Source: Ibid., 728–731.

Reverend John Francis, 1877

Question. You have been in charge of the mission-schools here?—Answer. Yes, sir. . . .

Q. Will you state, from your intercourse with the Chinese, what is their general character?—A. I find the Chinese to be just like other people. I cannot perceive any difference at all. When we bring religious truths to bear upon them they appreciate and exemplify religious principles just like other people. I have been to some extent connected with almost all nationalities in both hemispheres; I hold the office of a minister, and I am not able to point out any differences between a

Chinese and other nationalities, Welsh, Irish, Scotch, &c. When I bring the truth to bear upon their intellects and hearts, the effect is alike.

Q. What is their general character as members of society?—A. All our young men with whom we have been connected have proved themselves, with very few exceptions, to be honorable, just, reasonable, and honest in their character and in their dealings with us. A number of them are in different occupations in the city, photograph galleries, and other occupations. I find there is a demand for our young men, and we are not able to supply that demand. I think the same is felt by other missions. Our Christian community, our converts, are in demand. The people want them in their service and in their employ. . . .

Q. Would not your work be facilitated to a great extent if the Chinese were permitted to attend our schools and get an English education?—A. Certainly; it would take away a great deal of labor that we are now obliged to perform. We could instruct them in the Christian religion at once, if they were to come prepared to read the scriptures, and it would save a great deal of time. I must say that it is amazing to me that in this Christian America (I am a British subject) the privileges of education are not secured to all alike.

Source: Ibid., 484–488.

THE CHINESE VIEW: CHUNG WAI HSIN PAO

But suppose we admit that the party favoring Chinese immigration in California is largely in the minority! . . .

Congress cannot and will not, throw aside the testimony obtained by the Congressional Commission of Inquiry of 1876, by which your charges and allegations were utterly disproved. Men of unimpeachable character, high standing in the community, holding positions of trust, having large interests at stake, ministers of the gospel, missionaries, judges, lawyers and merchants in large number, who have resided in California ten, twenty, and thirty years, who have had intercourse with the Chinese most of their time, spoke of facts that came under their actual observation, and affirmed their truth under oath; a testimony of eyewitnesses, so emphatic, so unexceptionable is altogether invincible. The anti-Chinese testimony, on the contrary, was conspicuous for its glaring contradictions and the paucity of its high-order witnesses, few of whom could claim a long residence in the State and large commercial transactions with the Chinese. Police officers, detectives, laborers, reporters of newspapers made up in large measure, the number of those who testified against the Chinese. . . .

But we wish to press this matter still further. If, as you affirm, the people of California are practically a unit on this question, or, if your former testimony taken by the Congressional Committee is unassailable, what need was there of strengthening your position by holding another inquiry into the Chinese question through the friendly services of the Congressional Committee on Labor during a most exciting State canvass? And why were you so afraid to admit the pro-

Chinese testimony. . . . It is for you to reconcile this action with your boastful declaration that the people of California are unanimously and unalterably opposed to Chinese immigration.

We too sympathize with the white workingman who suffers poverty from crushing opposition or even competition. If, therefore, it were true that the presence of the Chinese in California is a block to the prosperous advancement of our working-classes, we would not raise our voice against this unchristian and inhuman crusade. But it is not. . . .

And shall a class of industrious emigrants, who have assisted in creating new industries, in building railroads, reclaiming swamp lands, opening new agricultural districts, be excluded from our country, driven from cities and towns, as they now propose to do in California, in conformity with Article XIX of the New Constitution, regardless of the existing treaty with China? Who are they that make this infamous demand? For the greater part they are foreigners, a large number of whom came but yesterday from a land of oppression, in abject poverty and ignorance; who have been endowed with political rights and privileges by the excessive magnanimity of the American Government. Yet, incredible as it may appear, they are so selfish, so ungrateful, so insolent, as to demand from the same beneficent government, that it shall refuse to the Chinese even a small share of that hospitality which has been liberally accorded to them; and without stopping to reflect that this is a national question, on which the voice of the other States must also be heard.

Source: Chung Wai Hsin Pao, "The Pro-Chinese Minority of California: To the American People, President and Congress. Reply to Governor Irwin's Circular Regarding the Vote of California Against Chinese Immigration," broadside (San Francisco, 1879).

WILLIAM LLOYD GARRISON, "LETTER TO THE EDITOR," 1879

Whatever inevitably tends to the subversion of the fundamental principles of this Government as set forth in the Declaration of Independence and the Constitution of the United States, or is sure to add a fresh stain of caste proscription to the many that have sullied our National character, should at once arrest the attention, and in some form elicit the indignant protest, of every lover of his country, every friend of the whole human race; for

"He who allows oppression shares the crime."

A case strikingly in point is pending at this hour in the passage of an act through Congress, summarily abrogating our present equitable and advantageous treaty with China, and forbidding under pains and penalties any vessel from bringing to these shores, at one time, more than fifteen Chinese, whether as visitors or immigrants, whether the most cultured or the most ignorant. . . .

Really, it is difficult in this case which is the greater, its absurdity or injustice. We have allowed all other peoples to take up their abode with us, notwithstanding their ignorance, destitution, unfortunate training, and difference of race;

and they have come by the million—Englishmen, Irishmen, Scotchmen, Frenchmen, Germans, Scandinavians, Italians, Africans, etc., etc.; so that in the aggregate they constitute a formidable portion of the population. We must either drive out these, or keep any more of them [from] seeking a refuge here, or else keep the barrier down and let the Chinese find an equal entrance, and be protected in the enjoyment of equal rights and privileges. . . .

The debate on the question of Chinese immigration in the United States Senate yesterday—to judge from the report of it in this morning's journals—was, with one or two honorable exceptions, most disgraceful to all who participated in it, and displayed a demogogical, partisan rivalry between Republican and Democratic Senators as to who should the most strongly cater to the brutal, persecuting spirit which for the time being is so rampant in California under the leadership of that most ignorant, profane, strike-engendering and besotted declaimer Denis Kearney—himself a foreigner, or of foreign descent, and much more entitled to be in a lunatic asylum than running at large. . . .

This is the spirit of caste; black versus white. It is essentially the same everywhere—vulgar, conceited and contemptible.

Source: New York Tribune, February 15, 1879.

THE CHINESE EXCLUSION ACT, MAY 6, 1882

Be it enacted. &c., That from and after the expiration of ninety days next after passage of this act, and until the expiration of ten years next after the passage of this act, the coming of Chinese laborers to the United States be, and the same is hereby suspended; and during such suspension it shall not be lawful for any Chinese laborer to come, or having so come after the expiration of said ninety days, to remain within the United States.

Sec. 2. That any master of any vessel, of whatever nationality, who shall knowingly on such vessel bring within the jurisdiction of the United States, and permit to be landed, any Chinese laborer from any foreign port or place shall be deemed guilty of a misdemeanor, and on conviction thereof shall be punished by a fine of not more than $500 for each and every such Chinese laborer so brought, and may be also imprisoned for a term not exceeding one year.

Sec. 4. That in order to the faithful execution articles 1 and 2 of the treaty of the United States and the Empire of China ratified July 19, 1881, in case any Chinese residing in the United States on the 17th day of November 1880, or shall have come into the same before the expiration of ninety days next after the passage of this act, shall depart therefrom, they shall, before such departure, cause themselves to be duly registered at a custom-house in the United States, and produce to the collector of the district at which they shall seek to re-enter the United States the certificate of such registration properly vised by the indorsement of the proper diplomatic representatives or consul of the United States as required in cases of passports by the fifth section of this act.

Sec. 16. That hereafter no State court or court of the United States shall admit Chinese to citizenship; and all laws in conflict with this act are hereby repealed.

Sec. 17. That the words "Chinese laborers," wherever used in this act, shall be construed to mean both skilled and unskilled laborers and Chinese employed in mining.

Source: U.S., *Statutes at Large*, 22: 58.

THE GEARY BILL AND ITS OPPONENTS, 1892

For over a century historians, social scientists, and policymakers have argued about why the Chinese did not assimilate into American society as other immigrant groups had. In the 1960s, many families that had passed six generations in the United States still spoke only Chinese in the home. Was this a product of Chinese culture or of the treatment Chinese had received when they arrived? Using comparisons with the assimilation of nineteenth-century Chinese in the more culturally tolerant countries of South America, Bernard Wong levels blame at the exclusion acts. According to Wong, the exclusion acts forced the Chinese into a separate history. In opposition was the Chinese Equal Rights League, formed in New York City in direct response to the exclusion acts.

THE GEARY BILL, MAY 5, 1892

Mr. GEARY. Mr. Speaker, I move to suspend the rules and pass the bill (H.R. 6185) to absolutely prohibit the coming of Chinese persons into the United States.

The SPEAKER. The bill will be read.

Be it enacted, etc. That from and after the passage of this act it shall be unlawful for any Chinese person or persons, whether subjects of the Chinese Empire or otherwise, as well those who are now within the limits of the United States, and those who may hereafter leave the United States and attempt to return as those who have never been here, or having been here, have departed from the United States (save and excepting only the following classes, that is to say: Such Chinese person or persons as may be duly accredited to the Government of the United States as minister plenipotentiary or other diplomatic representatives, consuls-general, consular and commercial agents, including other officers of the Chinese or other governments traveling upon the business of that Government, with their body and household servants), to come to or within, or to land at any port or place within the United States; and the coming of Chinese persons of the United States, whether for the purpose of transit only or otherwise, excepting the classes hereinbefore specifically described and excepted from and after the passage of this act, be, and the same is hereby, prohibited. . . .

Sec. 7. That any Chinese person, or persons of Chinese descent, entering the United States or any of its Territories by crossing its boundary lines, or entering therein in any other manner whatever contrary to the provisions of this act, or found unlawfully in the United States or its Territories, may be arrested . . . , and when convicted upon a hearing, and found and adjudged to be one not lawfully entitled to be or remain in the United States, such person shall be imprisoned in a penitentiary for a term of not exceeding five years, and at the expiration of such term of imprisonment be removed from the United States to the country from whence he came: Provided, That when Chinese persons found unlawfully in the United States shall have come into the United States from China by way of contiguous foreign territory they shall be returned to China. . . .

Sec. 12. That it shall be the duty of all Chinese persons within the limits of the United States, at the time of the passage of this act, to apply to the commissioner of internal revenue of their respective districts within one year after the passage of this act for a certificate of residence, and any Chinese person . . . who shall fail or refuse to comply with the provisions of this act, or who, within one year after the passage hereof, shall be found without such certificate of residence, shall be adjudged by the court before whom he may be brought as being unlawfully within the limits of the United States and subject to the same fines and penalties as though he had unlawfully come into the United States in the first instance.

Source: Congressional Record, February 18, 1892, vol. 23, 52nd Congress, 1st Session, 2911.

New York Chinese Fight the Geary Bill

To the American People, Friends of Humanity: —

We, the members of the Chinese Equal Rights League in the United States, who have adopted this country and its customs in the main, are at this moment engaged in a perilous struggle in which our dearest rights as men and residents are involved. Doubtless the reading public is acquainted with the fact that during the last session of the Fifty-second Congress, a Bill was passed, styled the "Geary Bill" or "Chinese Registration Act," in which the attempt is made to humiliate every Chinaman, regardless of his moral, intellectual and material standing in the community, neither his long residence in the country is considered. This mean and unjust Act discriminating between foreign residents from different countries has traversed and contraversed the fundamental principles of common law.

As residents of the United States we claim a common manhood with all other nationalities, and believe we should have that manhood recognized according to the principles of common humanity and American freedom. This monstrous and inhuman measure is a blot upon the civilization of the Western World, and is destined to retard the progress already made by the good people of this country in the East in art, science, commerce and religion.

We appeal to the humane, liberty-loving sentiment of the American people, who are lovers of equal rights and even-handed justice, a people from who sprung such illustrious characters as Washington, Jefferson, Clay, Sumner, lastly Lincoln, the citizen of the world, the friend of humanity and the champion of freedom: such illustrious warriors as Sherman, Sheridan, Logan and Grant, whose deeds of valor in the cause of freedom are to be seen in the grand march of American development—a development which merits the emulation of the nations of the earth. Must this growth be retarded simply on account of the doings of a misguided element who have suffered their feelings to control reason, encouraging a prejudice fiendish in its nature and purpose against a class of people who are industrious, law-abiding and honest? Can there be found a more inoffensive class in the body politic? not that we are cowards, but because we believe that mildness and simplicity should be the controling element in the character of a great man as well as in a great race of people. We have and are still paying our portion of government taxation, thereby assisting in supporting the Government, and thereby sharing an equal part in the support of the nation.

We, therefore, appeal for an equal chance in the race of life in this our adopted home—a large number of us have spent almost our entire lives in this country and claim no other but this as ours. Our motto is *"Character and fitness should be the requirement of all who are desirous of becoming citizens of the American Republic."*

. . . Our interest is here, because our homes, our families and our all are here. America is our home through long residence. Why, then, should we not consider your welfare ours? Chinese immigration, as well as Irish, Italian and other immigration, cannot be stopped by the persecution of our law-abiding citizens in the United States.

Treat us as men, and we will do our duty as men, and will aid you to stop this obnoxious evil that threatens the welfare of this Republic. We do not want any more Chinese here than you do. The scarcer the Chinese here, the better would be our conditions among you.

Source: "Appeal of the Chinese Equal Rights League to the People of the United States for Equality of Manhood," pamphlet (New York: Chinese Equal Rights League, 1892), 2.

Among supporters of the Chinese were the Industrial Workers of the World, often called the Wobblies. Known for their militant strikes and industrial sabotage along the Pacific Coast from Chile to Canada, the Wobblies believed that Asians could be organized into unions like other workers in the West.

THE WOBBLIES DEFEND THE CHINESE AND JAPANESE WORKER, 1908

The Oriental exclusion question has received so much attention and caused us so much discussion, especially on the Pacific coast, that it is well for us to look for the cause of all this agitation.

So far as is known, the Industrial Workers of the World is the only organization that has ever done any organizing among the Japanese and Chinese in this country. . . . The Japanese and Chinese can be organized as rapidly as any other nationality, and when once pledged to stand with you, no fear or doubt need to be entertained as to them, during labor trouble. But some one will say, Why organize them when we can keep them out of this country? The workers cannot keep them out, because the working class does not compose the organized or dominant part of society. The organized part of society that controls today is the employing class, and it is at their will and desire that exclusion or admittance will be regulated. . . .

EXCLUSION IS IN THE INTEREST OF THE MIDDLE CLASS.

At this point let us see why all this agitation. The greater number of the Orientals that have been coming to this country for some time are small business men. In fact, they are pretty much the "Jew Merchant" of the Orient, and when they enter the business field, their shrewdness, coupled with their keen perception of criminal commercialism, spells ruin to all competitors. The little American cock-roacher sees the handwriting on the wall. I have not the space here to quote the many instances repeatedly published by the capitalist papers as to the closing of a "Jap" restaurant because of its being so filthy, etc.; of the "pure food inspector" finding the milk diluted, etc., etc. But the truth of all this is the shifting economic position of the little bourgeois American who secures this persecution in behalf of his own material interest. But the Japanese soon learn this, and then they become equal to the occasion. These people are entering every business of the middle class, and our little American cock-roach merchant sees his finish, unless he can create some disturbance of some kind, and thereby drag the working class into a middle-class fight. This dodge has been worked on the wage slaves many times by the bourgeois, but it remains to be seen whether the dastardly trick can be turned by this dying class in the twentieth century. . . .

We of the Industrial Workers of the World have organized Japanese and Chinese, and the United Mine Workers of America have organized Japanese in the coal fields of Wyoming. This is proof that they can be organized. . . .

Source: J. H. Walsh, "Japanese and Chinese Exclusion or Industrial Organization?" *Industrial Union Bulletin*, April 11, 1908.

Chapter 4

DAM HETCH HETCHY?

Before the late nineteenth century, few Americans worried about conserving natural resources or preserving wilderness areas. European settlers of the United States thought of how to find the labor, the capital, and the technology to exploit the seemingly inexhaustible natural resources of the continent. Wilderness, visualized as forest or mountain or animals or native Americans, was something to overcome, push back, civilize. When Henry David Thoreau moved to the semi-wilderness of Walden Pond in 1845, only a few close friends were interested: few others read the book he wrote or attended the lectures he delivered on his experience.

Toward the end of the nineteenth century, however, the massive impact of industrialism awakened both a practical concern about the exhaustion of critical resources such as lumber, soil, and water and a determination on romantic or aesthetic grounds to preserve remaining wilderness in its purity and beauty. Although deeply attached to the idea of nature itself as a testing ground for "the strenuous life," as a political leader Theodore Roosevelt emphasized the harder logic of conservation of natural resources not so that they could be kept forever in their pristine form but so that American industry could carefully and rationally exploit them. He made conservation a national movement, establishing by presidential decrees national parks, wildlife refuges, and monuments, setting aside hundreds of millions of acres as national forests and nationally controlled mineral lands, and putting federal land and water policy on a solid and coherent basis. In thus conserving natural resources, Roosevelt also preserved many wilderness areas. That preservation as an act of respect for nature differed from conservation for the sake of use. That the two motives could even come into direct conflict with each other became apparent in the controversy over the proposed damming of the Hetch Hetchy Valley.

Fresh water had always been in short supply in San Francisco, and the city's leaders had long dreamed of flooding the nearby Hetch Hetchy Valley by damming the Tuolumne River to provide water and hydroelectric power for the city. But the act creating Yosemite National Park had included the Hetch Hetchy Valley within its borders. San Francisco's case for the watershed languished until the great earthquake of 1906 publicized the city's water shortage and engendered national sympathy for its plight. In May 1908, the secretary of the interior approved the city's application for the flooding of Hetch Hetchy. This initiated a five-year controversy that educated a national audience in the finer points of wilderness preservation and divided old allies in the conservation movement.

THEODORE ROOSEVELT
CHAMPIONS CONSERVATION

Roosevelt in his public pronouncements stressed the utility of conservation while attempting as well to preserve wilderness areas for their inherent virtues.

THEODORE ROOSEVELT, FIRST ANNUAL MESSAGE TO CONGRESS, DECEMBER 3, 1901

Public opinion throughout the United States has moved steadily toward a just appreciation of the value of forests, whether planted or of natural growth. The great part played by them in the creation and maintenance of the national wealth is now more fully realized than ever before.

Wise forest protection does not mean the withdrawal of forest resources, whether of wood, water, or grass, from contributing their full share to the welfare of the people, but, on the contrary, gives the assurance of larger and more certain supplies. The fundamental idea of forestry is the perpetuation of forests by use. Forest protection is not an end of itself; it is a means to increase and sustain the resources of our country and the industries which depend upon them. The preservation of our forests is an imperative business necessity. We have come to see clearly that whatever destroys the forest, except to make way for agriculture, threatens our well-being.

The practical usefulness of the national forest reserves to the mining, grazing, irrigation, and other interests of the regions in which the reserves lie has led to a widespread demand by the people of the West for their protection and extension. The forest reserves will inevitably be of still greater use in the future than in the past. Additions should be made to them whenever practicable, and their usefulness should be increased by a thoroughly businesslike management. . . .

The wise administration of the forest reserves will be not less helpful to the interests which depend on water than to those which depend on wood and grass. The water supply itself depends upon the forest. In the arid region it is water, not land, which measures production. The western half of the United States would sustain a population greater than that of our whole country today if the waters that now run to waste were saved and used for irrigation. The forest and water problems are perhaps the most vital internal questions of the United States.

Certain of the forest reserves should also be made preserves for the wild forest creatures. All of the reserves should be better protected from fires. Many of them need special protection because of the great injury done by livestock, above all by sheep. The increase in deer, elk, and other animals in the Yellowstone Park shows what may be expected when other mountain forests are properly protected by law and properly guarded. Some of these areas have been so denuded of surface vegetation by overgrazing that the ground breeding birds, including grouse and quail, and many mammals, including deer, have been exterminated or driven away. At the same time the water-storing capacity of the surface has been decreased or destroyed, thus promoting floods in times of rain and diminishing the flow of streams between rains.

In cases where natural conditions have been restored for a few years, vegetation has again carpeted the ground, birds and deer are coming back, and hundreds of persons, especially from the immediate neighborhood, come each summer to enjoy the privilege of camping. Some at least of the forest reserves should afford perpetual protection to the native fauna and flora, safe havens of refuge to our rapidly diminishing wild animals of the larger kinds, and free camping grounds for the ever-increasing numbers of men and women who have learned to find rest, health, and recreation in the splendid forests and flower-clad meadows of our mountains. The forest reserves should be set apart forever for the use and benefit of our people as a whole and not sacrificed to the shortsighted greed of a few.

The forests are natural reservoirs. By restraining the streams in flood and replenishing them in drought they make possible the use of waters otherwise wasted. They prevent the soil from washing, and so protect the storage reservoirs from filling up with silt. Forest conservation is therefore an essential condition of water conservation.

The forests alone cannot, however, fully regulate and conserve the waters of the arid region. Great storage works are necessary to equalize the flow of streams and to save the flood waters. Their construction has been conclusively shown to be an undertaking too vast for private effort. Nor can it be best accomplished by the individual states acting alone. Far-reaching interstate problems are involved; and the resources of single states would often be inadequate. It is properly a national function, at least in some of its features. It is as right for the national government to make the streams and rivers of the arid region useful by engineering works for water storage as to make useful the rivers and harbors of the humid region by engineering works of another kind. The storing of the floods in reservoirs at the headwaters of our rivers is but an enlargement of our present policy of river control, under which levees are built on the lower reaches of the same streams.

The government should construct and maintain these reservoirs as it does other public works. Where their purpose is to regulate the flow of streams, the water should be turned freely into the channels in the dry season to take the same course under the same laws as the natural flow.

Source: James D. Richardson, *A Compilation of the Messages and Papers of the Presidents, 1789–1908* (Washington: Bureau of National Literature and Art, 1908), X: 431–434.

JOHN MUIR DESCRIBES HETCH HETCHY

John Muir once characterized himself as a "poetico-trampo-geologist-bot. and ornith-natural, etc.!—!—!—!." Born in Scotland in 1838, he had moved with his family to frontier Wisconsin in 1849. The wilderness his family labored to destroy he preferred to the civilization they were carving out of it. Muir spent two eye-opening years at the University of Wisconsin learning about the natural world and abandoning his family's Calvinist religion before leaving for what he called "the University of the Wilderness." His first semester there was a thousand-mile hike to the Gulf of Mexico. Then, sailing to San Francisco, he headed out of town toward "any place that is wild," eventually camping year round in the Yosemite Valley, which inspired his most important writings and his most famous political battle.

JOHN MUIR, THE ENDANGERED VALLEY:
THE HETCH-HETCHY VALLEY IN THE YOSEMITE NATIONAL PARK

The fame of the Merced Yosemite has spread far and wide, while Hetch-Hetchy, the Tuolumne Yosemite, has until recently remained comparatively unknown, notwithstanding it is a wonderfully exact counterpart of the famous valley. As the Merced [River] flows in tranquil beauty through Yosemite, so does the Tuolumne through Hetch-Hetchy. The floor of Yosemite is about 4,000 feet above the sea, and that of Hetch-Hetchy about 3,700, while in both the walls are of gray granite, very high, and rise precipitously out of flowery gardens and groves. Furthermore, the two wonderful valleys occupy the same relative positions on the flank of the Sierra, were formed by the same forces in the same kind of granite, and have similar waterfalls, sculpture, and vegetation. Hetch-Hetchy lies in a northwesterly direction from Yosemite at a distance of about eighteen miles, and is now easily accessible by a trail and wagon-road from the Big Oak Flat road at Sequoia.

The most strikingly picturesque rock in the valley is a majestic pyramid over 2,000 feet in height which is called by the Indians "Kolana." It is the outermost of a group like the Cathedral Rocks of Yosemite and occupies the same relative position on the south wall. Facing Kolana on the north side of the valley there is a massive sheer rock like the Yosemite El Capitan about 1,900 feet high, and over its brow flows a stream that makes the most beautiful fall I have ever seen. The Indian name for it is "Tueeulala." From the edge of the cliff it is perfectly free in the air for a thousand feet, then breaks up into a ragged sheet of cascades among the boulders of an earthquake talus. It is in all its glory in June, when the snow is melting fast, but fades and vanishes toward the end of summer. The only fall I know with which it may fairly be compared is the Yosemite Bridal Veil; but it excels even that favorite fall both in height and fineness of fairy airy beauty and behavior. Lowlanders are apt to suppose that mountain streams in their wild career over cliffs lose control of themselves and tumble in a noisy chaos of mist and spray. On the contrary, on no part of their travels are they more harmonious and self-controlled. Imagine yourself in Hetch-Hetchy on a sunny day in June, standing waist-deep in grass and flowers (as I have oftentimes stood), while the great pines sway dreamily with scarce perceptible motion. Looking northward across the valley you see a plain gray granite cliff rising abruptly out of the gardens and groves to a height of 1,800 feet, and in front of it Tueeulala's silvery scarf burning with irised sun-fire in every fiber. Approaching the brink of the rock, her waters flow swiftly, and in the first white outburst of the stream at the head of the fall there is abundance of visible energy, but it is speedily hushed and concealed in divine repose; and its tranquil progress to the base of the cliff is like that of downy feathers in a still room. Now observe the fineness and marvelous distinctness of the various sun-illumined fabrics into which the water is woven: they sift and float from form to form down the face of that grand rock. . . . Near the head of the fall you see groups of booming comet-like masses, their solid white heads separate, their tails like combed silk interlacing among delicate shadows, ever forming and dissolving, worn out by friction in their rush through the air. Most of these vanish a few hundred feet below the summit, changing to the varied forms of cloudlike drapery. Near the bottom the width of the fall has increased from about twenty-five to a hundred feet, and is composed of yet finer tissue, fold over fold—air, water, and sunbeams woven into irised robes that spirits might wear. . . .

The floor of the valley is about three and a half miles long, half a mile wide, and is partly separated by a bar of glacier-polished granite across which the river breaks in rapids. The lower part is mostly a grassy, flowery meadow, with the trees confined to the sides and the river-banks. The upper forested part is charmingly diversified with groves of the large and picturesque California live-oak, and the noble yellow pine, which here attains a height of more than two hundred feet, growing well apart in small groves or singly, allowing each tree to be seen in all its beauty and grandeur. . . .

Dam Hetch-Hetchy! As well dam for water-tanks the people's cathedrals and churches, for no holier temple has ever been consecrated by the heart of man.

Source: "Let Everyone Help to Save the Famous Hetch-Hetchy Valley," pamphlet (np: November 1909).

CORRESPONDENCE BETWEEN JOHN MUIR AND THEODORE ROOSEVELT

Roosevelt found the Hetch Hetchy issue "one of those cases where I was extremely doubtful." Muir and other friends opposed the dam, but Roosevelt's closest advisors on environmental issues, chief forester and close friend Gifford Pinchot and Secretary of the Interior James R. Garfield,

*favored the city's application as "the highest use to which [the] water
. . . can be put." Roosevelt vacillated on the issue, but in his eighth annual message in December 1908 he asserted that Yosemite, like Yellowstone, "should be a great national playground. . . . All wild things should
be protected and the scenery kept wholly unmarred."*

MUIR TO ROOSEVELT, APRIL 21, 1907

To Theodore Roosevelt

April 21, 1907

DEAR MR. PRESIDENT:

I am anxious that the Yosemite National Park may be saved from all sorts of
commercialism and marks of man's work other than the roads, hotels, etc., required to make its wonders and blessings available. For as far as I have seen there
is not in all the wonderful Sierra, or indeed in the world, another so grand and
wonderful and useful a block of Nature's mountain handiwork.

There is now under consideration, as doubtless you well know, an application of San Francisco supervisors for the use of the Hetch-Hetchy Valley and
Lake Eleanor as storage reservoirs for a city water supply. This application
should, I think, be denied, especially the Hetch-Hetchy part, for this Valley, as
you will see by the inclosed description, is a counterpart of Yosemite, and one of
the most sublime and beautiful and important features of the Park, and to dam and
submerge it would be hardly less destructive and deplorable in its effect on the
Park in general than would be the damming of Yosemite itself. For its falls and
groves and delightful camp-grounds are surpassed or equaled only in Yosemite,
and furthermore it is the hall of entrance to the grand Tuolumne Cañon, which
opens a wonderful way to the magnificent Tuolumne Meadows, the focus of pleasure travel in the Park and the grand central camp-ground. If Hetch-Hetchy
should be submerged, as proposed, to a depth of one hundred and seventy-five
feet, not only would the Meadows be made utterly inaccessible along the
Tuolumne, but this glorious cañon way to the High Sierra would be blocked.

I am heartily in favor of a Sierra or even a Tuolumne water supply for San
Francisco, but all the water required can be obtained from sources outside the
Park, leaving the twin valleys, Hetch-Hetchy and Yosemite, to the use they were
intended for when the Park was established. For every argument advanced for
making one into a reservoir would apply with equal force to the other, excepting
the cost of the required dam.

The few promoters of the present scheme are not unknown around the
boundaries of the Park, for some of them have been trying to break through for
years. However able they may be as capitalists, engineers, lawyers, or even philanthropists, none of the statements they have made descriptive of Hetch-Hetchy
dammed or undammed is true, but they all show forth the proud sort of confidence that comes of a good, sound, substantial, irrefragable ignorance.

For example, the capitalist Mr. James D. Phelan says, "There are a thousand places in the Sierra equally as beautiful as Hetch-Hetchy: it is inaccessible nine months of the year, and is an unlivable place the other three months because of mosquitoes." On the contrary, there is not another of its kind in all the Park excepting Yosemite. It is accessible all the year, and is not more mosquitoful than Yosemite. "The conversion of Hetch-Hetchy into a reservoir will simply mean a lake instead of a meadow." But Hetch-Hetchy is not a meadow: it is a Yosemite Valley. . . . These sacred mountain temples are the holiest ground that the heart of man has consecrated, and it behooves us all faithfully to do our part in seeing that our wild mountain parks are passed on unspoiled to those who come after us, for they are national properties in which every man has a right and interest.

I pray therefore that the people of California be granted time to be heard before this reservoir question is decided, for I believe that as soon as light is cast upon it, nine tenths or more of even the citizens of San Francisco would be opposed to it. And what the public opinion of the world would be may be guessed by the case of the Niagara Falls.

Faithfully and devotedly yours

JOHN MUIR

O for a tranquil camp hour with you like those beneath the sequoias in memorable 1903!

Source: William F. Bade, *The Life and Letters of John Muir* (Boston: Houghton Mifflin, 1924), II: 417–420.

ROOSEVELT TO MUIR, SEPTEMBER 16, 1907

Roosevelt MSS.

TO JOHN MUIR

September 16, 1907

My dear Mr. Muir: I gather that Garfield and Pinchot are rather favorable to the Hetch Hetchy plan, but not definitely so. I have sent them your letter with a request for a report upon it. I will do everything in my power to protect not only the Yosemite, which we have already protected, but other similar great natural beauties of this country; but you must remember that it is out of the question permanently to protect them unless we have a certain degree of friendliness toward them on the part of the people of the State in which they are situated; and if they are used so as to interfere with the permanent material development of the State instead of helping the permanent material development, the result will be bad. I would not have any difficulty at all if, as you say, nine tenths of the citizens took ground against the Hetch Hetchy project; but so far everyone . . . has been for it and I have been in the disagreeable position of seeming to interfere with the development of the State for the sake of keeping a valley, which apparently hardly anyone wanted to have kept, under national control.

I wish I could see you in person; and how I do wish I were again with you camping out under those great sequoias or under the silver firs.

Faithfully yours

THEODORE ROOSEVELT

Source: Elting Morison et al., eds., *The Letters of Theodore Roosevelt* (Cambridge: Harvard University Press, 1952), V: 793.

LOBBYING AGAINST THE DAM

For five years until the final decision in 1913, Muir and his allies led the first major lobbying effort on an environmental issue. The Department of the Interior and its San Francisco allies responded with an engineering report, publicity of their own, and quiet but effective lobbying in Congress and in the executive branch.

LOBBYING EFFORTS TO SAVE HETCH HETCHY

"HOW TO HELP TO PRESERVE THE HETCH-HETCHY VALLEY AND THE YOSEMITE PARK"

1. Write at once to Hon. Richard A. Ballinger, Secretary of the Interior, Washington, D.C., requesting him to revoke the Garfield permit to flood the Hetch-Hetchy Valley.

2. Send a copy of the letter to President William H. Taft.

3. See personally if possible, or write to, the Senators and Congressmen from your State, and as many others as you can reach, requesting them to vigorously oppose any bill having for its object the confirmation of the Garfield permit to flood Hetch-Hetchy Valley, and request them to favor legislation designed to protect our parks from invasion, and particularly to favor improving the Yosemite Park. After December 1, 1909, address them either "Senate Chamber" or "House of Representatives," Washington, D.C.

4. After December 1st write to each member of the Public Lands Committees of both the Senate and the House, Washington, D.C., requesting them to oppose any and all legislation having for its object the destruction of the Hetch-Hetchy Valley and to favor any legislation designed to protect the parks. Write to all if you can, but if you cannot, at least write to the Chairman of each committee. (The names of the members of the committees will be found on the opposite page.)

5. Get as many of your friends as possible to write. Remember! every letter and every protest counts.

6. Interest your newspapers and get them to publish editorials and news items and send copies to your Senators and Representatives.

7. Send the names and addresses of any persons who would be interested in receiving this pamphlet to "Society for the Preservation of National Parks, 302 Mills Building, San Francisco, Cal."

EDITORS are respectfully requested to write brief editorials and news items informing the public and calling on them to write to their Congressmen and Senators and protest.

CLUBS should send copies of resolutions they may adopt to President Taft, Secretary Ballinger, and each member of the Public Lands Committees, and the Senators and Representatives from their State.

FUNDS ARE NEEDED to carry on this fight. A few have generously carried the burden of expense connected with the issuance of this literature, but more money is required to spread information. Those who would like to render pecuniary assistance may send their contributions to JOHN MUIR, President of Society for the Preservation of National Parks, 302 MILLS BUILDING, SAN FRANCISCO, CAL.

WHERE TO OBTAIN INFORMATION CONCERNING THE PROPOSED UNNECESSARY
DESTRUCTION OF THE FINEST HALF OF THE
YOSEMITE NATIONAL PARK.

[List of articles]

[List of members of Public Lands Committees
in Senate and House of Representatives]

It is particularly urgent that you impress the members of the Public Lands Committees from your State with the importance of *opposing* any bill granting the Hetch-Hetchy Valley to San Francisco. See them personally if possible, write to them and send resolutions to them. After December 1st address them, "Senate Chamber" or "House of Representatives," Washington, D.C.

HON................................

House of Representatives or Senate Chamber, (as the case may be) Washington, D.C.

SIR:—Our national parks are already too few in number. We are vitally interested in preserving intact those now existing. We earnestly protest against the destruction of any of the wonderful scenery of the Yosemite National Park and urge you to oppose any bill which will permit San Francisco to use Hetch-Hetchy as a municipal water tank. Strengthen our park laws instead of allowing them to be overridden.

Very truly,

....

(Write letters similar to the foregoing in your own language and in accordance with your own ideas.)

Source: "Let Everyone Help to Save the Famous Hetch-Hetchy Valley."

ARMY ENGINEERS' REPORT

CONCLUSIONS.

The board is of the opinion that there are several sources of water supply that could be obtained and used by the city of San Francisco and adjacent communities to supplement the near-by supplies as the necessity develops. From any one of these sources the water is sufficient in quantity and is, or can be made, suitable in quality, while the engineering difficulties are not insurmountable. The determining factor is principally one of cost.

The project proposed by the city of San Francisco, known as the Hetch Hetchy project, is about $20,000,000 cheaper than any other feasible project for furnishing an adequate supply. . . .

The Hetch Hetchy project has the additional advantage of permitting the development of a greater amount of water power than any other. . . .

The Valley of the San Joaquin has less rainfall and less run-off from its rivers than the Valley of the Sacramento. The Tuolumne River could if not used for city supply be used to irrigate a large amount of fertile land, as could almost any river in the Valley of California if means are found economically to store the water.

The board believes that on account of the fertility of the lands under irrigation and their aridness without water the necessity of preserving all available water in the Valley of California will sooner or later make the demand for the use of Hetch Hetchy as a reservoir practically irresistible. The board does not think that a delay of a few years in transforming the Hetch Hetchy Valley into a reservoir is of importance, and therefore does not think it necessary to require delaying construction of this reservoir until [other] sources have been fully developed.

The board believes that the regulations proposed by the city will be found sufficient to protect the waters from pollution, and that these regulations will tend toward the protection of campers and others using the park and will not be onerous upon them. It recommends, however, that the permit to the city require the city to take other means, such as filtration, to purify its water supply if these regulations are ever deemed insufficient.

The construction of reservoirs, especially the Hetch Hetchy, will destroy a few camping grounds in the park. The construction of the proposed trails will, however, render accessible other parts of the park not now readily reached, and the number of camping places within the park is large.

Source: Hetch Hetchy Valley. Report of Advisory Board of Army Engineers to the Secretary of the Interior, February 13, 1913 (Washington, 1913), 50–51.

CONGRESSIONAL HEARINGS ON HETCH HETCHY

Although opponents of the dam generated louder public support, the California congressional delegation had worked far more effectively in

Washington. At the hearings before the House Committee on the Public Lands, supporters of the dam called as their star witness the man of whom Theodore Roosevelt had once said "in all forestry matters I have put my conscience in the keeping of Gifford Pinchot." Seeing the issue as a test of his hard-edged rational understanding of the use of resources against Muir's romantic opposition to development, Pinchot exerted a powerful influence.

TESTIMONY OF GIFFORD PINCHOT, JUNE 25, 1913

Mr. PINCHOT. Mr. Chairman and gentlemen of the committee, my testimony will be very short. I presume that you very seldom have the opportunity of passing upon any measure before the Committee on the Public Lands which has been so thoroughly thrashed out as this one. This question has been up now, I should say, more than 10 years, and the reasons for and against the proposition have . . . been discussed over and over again. . . . So we come now face to face with the perfectly clean question of what is the best use to which this water that flows out of the Sierras can be put. As we all know, there is no use of water that is higher than the domestic use. Then, if there is, as the engineers tell us, no other source of supply that is anything like so reasonably available as this one; if this is the best, and, within reasonable limits of cost, the only means of supplying San Francisco with water, we come straight to the question of whether the advantage of leaving this valley in a state of nature is greater than the advantage of using it for the benefit of the city of San Francisco.

Now, the fundamental principle of the whole conservation policy is that of use, to take every part of the land and its resources and put it to that use in which it will best serve the most people; and I think there can be no question at all but that in this case we have an instance in which all weighty considerations demand the passage of the bill. There are, of course, a very large number of incidental changes that will arise after the passage of the bill. The construction of roads, trails, and telephone systems which will follow the passage of this bill will be a very important help in the park and forest reserves. The national forest telephone system and the roads and trails to which this bill will lead will form an important additional help in fighting fire in the forest reserves. As has already been set forth by the two Secretaries, the presence of these additional means of communication will mean that the national forest and the national park will be visited by very large numbers of people who can not visit them now. I think that the men who assert that it is better to leave a piece of natural scenery in its natural condition have rather the better of the argument, and I believe if we had nothing else to consider than the delight of the few men and women who would yearly go into the Hetch Hetchy Valley, then it should be left in its natural condition. But the considerations on the other side of the question to my mind are simply overwhelming, and so much so that I have never been able to see that there was any reasonable argument against the use of this water supply by the city of San Francisco, provided the bill was a reasonable bill.

Mr. RAKER [Congressman]. Taking the scenic beauty of the park as it now stands, and the fact that the valley is sometimes swamped along in June and July, is it not a fact that if a beautiful dam is put there, as is contemplated, and as the picture is given by the engineers, with the roads contemplated around the reservoir and with other trails, it will be more beautiful than it is now, and give more opportunity for the use of the park?

Mr. PINCHOT. Whether it will be more beautiful, I doubt, but the use of the park will be enormously increased. I think there is no doubt about that.

Mr. RAKER. In other words, to put it a different way, there will be more beauty accessible than there is now?

Mr. PINCHOT. Much more beauty will be accessible than now.

Mr. RAKER. And by putting in roads and trails the Government, as well as the citizens of the Government, will get more pleasure out of it than at the present time?

Mr. PINCHOT. You might say from the standpoint of enjoyment of beauty and the greatest good to the greatest number, they will be conserved by the passage of this bill, and there will be a great deal more use of the beauty of the park than there is now.

Mr. RAKER. Have you seen Mr. John Muir's criticism of the bill? You know him?

Mr. PINCHOT. Yes, sir; I know him very well. He is an old and a very good friend of mine. I have never been able to agree with him in his attitude toward the Sierras for the reason that my point of view has never appealed to him at all. When I became Forester and denied the right to exclude sheep and cows from the Sierras, Mr. Muir thought I had made a great mistake, because I allowed the use by an acquired right of a large number of people to interfere with what would have been the utmost beauty of the forest. In this case I think he has unduly given away to beauty as against use.

Mr. RAKER. Would that be practically the same as to the position of the Sierras Club?

Mr. PINCHOT. I am told that there is a very considerable difference of opinion in the club on this subject.

Mr. RAKER. Among themselves?

Mr. PINCHOT. Yes, sir.

Mr. RAKER. You think then, as a matter of fact, that the provisions of this bill carried out would relieve the situation; in other words, that there is no valid objection which they could make?

Mr. PINCHOT. That is my judgment. . . .

Mr. GRAHAM [Congressman]. Have you been in the Hetch Hetchy Valley yourself?

Mr. PINCHOT. I never have; I have been in the Yosemite.

Mr. GRAHAM. I am much interested in knowing from the purely scenic point of view what the character of the land is and what the scenic beauty consists of in the 100 or 150 feet nearest the water level? What scenic beauty would be destroyed by raising the level of the lake 100 or 150 feet?

Mr. PINCHOT. The water would cover a large part of the slope of broken rock at the foot of the cliffs, and according to the claims of the opponents of the bill it would replace a meadow with a lake and would result in reducing the height of the cliffs.

Mr. GRAHAM. When this matter was up before I received a great many telegrams, most of them from ladies in my district, protesting against any interference with the beauty of the valley, and I wondered if the place was inaccessible, whether they spoke from observation or whether they had been influenced in some other way?

Mr. PINCHOT. A very small number of people have been in the valley.

Mr. GRAHAM. What is the means of getting in there now?

Mr. PINCHOT. There is a pack trail, a journey of a day or a day and a half from Yosemite, is it not, Mr. Long?

Mr. LONG [Congressman]. Yes, sir; 9 miles over a trail.

Mr. GRAHAM. Would the raising of the water level facilitate the making of roads at the higher level?

Mr. PINCHOT. I think it would be more expensive, but that is a question for San Francisco.

There is a lake in the upper end of the Yosemite called Mirror Lake which reproduces to a certain extent the same features which this lake would have, and that is one of the most visited scenic beauties in the Yosemite.

Mr. RAKER. One of the beauties of Lake Louise is that very thing—the reflection from the mountains and the height of the lake puts an addition to its beauty that nothing else could accomplish. I am speaking of the same thing that Mr. Pinchot speaks of in regard to Mirror Lake. This would have the same effect.

Mr. TAYLOR [Congressman]. Do you feel, in view of the necessities and of the higher use of the city of San Francisco, that this committee would be justified at this time in doing what the nature lovers of the United States are liable to look upon as undue rushing of this measure in putting it through at this time? In other words, there are in my State, and, I suppose, in every other State, a large number of very good people—ladies and clubs and other people—who have memorialized and written us time and time again—I think I have 200 such communications—protesting against this measure on the ground of the destruction of the scenic beauty of what they contend belongs to all the people of the United States, who, if they had an opportunity possibly to study this bill and to realize more fully the necessities, would become placated or satisfied. I think we could appeal to them in that way. Do you feel that the necessities of the situation warrant us now in pushing this bill through Congress without giving them an opportunity; would they look upon it incredulously?

Mr. PINCHOT. They have had ample opportunity; this bill has been up for discussion 10 years.

Mr. TAYLOR. They have always succeeded in defeating it before?

Mr. PINCHOT. The arguments against it have been made over and over again; there will be nothing new.

Mr. TAYLOR. Will they or will they not think that there is nothing new presented on behalf of San Francisco that would warrant the passage of the measure?

Mr. PINCHOT. That is a matter of opinion. I am well satisfied nothing new will be presented at this time except the agreement of the former opponents of the bill.

Mr. TAYLOR. Are you thoroughly and heartily in favor of the measure?

Mr. PINCHOT. I am thoroughly and heartily in favor of it. I am in favor of reporting the bill now before the committee and passing it at this session.

Mr. TAYLOR. You feel that the wishes of these people should be disregarded?

Mr. PINCHOT. I think their protests have already been presented and that their case is not a good one. . . .

The CHAIRMAN. You are aware that there are other private companies out there seeking to sell [water] to San Francisco?

Mr. PINCHOT. I have long been aware of that.

The CHAIRMAN. Have you had occasion to compare the relative merits of the different proposals?

Mr. PINCHOT. I must answer that question by saying that I am not an expert in the matter, and I simply accept the opinions of the engineers, who are experts and who know better than I do.

The CHAIRMAN. It has been examined by a number of Army engineers and others?

Mr. PINCHOT. Yes, sir.

The CHAIRMAN. Have you had occasion to examine their reports?

Mr. PINCHOT. To some extent.

The CHAIRMAN. What was the conclusion you reached?

Mr. PINCHOT. That the conclusions of the board stated on pages 50 and 51 of the report were correct.

The CHAIRMAN. That shows that this project would be the most economical by about $20,000,000?

Mr. PINCHOT. That, I understand, is only for the construction work and does not take into consideration the cost of acquiring water rights on other streams.

The CHAIRMAN. Which would make it very much greater?

Mr. PINCHOT. Yes, sir.

The CHAIRMAN. As between the patriotic and good citizens who think that this ought to be kept sacred in its natural state and the beneficial use to these irrigation people and to the city there can be no question as to the proper thing for this committee to do?

Mr. PINCHOT. None whatever in my mind.

The CHAIRMAN. To indulge them would be to waste the waters of the entire river and let them flow idly to the sea, would it not?

Mr. PINCHOT. The situation in California is such that it is important to save the waste of water; it is all necessary, and ultimately all will be used. The most they could hope to accomplish would be to delay the development of this water supply. . . .

The CHAIRMAN. I know you have given a great deal of attention to these matters, and I would like to know what you think of this bill from the standpoint of properly preserving the rights of the Federal Government in the matter of the power which is granted?

Mr. PINCHOT. I think they are very well safeguarded. As I understand it, no charge is to be made for the power San Francisco uses for its own purposes; but as to power which it may dispose of commercially—that is, requires somebody else to pay for—the Government would get the benefit of the usual charge which is made in all other commercial cases.

The CHAIRMAN. Have you examined the bill sufficiently to say whether you approve of the provisions in reference to that particular point?

Mr. PINCHOT. In its present form it seems very good to me.

Mr. TAYLOR. Ought there not to be some provision in the bill regarding the rates or charges?

Mr. PINCHOT. I think it decidedly unwise to fix rates in this kind of a bill.

Mr. TAYLOR. Ought we not to reserve such power in Congress?

Mr. PINCHOT. Congress would always have the right, I judge, to fix the rates if it chose to avail itself of that right, but the bill simply authorizes the Secretary of the Interior to do that for Congress.

Source: Hetch Hetchy Dam Site. Hearings Before the Committee on the Public Lands, House of Representatives, 63rd Congress, 1st Session (Washington, 1913), 25–33.

PUBLIC OR PRIVATE POWER?

Cutting across issues of conservation and preservation was the question of the relative merits of private and public power. The conservation movement had always stressed the contrast between private greed and public good. A number of congressmen like George W. Norris of Nebraska as well as other influential figures were drawn to support the dam because it would be a public facility owned by the city of San Francisco. William Kent, a California congressman and member of the Committee on the Public Lands, was famous as a preserver of wilderness. Donating to the nation a magnificent stand of redwoods just outside San Francisco, the wealthy Kent had insisted that it be named Muir Woods in honor of John Muir. Now despite his love of wilderness, Kent supported San Francisco's claim to the Hetch Hetchy Valley because, like Norris, he feared the growing power of the Pacific Gas and Electric

Company and thought that municipal ownership of Hetch Hetchy would encourage public ownership of utilities. Old arguments and new mixed in strange ways. The advocates of flooding the valley prevailed when President Woodrow Wilson signed congressional enabling legislation in 1913.

GEORGE W. NORRIS ARGUES AGAINST
THE POWER COMPANIES

A part of the national park preserves and on the fringes of the natural glories of Yosemite National Park in the California Sierras is known as the Hetch Hetchy watershed.

Among other assignments which fell to me when I entered the United States Senate in 1913 was one to the Public Lands Committee.

It had before it the bitterly controversial issue of developing the water and power resources of the Hetch Hetchy watershed for the benefit of the people of the city and county of San Francisco.

There could be, in my judgment, no better example of the slow and painful processes through which the American people ultimately in their wisdom may come into the full benefits of some of the great natural wealth which belongs to them.

Now, thirty years later—three full decades—the powerfully intrenched private interests which prevented San Franciscans from enjoying what belongs to them still thwart the express will of the American Congress, the clear-cut mandates of the federal courts, and the Department of the Interior, under both conservative and liberal administrations. Strangely, these forces flaunt their defiance seemingly with the approval and support of the government of the city of San Francisco, and indirectly its people, for whom the project was undertaken and to whom Congress granted rights with certain sound limitations. . . .

I reached the conclusion, after listening intently to all the evidence, that the beauty of the region would not be injured in any sense by the construction of O'Shaughnessy Dam. If anything, a lake would accentuate its loveliness. . . .

I could come to no other decision than that, if we believed in the conservation of natural resources in America, the construction of a dam so magnificently located and so promisingly useful could not be opposed. I did not then recognize the inspiration, in other quarters, for a newly awakened interest in nature.

Through months of fight which flared and flamed to new bitterness, the project embraced in the House Resolution 242 finally won approval and became known as the Raker Act.

A simple eleven-line clause—Section 6—was the center of a savage battle continuing for months until the bill became law on December 19, 1913. Constantly through a period of thirty years since that day, that fight has gone on.

It would never have begun if Section 6 had not dedicated the power developed by Hetch Hetchy to public benefit.

The section reads:

> The grantee [the city and county of San Francisco] is prohibited from ever selling or letting to any corporation or individual, except a municipality or municipal water district or irrigation district, the right to sell or sublet the water or the electric energy sold or given to it or him by said grant; provided that the rights hereby granted shall not be sold, assigned or transferred to any private person, corporation or association, and in case of any attempt to sell, assign, transfer or convey this grant shall revert to the government of the United States.

It is this language which dedicates Hetch Hetchy to the use and benefit of the people. It was this language which also inspired the savage opposition of private utilities to the proposed development in the early years of the Wilson administration. The will and purpose of the Congress was clear and unmistakable.

I am certain that, had it not been for Section 6 under which San Francisco was given valuable rights in a national park reserve and the Stanislaus National Forest to obtain both a water and a power supply, the Sixty-third Congress, and possibly any succeeding Congress, would not have given approval. I am equally certain that, in the absence of this restriction, there would have been no fight by the privately owned utilities.

In Congress itself, then in the courts, and through one municipal election after another, sometimes subtly under cover and on other occasions out in the open, the battle went on unnoted by millions of Americans.

In the House discussion Congressman Raker bluntly said it was the purpose of his bill to have San Francisco supply electric power and water to its own people. In the Senate, speaking in defense of the safeguard provided by Section 6, a colleague, Senator Key Pittman, told the members the bill "provides absolutely that neither this water nor this power can ever fall into the hands of a monopoly."

And in the course of the debate, speaking in similar vein to many others, I said:

"This bill is not giving to a private corporation any power. It is giving to the people of this locality of San Francisco the right to use a cheap power when it is developed. . . . Why do we want to develop water power? Will we give it to the public or to a private individual or corporation? Here is an instance where we are going to give it directly to the people, if we pass this bill. It is going to come into competition with power companies and corporations that have, or will have, if this bill is defeated, almost a monopoly, not only in San Francisco, but throughout the greater portion of California."

I underestimated the resourcefulness of the Pacific Gas and Electric Company.

When I spoke so hopefully and so confidently (not only I but many others) it was incredible that a great utility could control the policies of city government in San Francisco, [and] with all of the resources at its command could battle through the courts to defeat—only to stave off that defeat by delaying rear-guard actions, and then reappear in the halls of Congress itself to renew the fight, and at all times and under all circumstances continue to defeat the original purpose and spirit of Hetch Hetchy.

But it has done all this. . . .

It was not until 1925, more than a decade after the congressional authorization had been given, that Hetch Hetchy electric capacities were developed to furnish any substantial amount of electricity.

But from the beginning the city made no substantial effort to comply with the restrictions imposed by Congress, and openly violated the limitations in Section 6 by selling its power to private companies for resale to the consumer.

Source: Fighting Liberal, The Autobiography of George W. Norris (Lincoln: University of Nebraska Press, 1972), 162–166.

Chapter 5

HOW AMERICA FOUGHT
ITS FIRST DRUG WAR:
THE HARRISON ACT*

In the twentieth century the United States has fought at least three wars on drugs. The first, between 1905 and 1920, outlawed opium-based products. In the second, President Richard Nixon in the early 1970s declared war on marijuana and LSD, which were seen as central to the hippie counterculture of the 1960s and to a breakdown of morale among American soldiers in Vietnam. The current war on drugs began in the 1980s and still rages. The documents in this chapter concern the earliest set of decisions that made narcotics illegal and criminalized their users.

Medicines based in opium and coca have a long history in the United States. Marketed under names like "laudanum" and "black drop," narcotic preparations were an important part of medical treatment in the eighteenth and nineteenth century. Lacking good explanations or cures for the mysterious and deadly diseases that bedeviled Americans before the Civil War, physicians relied on orally administered crude opium products to stop pain, reduce anxiety, and stimulate a patient's immune system. Despite being freely available without prescription, narcotics were not a major problem. Mild in effect and expensive, imported crude opium never threatened to displace alcohol as the nation's main social lubricant.

During the middle of the nineteenth century, advances in chemistry and the growing availability of hypodermic needles increased the importation and use of new and powerful narcotics. As early as 1832 Rosengarten & Company (now Merck Pharmaceuticals) had begun manufacturing purified morphine salts. By

*Research for this chapter by Anthony Marcus was assisted by the study "Heroin in the 21st Century," funded by the National Institute on Drug Abuse. He thanks Kate McCoy for suggesting the idea, Jim Baumhol for bibliographic leads, and Ric Curtis for useful commentary.

midcentury, chemists were isolating the active ingredient in coca leaves and began manufacturing cocaine. Finally in 1898, a German chemist working for Bayer & Company isolated a drug based in opium that was soon marketed under the name "heroin."

These new chemicals rapidly became far more popular in the United States with its powerful anti-alcohol tradition than in Europe, initiating a continuing drug problem that David Musto has labeled "the American disease." By the turn of the century narcotics were everywhere. Advertisements promoted their wondrous properties; patent medicines for everything from headaches and hay fever to the common cold contained narcotics. They were used as a substitute for alcohol by middle-class women who did not want to appear intemperate or unladylike, by religious folk who had vowed not to drink alcohol, and by black people who could not buy alcohol in southern dry counties. Narcotics soothed infants' teething pains, laborers' fatigue, and women's menstrual cramps and the "vapors" supposedly caused by constricting garments. Such drugs were so much a part of daily life that until 1903, when caffeine was substituted, Coca-Cola contained cocaine.

As the nation's attraction to narcotics deepened, so too did the struggle to eliminate them. In the first decades of the twentieth century, Progressive Era social planning and reform along with the beginnings of modern medicine and the growth of the United States as an international power produced a demand for narcotics control and an end to patent medicine "quackery."

In 1906 Congress, in the Pure Food and Drug Act, made it a crime to transport products for human consumption across state lines without labels indicating the presence of opiates. In 1909, the importing of opium for smoking, popular with Chinese-Americans on the West Coast, was banned. In 1913, the American Medical Association (AMA), as part of a drive to professionalize medicine and separate legitimate doctors from "opium quacks" and "charlatans," established its Propaganda Department "to gather and disseminate information concerning health fraud and quackery." In this same period police departments throughout the South switched from .32 caliber to .38 caliber revolvers, claiming that blacks on cocaine were not affected by the smaller bullets.

Between December 1911 and June 1914, a series of international conferences addressing trafficking in narcotics took place at the Hague in the Netherlands at the initiative of the United States. There major opium exporting countries like Germany, Switzerland, and Turkey refused to sacrifice their lucrative trade. The United States persuaded the narcotic-producing countries of Latin America to cooperate, but Germany demanded that Washington write its own domestic legislation before trying to impose its will on other nations. Out of this emerged the Harrison Act of 1914.

Although the Harrison Act was only a revenue act requiring the registration and taxation of sales or prescription of narcotics, it established the precedent for government control of opiates and created a public record, making physicians and pharmacists accountable. This critical first decision prepared the way for *U.S. vs.*

Doremus and *Webb vs. U.S.,* the 1919 Supreme Court decisions that upheld the government's criminalizing of opiate prescriptions for the relief of addicts. Soon after the *Webb* decision, physicians began being arrested and imprisoned for prescribing opiates to their addicted patients. Many cities set up heroin maintenance clinics to deal with the public health crisis that had been created by prohibition. But the federal government had not outlawed opium to enable municipal governments to continue maintaining "dope fiends." Within four years federal authorities closed all the clinics, and heroin, cocaine, and the people who used them were driven into the world of crime and violence where they remain today.

DOPE FIENDS AND QUACKS

In 1905 and 1906 Samuel Hopkins Adams, one of the important jour-
nalists of the Progressive Era, wrote for Collier's *magazine "The Great*
American Fraud" series, articles exposing patent medicine fraud and
a variety of other "quackery." Written while Congress was debating
the Pure Food and Drug Act, these articles sought to warn people of the
dangers of narcotics in over-the-counter medications and to check the
influence of the powerful patent medicine interests in Congress.

Drug Frauds

Gullible America will spend this year some seventy-five millions of dollars in the purchase of patent medicines. In consideration of this sum it will swallow huge quantities of alcohol, an appalling amount of opiates and narcotics, a wide assortment of varied drugs ranging from powerful and dangerous heart depressants to insidious liver simulants; and, far in excess of all other ingredients, undiluted fraud. For fraud, exploited by the skillfulest of advertising bunco men, is the basis of the trade. Should the newspapers, the magazines and the medical journal refuse their pages to this class of advertisements, the patent medicine business in five years would be as scandalously historic as the South Sea Bubble, and the nation would be richer not only in lives and money, but in drunkards and drug-fiends saved. . . .

At the bottom of the noisome pit of charlatanry crawl the drug habit specialists. They are the scavengers, delving amid the carrion of the fraudulent nostrum business for their profits. The human wrecks made by the opium and cocaine laden secret patent medicines come to them for cure, and are wrung dry of the last drop of blood. By comparison with these leeches of the uttermost slime, the regular patent medicine faker is a pattern of righteousness. He can find something to say for himself, at least. The leading citizen of Columbus will advocate the faith-cure virtues of his Peruna with a twinkle in his eye; the highly respectable legal light who is now president of Chicago's University Club will manage to defend, with smug lawyer talk, the dollars he made out of Liquozone; even the menacing trade of the Antikamnia folk is excused (by the owners) on the ground that it does give relief in certain cases. But the creatures who prey upon drug fiends are confessedly beyond the pale. They deliberately foster the most dreadful forms of slavery, for their own profit. They have discovered a money-making villainy worse than murder, for which, apparently, there is no legal penalty. Equally deep in degradation I would rank those thugs who, as "specialists" in private diseases, ruin the lives of men and extort their pay by daring blackmail.

The drink curers are on a somewhat different plane. They are swindlers, not panderers. Time was when the "cures" for alcoholism consisted in the substitution of the worse morphine or cocaine habits for the drink habit. This is done, if at all, very little now. The "alcoholists" give some "bracer" or slow emetic, and try to persuade the victim that he is cured, long enough to get their pay. I group them with the drug cure wretches, because they prey on the same class, though with a less degree of viciousness. They may be compared to the petty shore thieves who furtively strip the bodies of the drowned; the opium-morphine-cocaine-cure quacks are the wreckers who lure their victims to destruction by false signals.

No Effort is Made to Save a Patient

No more vivid illustration of the value of the patent medicine clause in the Pure Food law, requiring that the amount of habit-forming drug in any medicine be stated on the label, could be found than is furnished by the "drug habit" cures. Practically all of these advertised remedies are simply the drug itself in concealed form. No effort is made to save the patient. The whole purpose is to substitute for the slavery to the drug purchased of the corner pharmacist the slavery to the same drug, disguised, purchased at a much larger price from the "Doctor" or "Institute" or "Society." Here is a typical report from a victim: "When I tried to stop the remedy, I found I could not, and it was worse than the morphine itself. I then went back to plain morphine, but found that I required *twice as much* as before I took the cure. That is what the morphine cure did for me.". . .

Investigations into the mail order drug cures have been made on the basis of a pretended morphine addiction. In every case the "remedy" sent me to cure the morphine habit has been a morphine solution. Sometimes the morphine was mixed with other drugs, to produce greater effect and fasten more firmly upon the unfortunate the *habit* of the *remedy,* as a substitute for the original drug habit. All these concerns advertise to cure also the cocaine habit, the chloral habit, the opium habit, etc. As they covertly give morphine to their morphine victims, it is a just inference that they treat the cocaine habit with disguised cocaine, the opium habit with concealed opium, the chloral habit with hidden chloral, and so throughout the list. . . .

I am invited to *cure* myself by taking this stuff *four times* a day. If I lived through the first dose [of 2.2 grains] the second would kill me, or any of my readers who is not a morphine fiend. The ordinary dose is 1/8 of a grain, heavy dose 1/4 of a grain. But the Richie Company supposes I can stand more, so they endeavor to foist their concoction upon me in place of my supposed addiction. How does this comport with their "No substitution" claim? This and other questions I put in writing to the Rev. Dr. Richie. He has not answered it. His silence is not surprising. It is the part of wisdom—or, at least, caution. I'm not certain just how to place this reverend gentleman. It may be that he has been fooled into believing in the "Richie cure," and that he is an exemplar of a type of asininity so baneful and deadly that its possessor ought, for the sake of the public, to be permanently established in an asylum for the dangerously imbecile. But I think not. I think he can not be ignorant of his traffic in ruined lives. This alternative implies flat criminality. Nor has the divinity doctor always eluded the clutch of the law. He has been convicted and fined for practising medicine without a license. . . .

Source: Samuel Hopkins Adams, "The Great American Fraud," *Collier's,* October 7, 1905 and September 22, 1906.

THE HARRISON ACT AND ITS DISCONTENTS

The Harrison Act was passed late in 1914. Few people really knew what effect it would have. Some doctors believed that it was necessary to professionalize medicine and drive irresponsible opium quacks out of business. A Boston medical journal reflected a common belief among physicians that powerful narcotics like morphine should be prescribed only by trained professional doctors. It viewed the Harrison Act as a minor annoyance that provided necessary protections against the dangers of drug abuse. New York, on the other hand, had many more narcotic addicts than Boston, which may explain why a New York medical journal disagreed, worrying that the law could lead to a connection between drugs and violence. And soon many doctors and public health officials came to believe that control of narcotics was itself part of the problem, as several articles in the December 1917 American Medicine *argued.*

THE HARRISON ACT, 1914

CHAP. 1.—An Act To provide for the registration of, with collectors of internal revenue, and to impose a special tax upon all persons who produce, import, manufacture, compound, deal in, dispense, sell, distribute, or give away opium or coca leaves, their salts, derivatives, or preparations, and for other purposes.

Be it enacted by the Senate and House of Representatives of the United States of America in Congress assembled, That on and after the first day of March, nineteen hundred and fifteen, every person who produces, imports, manufactures, compounds, deals in, dispenses, sells, distributes, or gives away opium or coca leaves or any compound, manufacture, salt, derivative, or preparation thereof, shall register with the collector of internal revenue of the district his name or style, place of business, and place or places where such business is to be carried on: *Provided,* That the office, or if none, then the residence of any person shall be considered for the purposes of this Act to be his place of business. At the time of such registry and on or before the first day of July, annually thereafter, every person who produces, imports, manufactures, compounds, deals in, dispenses, sells, distributes, or gives away any of the aforesaid drugs shall pay to the said collector a special tax at the rate of $1 per annum. . . .

SEC. 2. That it shall be unlawful for any person to sell, barter, exchange, or give away any of the aforesaid drugs except in pursuance of a written order of the person to whom such article is sold, bartered, exchanged, or given, on a form to be issued in blank for that purpose by the Commissioner of Internal Revenue. Every person who shall accept any such order, and in pursuance thereof shall sell, barter, exchange, or give away any of the aforesaid drugs, shall preserve such order for a period of two years in such a way as to be readily accessible to inspection by any officer, agent, or employee of the Treasury Department duly authorized for that purpose, and the State, Territorial, District, municipal, and insular officials named in section five of this Act. Every person who shall give an order as herein provided to any other person for any of the aforesaid drugs shall, at or before the time of giving such order, make or cause to be made a duplicate thereof on a form to be issued in blank for that purpose by the Commissioner of Internal Revenue, and in case of the acceptance of such order, shall preserve such duplicate for said period of two years in such a way as to be readily accessible to inspection by the officers, agents, employees, and officials hereinbefore mentioned. Nothing contained in this section shall apply—

(a) To the dispensing or distribution of any of the aforesaid drugs to a patient by a physician, dentist, or veterinary surgeon registered under this Act in the course of his professional practice only: *Provided,* That such physician, dentist, or veterinary surgeon shall keep a record of all such drugs dispensed or distributed, showing the amount dispensed or distributed, the date, and the name and address of the patient to whom such drugs are dispensed or distributed, except such as may be dispensed or distributed to a patient upon whom such physician, dentist or veterinary surgeon shall personally attend; and such record shall be kept for a period of two years from the date of dispensing or distributing such drugs, subject to inspection, as provided in this Act. . . .

SEC. 3. That any person who shall be registered in any internal-revenue district under the provisions of section one of this Act shall, whenever required so to do by the collector of the district, render to the said collector a true and correct statement or return, verified by affidavit, setting forth the quantity of the aforesaid drugs received by him in said internal-revenue district during such period immediately preceding the demand of the collector, not exceeding three months, as the said collector may fix and determine; the names of the persons from whom the said drugs were received; the quantity in each instance received from each of such persons, and the date when received. . . .

SEC. 8. That it shall be unlawful for any person not registered under the provisions of this Act, and who has not paid the special tax provided for by this Act, to have in his possession or under his control any of the aforesaid drugs; and such possession or control shall be presumptive evidence of a violation of this section, and also of a violation of the provisions of section one of this Act. . . .

SEC. 9. That any person who violates or fails to comply with any of the requirements of this Act shall, on conviction, be fined not more than $2,000 or be imprisoned not more than five years, or both, in the discretion of the court.

Source: U.S., *Statutes at Large,* 38: 785–789.

A SLIGHT ANNOYANCE TO CHECK A GREAT EVIL:
A BOSTON MEDICAL JOURNAL

The provisions of the federal act regulating the dispensing and distribution of narcotic drugs, which went into effect March 1, 1915, were summarized in an insert in the JOURNAL of Feb. 18, 1915, and editorial comment followed in the issue of March 4, 1915. The profession has become accustomed to the slight annoyance caused by the necessary registration, with its attendant small fee, and has coöperated heartily in checking a great evil—the abuse of narcotics. From those who have been entrusted with the enforcement of the act we learn that druggists are very generally obeying the law, that the peddling of morphine and cocaine by vendors who had purchased the drugs on prescriptions from irregular practitioners of medicine has been very nearly abolished in this neighborhood, but that there are still unprincipled physicians who are making money in the following fashion: A morphine eater consults a physician whose name has been given him by another addict and says, "Doctor, I am a morphine user. Will you prescribe for me?" "How much morphine are you accustomed to use?" "About ten grains a day." The doctor makes out a prescription for a dram of morphine and counsels the patient to use only so much as he directs. Whereupon the drug user departs to have his prescription filled and another unfortunate mortal with a craving takes his place. Naturally this is not the *lawful practice of medicine* within the meaning of the language of the act. To gather proof that the law is being evaded by this particular method of prescribing is by no means easy of accomplishment, and the federal authorities need, and should have, any assistance the right minded members of the profession can give in bringing to justice those who are thus stultifying themselves and their calling.

Source: "The First Year of the Harrison Narcotic Act," *Boston Medical and Surgical Journal,* March 23, 1916: 434.

THE HARRISON ACT LEADS TO VIOLENCE:
A NEW YORK MEDICAL JOURNAL

As was expected generally by the press, medical and other, the immediate effects of the Harrison antinarcotic law were seen in the flocking of drug habitués to hospitals and sanatoriums. Sporadic crimes of violence were reported too, due usually to desperate efforts by addicts to obtain drugs, but occasionally to a delirious state induced by sudden withdrawal of the stimulant.

The really serious results of this legislation, however, will only appear gradually and will not always be recognized as such. These will be the failures of promising careers, the disrupting of happy families, the commission of crimes which will never be traced to their real cause, and the influx into hospitals for the mentally disordered of many who would otherwise live socially competent lives.

To understand this, we must remember that drugs, especially opium and its preparations, in the vast majority of cases represent for the individual a compromise with life, an adjustment with the scheme of things which is not to be lightly destroyed. In the life of everyone there are conflicts of desire and duty, of pleasure and reality. In some cases the instinctive demands are so much at variance with the social requirements that a normal adjustment appears impossible and the individual takes refuge in a drug habit wherein his real personality is so stupefied that he can satisfy his subconscious cravings in a world of fantasy and day dreaming. Remove this aid to adjustment, however, upon which he has leaned for many years, and he finds it necessary to harmonize himself all over again with a complex social organization. Having passed by this time the malleable period of his development, he finds himself unable to make this adjustment and his reaction will be antisocial.

We must face the fact then that the erstwhile drug habitué is not a well man when he has overcome the first fierce craving for the drug. The mental side of the picture should be studied as well as the physical, and the physician should be ready to help him to readjust himself to the world of sober reality, to sublimate his subconscious desires, and to occupy his social niche unsupported by artificial stimuli.

Source: "Mental Sequelae of the Harrison Law," *New York Medical Journal*, May 15, 1915: 1014.

DRUG CONTROL AND CRIME

SOME VIEWS ON DRUG ADDICTION—PERSONAL AND LEGAL

BY

A PROMINENT MEMBER OF THE NEW YORK BAR

A half dozen years ago I had a long, severe attack of gall-stones and inflammation of the gall-bladder. I suffered so much pain that the physicians gave me morphine for nearly a year. When I got better I tried my very best to get along without the drug, but could not. I came to a physician in New York for treatment who had made a special study of drug addiction and is a recognized authority on that subject. However, he could not help me at that time on account of a recurrence of my gall-bladder inflammation with severe jaundice and fever.

Since that time I have tried repeatedly to stop and reduce the quantity of the drug, but have found it impossible because of the physical pain and exhaustion due to the lack of the drug. This is unbearable. I have since then kept my daily amount of morphine medication at a minimum which permitted me to work and to maintain good health and bodily function. The idea which I have heard so often expressed, that addicts tend to increase their daily intake of narcotic, is certainly untrue in my case, and there seems to me no reason nor temptation to do so. I have simply found the smallest amount which would keep me from physical suffering, and have experienced no difficulty in maintaining that dosage, except in occasional emergencies of gall-bladder attacks or other crises, after which I found it a simple matter to discontinue the excess dosage. As I have never experienced the slightest pleasurable or sensually enjoyable sensations from the administration of morphine, there seems to me no foundation for this prevalent idea of tendency to increase. It may be true of the degenerate who has become addicted, but it certainly is untrue in my case, and must be untrue of the thousands like me whose misfortune it has been to become afflicted with this condition.

Recently I have again consulted specialists, and it seems that with my condition, I must continue the administration of morphine for the present, and perhaps for the rest of my life. Physical conditions render present attempts to discontinue its use impractical, undesirable and dangerous.

Now what am I to do under the present "Drug Habit" laws of this State? I am a lawyer long past middle age—have held important state and judicial positions, and many positions of responsibility and trust. It would be ruinous to me if my addiction condition became public.

This law was enacted to control the drug traffic and to stop the evils which are connected to it. In many respects it is an excellent law, but the provisions which require the record of the name, age and residence of the addict to be filed in the Board of Health Office is outrageous. It does not affect the underworld, for they don't care and avoid registration by not going to those who have to register them. But see the position of a man who has a good reputation and standing in the community—forever recorded in the records of the State Board of Health as a "dope fiend," even though his condition is not the result of his own acts or desires and is absolutely beyond his control.

This part of the law which requires the recording of the name, age and residence of the addict should be repealed. The only effect of these provisions is to record the addict as what everybody considers a "dope fiend" or force him to go to the smugglers for his drug. He must either place his good name and social and economic position in constant jeopardy or in some way or other evade the law with its attendant penalty, and constant fear of detection. I should not be surprised if it finally develops to be the fact that a majority of decent sufferers from this condition have chosen the latter course as the lesser of evils. . . .

Conditions in New York today, affecting the honest addict, constitute in effect persecution of the sick. It is bad enough to be afflicted with this disease. Agonizing as gall-stone attacks have been, the physical suffering from lack of morphine in an addict is worse. Added to this is the knowledge that your name is on file at Albany, and perhaps elsewhere, as an addict. You know that disclosure of your condition will ruin you and disgrace your family. You are potentially subject to leakage from those records and the attendant possibilities of blackmail and other persecution. Such conditions tend to force and undoubtedly have forced many innocent and honest addicts of good social and economic standing to become criminals by obtaining their necessary opiate medicine through illegal channels.

Source: "Some Views On Drug Addiction—Personal and Legal. By a Prominent Member of the New York Bar," *American Medicine*, December 1917: 808–809.

SUPPLYING NARCOTICS BECOMES A CRIMINAL ACTIVITY

In 1919, the United States Supreme Court upheld a federal law criminalizing the prescription of opium for maintaining addicts. After the Court's decision, doctors faced several dilemmas. The Boston Medical and Surgical Journal *discussed some of these difficulties.*

WEBB VS. THE UNITED STATES OF AMERICA, MARCH 3, 1919

Orders for morphine, issued by a practising and registered physician to an habitual user, not in the course of professional treatment in the attempted cure of the habit, but for the purpose of providing the user with morphine sufficient to make him comfortable by maintaining his customary use, are not physician's prescriptions within the meaning of the exception in the Harrison Narcotic Drug Act of December 17, 1914 (38 Stat. at L. 785, chap.1, Comp. Stat. 1916, § 6287h), § 2, in favor of sales by dealers upon written prescriptions issued by registered physicians.

Source: U.S., *Statutes at Large*, 249: 497.

CAUTIONS FOR DOCTORS ON PRESCRIBING NARCOTICS

The attention of physicians is called to a pamphlet entitled "Enforcement of the Harrison Narcotic Law," which has been issued recently by the Commissioner of Internal Revenue. The recent decisions of the Supreme Court of the United States indicate the necessity for exercising the greatest care in carrying out the provisions of the Harrison Narcotic Law, as amended by the Revenue Act of 1918. It is important to know that it has been held unlawful for a physician to furnish a drug addict with narcotic drugs for the purpose of satisfying his appetite, and not in the course of regular professional practice of medicine and in the proper treatment of disease; a practitioner who issues an order under these circumstances, as well as the druggist who knowingly fills such an order, is judged to have committed an indictable offense. A physician must personally attend the addict and himself administer the dosage in order to show that he is practicing in good faith.

Physicians will undoubtedly be called upon to meet many cases which it will be difficult to solve in strict accordance with the Harrison Narcotic Act, for it is not to be expected that rules can be formulated to cover every specific case. In view of this fact, a number of suggestions have been set forth in this pamphlet which may be found of great practical value. In extraordinary cases which cannot be decided by the collector, a full and accurate statement of the facts should be submitted to the Bureau at once. In many cases involving the treatment of incurable diseases, aged and infirm addicts, and the ordinary addict, the following suggestions, which are subject to modification through further interpretation of the courts, may be helpful.

In the treatment of persons suffering from a proven incurable disease, such as cancer and advanced tuberculosis, it is deemed justifiable for the reputable physician, strictly for legitimate medical purposes, to prescribe narcotic drugs for the immediate need of these patients, provided he personally attends such patients. . . .

The chief difficulty in carrying out the Harrison Narcotic Act will be met in the case of the ordinary addict who is neither aged nor infirm nor suffering from an incurable disease. It should be borne in mind that mere addiction alone is not recognized as an incurable disease. It is a violation of the law for practitioners to furnish an addict with narcotics for the mere purpose of satisfying his cravings for the drug. There is being considered a project by which the United States Public Health Service will assist in the institutional care of these addicts, but there has as yet been no specific appropriation made by Congress for this purpose. It is thought that it would not be difficult under the management of a reputable physician appointed by the local authorities, to examine, register, and give regular treatment to these ordinary addicts by reducing the dosage to a minimum and encouraging the addict to enter a hospital, sanitarium, or institution for further treatment and cure. It is the opinion of the Bureau that the so-called reductive ambulatory treatment, where narcotics are furnished to an addict who controls the dosage himself, will not benefit or cure the patient and will often lead to illicit traffic. All peddlers, smugglers, manufacturers, wholesalers, retailers, practitioners, and other persons who wilfully violate the intent and provisions of this law will be prosecuted by the field officers of the Bureau in order to eliminate this menace from the country.

Source: "Enforcement of the Harrison Act," *Boston Medical and Surgical Journal*, November 13, 1919: 592–593.

CLINICS FOR ADDICTS?

In regions with many addicts, prohibition created a crisis for police, politicians, and public health officials along with doctors. In such cities as Jacksonville, Florida, Shreveport, Louisiana, Atlanta, Georgia and New York City, public health and law enforcement officials set up opium clinics that registered and treated addicts with maintenance doses. The New York City clinic was open from the spring of 1919 until March 1920. By 1921, however, virtually every maintenance clinic in the country had been closed by a combination of local anti-drug forces and federal pressure. One of the last holdouts was the Shreveport clinic, founded and run by the tenacious Dr. Willis P. Butler with the support of local law enforcement officials. Dr. Butler fought the state board of health, the federal government, and local tabloids to keep his clinic open for his more desperate patients. In 1923, under threat of a term in a federal prison, he allowed the clinic to close.

FEAR OUTBREAK BY MEN NEEDING DRUGS: *NEW YORK TIMES*

Following the arraignment yesterday of the six physicians and four druggists arrested under the Harrison Anti-Narcotic law, it was learned that agents of the Bureau of Internal Revenue, in a two months' investigation into the traffic in drugs in this city, had established that in the last year 1,500,000 prescriptions for the illicit procuring of narcotics had been issued and filled.

It was also ascertained that the Federal authorities have evidence that thirty physicians are in a sort of "drug ring" issuing prescriptions for narcotics for fees ranging from 25 cents to $4. The principal drug being dispensed in this city, according to the investigations of the Federal agents, is heroin, a derivative of opium, and one of the most destructive narcotic poisons. This drug is obtained through the regular channels at $12 to $15 an ounce and is retailed through the prescriptions at $60 to $75 an ounce.

The unscrupulous physicians writing the prescriptions are each issuing as many as 200 a day, the agents are prepared to prove, most of the doctors having no other practice. The investigations of the Government in New York have disclosed that 70 per cent of the drug addicts are less than twenty-five years old, and that included in the victims are a remarkably high percentage of discharged soldiers and sailors.

Further details of Tuesday night's raids, obtained yesterday, revealed that sixty-five signed and sworn confessions were given to the agents by the nearly 200 addicts who were gathered in the basement of Police Headquarters. One of the addicts, a young man in the grip of heroin, related to the agents how he went into a "strange" drug store on a chance that he might be able to get his drug.

"Got a prescription?" inquired the druggist, according to the man's story, "No? Well, wait a while, the doctor will be in here in a minute and he'll fix you up." In a short time a physician came in, he said, and he was "fixed up.". . .

In one of the drugstores ransacked in the raid the agents found a box containing 50,000 prescriptions for drugs, all dated within the last ten months. In another the records showed a year's dispensing of 100,000 orders for narcotics. Records seized at the physician's offices and retained by the police indicate, it is said, that 800 patients requiring drugs visited the six doctors regularly, one physician maintaining a card index of 200 daily patients.

As an aftermath of the raid, the Federal agents and the police were worried yesterday that somewhere in the city were 800 men deprived of drugs and likely to break out violently when the narcotic hunger became stronger. To cope with this situation a hurried consultation was held in the office of Health Commissioner Copeland, representatives of the Federal Government, New York State Narcotic Commission, and the Police Department participating.

To Open Clinic for Addicts.

As a result, the Bureau of Drug Addiction Clinic will be opened this morning at 9 o'clock in the Board of Health Building, 139 Centre Street, and until 5 o'clock drug addicts of the six arrested doctors will be supplied with drugs at cost. Health Commissioner Copeland said that yesterday between thirty-five and fifty addicts had telephoned his office seeking drugs, and that he had sent many of them to clinics. Commissioner Copeland emphasized that the clinic would be conducted to effect cures through gradual reduction of the amount of narcotic furnished.

"It was pointed out by the Police Department," said Dr. Copeland, "that this method of furnishing the drug will put the 'bootlegging physician' out of business, because the drug will be furnished at its real value and not at the exorbitant figure charged by the traffickers, but I wish to emphasize the fact that the Health Department does not desire to have every narcotic victim in the city report here for treatment. The purpose of the plan inaugurated tomorrow will be to take care of the unfortunate victims formerly ministered to by the arrested physicians.

"It is necessary to maintain this clinic because if the victims are permitted to roam about without the drugs they become dangerous. An example of this happened only a short time ago when an innocent man was shot and killed by a drug addict who had just looted a Madison Avenue jewelry shop. It is necessary to maintain this clinic because this raid and further raids, depriving the addicts of their drugs, will inevitably produce a wave of violent crime.

"I know that the drug habit is steadily on the increase and that at the present time there are between 150,000 and 200,000 drug addicts in this city. Many of these are men who have only recently been discharged from the army and navy."

"I think," continued the Commissioner, "that the advent of prohibition is going to produce a tremendous increase in drug addiction. When the whisky drinker can no longer have an alcoholic jag, he is going to have a drug jag. I am saying this, not from my personal opinion, but from the experience of an administrator of public health."

Source: New York Times, April 10, 1919.

Shreveport, Louisiana, was the site of a thriving morphine clinic that was suddenly closed at the cost of much suffering.

THE SHREVEPORT CLINIC

In the spring of 1919 a situation arose that had to be met. There were a large number of people living here who were using morphine—some because of suffering from incurable diseases, some from untreated or unsuccessfully treated physical conditions, which were presumably curable, and some because they had a morphine habit and either could not get the proper assistance to quit it, or did not try or want to quit. All of these people were in some manner obtaining the drug previously, but now the supply was almost suddenly stopped, and there was great suffering. It was impossible for anyone to tell then who the really deserving ones were, or to be absolutely sure just what situations had to be met.

There was a general inclination to be rather harsh, stern and unsympathizing with them at first; as the result of this attitude many addicts suffered terribly. Due to a fear or natural disinclination on the part of doctors and druggists to have anything to do with an addict no matter what else might be his trouble (and when it was found out that he was an addict, usually that was enough to cause the doctor to go no deeper into his case), many sick people were caused to suffer terribly, or to seek the peddler. These people began coming to the officers of the law and to the board of health officials begging for relief. On several occasions places were entered, doctors' offices robbed or hand bags stolen, and many physicians were appealed to for assistance.

To meet the situation our dispensary was started. Later, our institutional treatment department was opened. At first, our methods were rather crude and we had much difficulty trying to devise the best ways to handle these cases. Gradually improving, within a few months we established our system. Its success is due largely to the fact that we have cooperation, assistance, hearty approval and commendation of every branch of our government locally, including the City Judge, Police Department, City Commission Council, State Board Inspector, City and Parish Boards of Health, Sheriff and his department, City and Parish Medical Society, the U. S. Marshal, U. S. District Attorney and U. S. Judge. We believe it is doing a good work and that in a practical way it is solving our local narcotic situation. That is all that we intend for it to do as we believe that each community or part of the state should be able and be required to care for its problems of this character.

On or about the 15th of March, 1921, the Louisiana State Board of Health discontinued the narcotic dispensaries at New Orleans, Alexandria and Shreveport, Louisiana. The next day the narcotic work at Shreveport was continued under different supervision, but with practically the same personnel and methods. I consider that for me to have discontinued suddenly the dispensing of narcotics to our aged, infirm and incurable disease patients with no warning and no kind of provision being made for their care, would have been absolutely criminal and would have caused much terrible and needless suffering and undoubtedly would have caused several deaths. Therefore, under my own personal responsibility as a doctor and as parish [public health] physician I continued the work for a few days until the proper steps could be taken by our city government to pass an ordinance establishing a hospital for this service. This the City Commission Council did and our work has gone on uninterrupted.

Morphine is the drug of addiction almost exclusively, and we seldom see a heroin addict. Cocaine being not a habit former, but we believe merely a vice, is not allowed; and no one using it is put on the dispensary; its use, as a rule, is easily detected. There are three users of codeine, these being old cases of asthma and arthritis.

Only incurable cases and those in which after examination and investigation we think treatment not at present indicated are dispensed to. Curable cases are put into the institution for a cure as soon as practical. Each incurable case is examined and classified as such by from two to seven reputable physicians. . . .

The dispensing days are Monday, Tuesday, Thursday and Saturday, from 8.30 to 10.00 A. M., from 4.30 to 6.00 P. M. The dispensary is open every day from 8.00 A. M. until 6.00 P. M., with arrangements made to care for all worthy cases at any hour. The morphine is dispensed in solution, labeled properly, showing amount in grains and the price of same (6 cents a grain). The patient signs the register in the window in the presence of the dispenser, receives his supply, pays for it, steps aside, and the next one follows in line. There is no confusion and all is quiet and orderly. It is alright for a patient to appear at the dispensary in his working clothes, but he must be neat and show that he cares for his personal appearance. We insist that all who are able must work, and spend their first money for good food and decent clothes. No vagabonds or loafers are tolerated.

We go thoroughly into their history and finger-print them in order that we may not knowingly care for some criminal who is not worthy of our assistance. If a patient is temporarily down and out he is assisted to get on his feet and become decent and at least respectable looking. The patients call it "Our Dispensary" and appreciating what is being done for them they help to keep it clean. . . .

The amount of morphine dispensed to each patient is the smallest amount that we believe the patient can get along on and keep in drug balance. The dispensary is not intended as a treatment department for a cure, but only as a means of caring for the incurables, and those not at present curable or treatable, but who must have the medicine. There is no longer a systematic and a regular effort at reduction, but each case is judged separately, a certain amount decided on, and this may at times have to be increased or decreased according to the condition of the patient and the disease from which he suffers. If too much medicine is allowed there is a temptation to dispose of some; if too little, the tendency would be to buy more, so we try to be as accurate as possible at the same time being reasonable and fair with the patient. We believe that this has paid us. The officers say there is little or almost no peddling here, and we have had a number of patients voluntarily request that they be reduced a grain or so, and to actually assist us to cut them down to very small doses. The tendency of many is to go up and up, but when they see that we know their actual needs as well or better than they do, there is no trouble. . . .

While in the institution being cured everything possible is done to treat the patient properly, humanely and scientifically, the best that our facilities will permit. He is under absolute restraint, with nurses, attendants, and proper medical supervision. He is kept there as long as the director thinks necessary. His commitment is legal. Additional to this commitment he signs a request to be placed in the Parish jail to complete the treatment if, for any reason, this may be deemed necessary or advisable by the director. The director who is also the parish physician, treats him when placed in jail, employing as nearly as possible the same methods as used at the hospital. Several methods of treatment are employed at the hospital, but all are humane and very effective. The patients suffer little and gain rapidly in weight. . . .

Morphinism is the same everywhere, yet opinion differs as to what it really is. It is variously considered as a vice, a crime, a disease, a purely mental condition, a pathologic condition, something that can voluntarily and easily be quit by the user if he wants to quit it, and some say it is a sociologic and legal problem, while still others contend it is a medical problem primarily. No matter what different persons may call the condition, the patient is a sick person, and as such is entitled to and should have proper consideration, care, and treatment, either for the causes that are responsible for him being an addict, or for the addiction itself. There are thousands of addicts, many of them very poor and something has to be done for them, or with them, as the need is urgent. The fact that an addict cannot get his medicine in some legal way does not mean that he will not, or in many cases that he should not get it in some other way. If we fail to provide a legal way for the needy suffering to obtain relief, are we to blame them for seeking relief from some other source? They suffer with mental and physical troubles and should be given proper and humane consideration. They are as much in need of assistance as our insane patients are of proper asylum facilities, or are our surgical cases of a hospital.

The medicine can be gotten from the dispensary by these unfortunate cases for 6 cents a grain, allowing the patient to make a decent living. Would it be right to stop this and force these cases to a peddler, thereby enriching him, and making a pauper of the sufferer? If the patient goes to the average doctor his legitimate fee is more than the patient can afford to pay continuously, and the chances are many to one that as soon as the doctor finds out that he is an addict he will not even make a thorough examination to determine the causes of addiction, or to see if there is a real need for the drug, but he will very likely have nothing to do with the case at all, and let the patient go away in no better condition and with no more hope than he had before consulting him. The records will show that doctors are responsible for over 50 per cent of the cases of addiction in the beginning. Does the fact that a doctor will not assume this responsibility, or burden if he so chooses to call it, make a dispensary any less needed, or from a standpoint of right and necessity does it make the dispensary essential? The fact that we are not personally responsible for their addiction does not justify us in refusing to care for them, or to cure them of their addiction. . . .

I am sure that in this part of the country there is very little money spent, or real earnest effort made, on the part of the government to stop peddling, yet we know that our dispensary here has done more good along these lines than all other efforts combined.

I have never seen a patient who was forced into jail and forcefully treated (or rather mistreated) remain well when released. That method is inhuman and wrong. Some will say to throw him into jail and let him "kick it out," that he is not worth saving anyway. I believe that only those who are very ignorant of the whole matter will say this, or believe those who do say it. We have here just as good, refined, and deserving people who use opiates as there are in this state, and no one need feel that he is any better than they. . . .

To care for the incurables and to help the curable get well is our aim. In this city where we have several dozen incurable cases I do not believe it is possible to properly care for them without a well-conducted dispensary—one that has the hearty cooperation of all branches of the government, of the citizens, and of the medical fraternity as this dispensary has. There should be a venereal clinic in co-operation with the work, such as we have here, because many narcotic cases suffer with venereal diseases.

For old, infirm, incurable, or any other class of cases that are not treatable, I believe that a well-regulated dispensary, having a treatment institution to care for the curable cases, both run on honest, humane but practical and business-like principles with the cooperation of the whole community, is necessary.

It is our duty to show these patients the same consideration that we have for those suffering from other kinds of sickness.

Source: Willis P. Butler, M.D., "How One American City Is Meeting the Public Health Problems of Narcotic Drug Addiction," *American Medicine,* March 1922: 154–162.

Chapter 6

THE UNITED STATES GOES TO WAR AGAINST THE AXIS POWERS, 1917

Americans, including President Woodrow Wilson, had long assumed that those "great watery moats" of the Atlantic and Pacific protected their country from international troubles. But the European war that broke out in 1914 soon troubled Americans. A German victory might be the basis for an attempt at world domination and harm American interests. An Anglo-French victory, on the other hand, might freeze Americans out of vast markets in their growing empires.

The American public initially preferred neutrality, particularly when war orders stimulated an economic boom. Yet within three years the United States moved from determined neutrality to war. For over eighty years, historians have debated to what degree this effort was to defend democracy and Western civilization and to what extent it grew out of commercial and strategic interests that have led the country to its present world dominance. Scholars agree on a long list of causative factors, but assessing their relative importance is another matter.

Once the European powers became locked in trench warfare, the outcome depended heavily on denying the enemy access to the products of American industry and agriculture. Great Britain, the preeminent naval power, could establish blockades that were legitimate under international law of war: their ships could board neutral vessels to search for weapons, and if armaments were found could seize or sink ships after removing the crews and passengers. Germany's fragile submarines, which if they warned merchant ships were in danger of being outgunned or rammed, had little choice but to torpedo vessels without warning, violating international law. So whatever the Germans did harmed them. If American supplies continued to reach the Allies, they would lose the war of attrition. If their torpedoes killed Americans, they risked American intervention against them.

At the same time, American neutrality appeared to many observers as less neutral than it seemed. Americans and Britons had deep common cultural roots and sympathies coupled with vital economic relations. President Wilson and his closest advisers were very Anglophile, although their sympathies were muted by awareness that many Americans of Irish and German extraction were hostile to the British. The British enhanced the historical connection between the two nations through a sophisticated propaganda effort, while German efforts were awkward and unsuccessful. And British control of the ocean lanes made American prosperity dependent on trading with them and their allies. American entrance into the conflict some critics later attributed to the government's friendliness toward munitions makers and the bankers who had made loans to finance this trade in war supplies.

When the United States finally entered the war in April 1917, Wilson— despite an overwhelming vote in Congress for a declaration of war—was leading a divided people into the conflict, so prosecution of the war required a barrage of anti-German propaganda and the strenuous repression of dissent.

AMERICAN NEUTRALITY

President Wilson quickly declared the nation's neutrality and his secretary of state, the pacifist William Jennings Bryan, labored to maintain strictly neutral policies.

WILSON'S DECLARATION OF NEUTRALITY, AUGUST 19, 1914

The effect of the war upon the United States will depend upon what American citizens say and do. Every man who really loves America will act and speak in the true spirit of neutrality, which is the spirit of impartiality and fairness and friendliness to all concerned. The spirit of the nation in this critical matter will be determined largely by what individuals and society and those gathered in public meetings do and say, upon what newspapers and magazines contain, upon what ministers utter in their pulpits, and men proclaim as their opinions upon the street.

The people of the United States are drawn from many nations, and chiefly from the nations now at war. It is natural and inevitable that there should be the utmost variety of sympathy and desire among them with regard to the issues and circumstances of the conflict. Some will wish one nation, others another, to succeed in the momentous struggle. It will be easy to excite passion and difficult to allay it. Those responsible for exciting it will assume a heavy responsibility, responsibility for no less a thing than that the people of the United States, whose love of their country and whose loyalty to its government should unite them as Americans all, bound in honor and affection to think first of her and her interests, may be divided in camps of hostile opinion, hot against each other, involved in the war itself in impulse and opinion if not in action.

Such divisions amongst us would be fatal to our peace of mind and might seriously stand in the way of the proper performance of our duty as the one great nation at peace, the one people holding itself ready to play a part of impartial mediation and speak the counsels of peace and accommodation, not as a partisan, but as a friend.

I venture, therefore, my fellow countrymen, to speak a solemn word of warning to you against that deepest, most subtle, most essential breach of neutrality which may spring out of partisanship, out of passionately taking sides. The United States must be neutral in fact, as well as in name, during these days that are to try men's souls. We must be impartial in thought, as well as action, must put a curb upon our sentiments, as well as upon every transaction that might be construed as a preference of one party to the struggle before another.

Source: Message to Congress, 63rd Congress, 2nd Session, Senate Document No. 566 (Washington, 1914), 3–4.

SECRETARY OF STATE BRYAN'S OPPOSITION TO LOANS TO BELLIGERENTS, AUGUST 10, 1914

Bryan to President Woodrow Wilson,
August 10, 1914:

I beg to communicate to you an important matter which has come before the Department. Morgan Company of New York have asked whether there would be any objection to their making a loan to the French Government and also the Rothschilds—I suppose that is intended for the French Government. I have conferred with Mr. Lansing and he knows of no legal objection to financing this loan, but I have suggested to him the advisability of presenting to you an aspect of the case which is not legal but I believe to be consistent with our attitude in international matters. It is whether it would be advisable for this Government to take the position that it will not approve of any loan to a belligerent nation. The reasons that I would give in support of this proposition are:

First: Money is the worst of all contrabands because it commands everything else. The question of making loans contraband by international agreement has been discussed, but no action has been taken. I know of nothing that would do more to prevent war than an international agreement that neutral nations would not loan to belligerents. While such an agreement would be of great advantage, could we not by our example hasten the reaching of such an agreement? We are the one great nation which is not involved, and our refusal to loan to any belligerent would naturally tend to hasten a conclusion of the war. We are responsible for the use of our influence through example, and as we cannot tell what we can do until we try, the only way of testing our influence is to set the example and observe its effect. This is the fundamental reason in support of the suggestion submitted.

Second: There is a special and local reason, it seems to me, why this course would be advisable. Mr. Lansing observed in the discussion of the subject that a loan would be taken by those in sympathy with the country in whose behalf the loan was negotiated. If we approved of a loan to France we could not, of course, object to a loan to Great Britain, Germany, Russia, or to any other country, and if loans were made to these countries, our citizens would be divided into groups, each group loaning money to the country which it favors and this money could not be furnished without expressions of sympathy. These expressions of sympathy are disturbing enough when they do not rest upon pecuniary interests—they would be still more disturbing if each group was pecuniarily interested in the success of the nation to whom its members had loaned money.

Third: The powerful financial interests which would be connected with these loans would be tempted to use their influence through the newspapers to support the interests of the Government to which they had loaned because the value of the security would be directly affected by the result of the war. We would thus find our newspapers violently arrayed on one side or the other, each paper supporting a financial group and pecuniary interest. All of this influence would make it all the more difficult for us to maintain neutrality as our action on various questions that would arise would affect one side or the other and powerful financial interests would be thrown into the balance. . . .

As we cannot prevent American citizens going abroad at their own risk, so we cannot prevent dollars going abroad at the risk of the owners, but the influence of the Government is used to prevent American citizens from doing this. Would the Government not be justified in using its influence against the enlistment of the nation's dollars in a foreign war?

Source: Senate Hearings, 74th Congress, 2nd Session, "Munitions Industry Hearings," pt. 25, January 7, 8, 1936 (Washington, 1937), 7665–7666.

SECRETARY BRYAN, MESSAGES TO GREAT BRITAIN AND TO GERMANY, FEBRUARY 10, 1915

To Great Britain

The department has been advised . . . that the British Government . . . on January thirty-first explicitly authorized the use of neutral flags on British merchant vessels presumably for the purpose of avoiding recognition by German naval forces. The department's attention has also been directed to reports in the press that the captain of the *Lusitania,* acting upon orders or information received from the British authorities, raised the American flag as his vessel approached the British coasts, in order to escape anticipated attacks by German submarines. . . .

The formal declaration of such a policy of general misuse of a neutral's flag jeopardizes the vessels of the neutral visiting those waters in a peculiar degree by raising the presumption that they are of belligerent nationality regardless of the flag which they may carry.

In view of the announced purpose of the German Admiralty to engage in active naval operations in certain delimited sea areas adjacent to the coasts of Great Britain and Ireland, the Government of the United States would view with anxious solicitude any general use of the flag of the United States by British vessels traversing those waters.

To Germany

The Government of the United States, having had its attention directed to the proclamation of the German Admiralty issued on the fourth of February, that the waters surrounding Great Britain and Ireland, including the whole of the English Channel, are to be considered as comprised within the seat of war; that all enemy merchant vessels found in those waters after the eighteenth instant will be destroyed . . . and that neutral vessels expose themselves to danger within this zone of war because, in view of the misuse of neutral flags . . . , it may not be possible always to exempt neutral ships from attacks intended to strike enemy ships, feels it to be its duty to call the attention of the Imperial Government of Germany . . . to the very serious possibilities of the course of action apparently contemplated under that proclamation. . . .

If the commanders of German vessels of war should act upon the presumption that the flag of the United States was not being used in good faith and should destroy on the high seas an American vessel or the lives of American citizens, it would be difficult for the Government of the United States to view the act in any other light than as an indefensible violation of neutral rights.

Source: The Messages and Papers of Woodrow Wilson (New York: Review of Reviews Corporation, 1924), 220–224.

THE SINKING OF THE *LUSITANIA*

On May 7, 1915, a German U-boat sank the British liner, the Lusitania, *with the loss of 1,198 lives, among them 128 Americans. The German government's published warnings to Americans against traveling on the ship had been generally ignored, as was the presence aboard it of over eight thousand boxes of munitions destined for Allied armies. Americans, nonetheless, condemned German submarine policy. Bryan resigned as secretary of state rather than endorse Wilson's stiff note to the German government over the incident which he feared would bring the United States into the war. Robert Lansing replaced him as secretary of state.*

GERMAN WARNING IGNORED
NEW YORK TIMES

SAILS UNDISTURBED BY GERMAN WARNING

The advertisement signed by the German Embassy which appeared in yesterday's newspapers warning Americans not to travel on British steamships across the Atlantic, because they ran the risk of being torpedoed, was commented upon by the passengers on the Lusitania, but did not cause any of them to cancel their booking. On the contrary the big liner left at 12:30 o'clock with 1,388 passengers, which was the largest number carried eastbound by one ship this year.

When the attention of Captain W. T. Turner, commander of the Lusitania, was called to the warning, he laughed and said: "I wonder what the Germans will do next. Well, it doesn't seem as if they had scared many people from going on the ship by the look of the pier and the passenger list."

Source: New York Times, May 2, 1915.

EDITORIAL REACTION TO THE SINKING OF THE *LUSITANIA*

WAR BY ASSASSINATION

From our Department of State there must go to the Imperial Government at Berlin a demand that the Germans shall no longer make war like savages drunk with blood, that they shall cease to seek the attainment of their ends by the assassination of non-combatants and neutrals. In the history of wars there is no single deed comparable in its inhumanity and its horror to the destruction, without warning, by German torpedoes of the great steamship Lusitania, with more than 1,800 souls on board, and among them more than 100 Americans. . . .

The evidence of deliberation, of an intent to destroy this particular ship, is too nearly conclusive to be ignored. Upon the very day the Lusitania sailed the Imperial German Embassy at Washington caused to be published in the newspapers of this country an advertisement warning travelers that ships flying the flag of Great Britain were liable to destruction in the waters about the British Isles and that passengers "sailing in the war zone on ships of Great Britain or her allies do so at their own risk." There were other warnings. They were not heeded by the passengers who sailed on the Lusitania, simply because it was impossible for them to believe that a great civilized nation like Germany would wantonly destroy a merchant ship carrying only peaceable non-combatants. We have learned much about Germany since the war began, much that has shocked the world's sense of humanity, but this frightful deed was held to be within the domain of the incredible until it was perpetrated. It transcends in atrocity anything our Government could have apprehended at the time it issued its warning.

Source: New York Times, May 8, 1915.

THE ANGLO-AMERICAN CONNECTION

Wilson's policy of quietly permitting large bank loans to the belligerents amounted in practice to supplying credit to the Allies alone, since only they could hope to transport bulky American goods across the Atlantic. Meanwhile, British propagandists presented the Americans with a steady stream of interpretations of war issues that Germany could not match.

President Wilson's Policy on Loans to Belligerents

My dear Mr. Secretary [William Jennings Bryan]:

My opinion of this matter [loans to belligerents], compendiously stated, is that we should say that "Parties [the Wilson administration] would take no action either for or against such a transaction," but that this should be orally conveyed, so far as we are concerned, and not put in writing.

I hope this is also your own judgment of the matter.

Faithfully yours,

W. W.

Source: *Foreign Relations of the United States: The Lansing Papers* (Washington: GPO, 1939), I: 144.

British Propaganda: The U-boats

The annals of the sea contain many stories of disaster, from the loss of the *White Ship* to the sinking of the *Titanic* and the *Empress of Ireland*. We have all been accustomed from childhood to read with deep emotion the accounts of historic shipwrecks, the tragic details condensed by Byron into the stanza:

Then rose from sea to sky the wild farewell,
    Then shrieked the timid and stood still the brave,
Then some leaped overboard with dreadful yell,
    As eager to anticipate their grave;
And the sea yawned around her like a hell,
    And down she sucked with her the whirling wave,
As one who grapples with his enemy,
And strives to strangle him before he die.

Even more terrible than the stories of the disasters themselves are the accounts of the agonies endured by survivors drifting helplessly on rafts or in open boats, and dying, one by one, of hunger, thirst, and exposure. These things cannot but haunt the imagination, especially of a seafaring race. There have been those who have been tempted to question the beneficence of the Power which brings to pass, or permits, such horrors as have frequently been enacted on the treacherous sea.

But until the present war broke out it had occurred to no one to imagine that disasters due to "the act of God" would ever be reduplicated with cold deliberation by the act of man. Who could have conceived, at midsummer, 1914, that more destruction to the world's merchant shipping, and suffering to harmless seamen and passengers, would be caused within the next three years by the calculated policy of a so-called civilised power, than had been attributable in a century to perils naturally incident to the lives of those who go down to the sea in ships? This is the phenomenon with which we are face to face to-day—the callousness of man far outstripping in its ravages the heedless destructiveness of natural forces. It is an appalling picture, and one well calculated to give the final touch of bitterness to that loathing of the German idol—War—with which Germany has made it her business to inspire all reasonable men.

The following pages contain a sketch of the gradual decline, in Germany's employment of the U-boat, from honourable to dishonourable, and finally to atrocious, uses. The time has not yet come for an exhaustive history of her piratical career. Only a few of its more conspicuous episodes are here briefly recorded, but sufficient to show to what depths of infamy she has been dragged down by a false philosophy playing into the hands of an overweening national egoism. . . .

* * *

When in January, 1917, the German Government resolved upon its great gamble, and announced the policy of "unrestricted" U-boat warfare, it did not fail to disclaim even the restriction placed by international law upon the sinking of hospital ships. Its great aim was to reduce the world's tonnage, no matter to what ends the tonnage was applied. It accordingly announced that it held "conclusive proof" of the misuse of hospital ships for the transport of munitions and troops, and that therefore "the traffic of hospital ships . . . would no longer be tolerated.". . .

The *Asturias,* which had escaped destruction two years earlier, was the first victim. She was torpedoed without warning on the night of March 20, when she was steaming with all navigating lights and with all the proper distinguishing Red Cross signs brilliantly illuminated. Of the medical staff 14 lost their lives, including one female staff nurse, and of the ship's company 29, including one stewardess.

Ten days later (March 30) the *Gloucester Castle* was torpedoed without warning in mid-channel. All the wounded, however, were successfully removed from the ship.

On the evening of April 17, two ships, the *Donegal* and the *Lanfranc,* were torpedoed without warning, while transporting wounded to British ports, [suffering many casualties]. . . .

The German Government afterwards offered to call off its war on hospital ships on two impudent conditions: first, that all such ships should pursue a route to be prescribed by Germany; second, that a Spanish officer should sail in each ship to guarantee that it was applied to no improper uses. These proposals were naturally treated with contempt by the British Government. Since the sinking of the *Donegal* and the *Lanfranc,* hospital ships no longer carry any distinctive marks, as these were found simply to attract the pirates.

Source: William Archer, *The Pirate's Progress: A Short History of the U-Boat* (New York and London: Harpers, 1918), 1–3, 93–97.

THE UNITED STATES ENTERS THE WAR

In early 1917 events crowded upon one another, pressing the United States to enter the war. When the German government announced that unrestricted submarine warfare would resume on February 1, Wilson quickly severed diplomatic relations. German submarines soon torpedoed five American ships, killing several American citizens. British intelligence officers then made public a startling secret. Germany's foreign minister, Arthur Zimmermann, had promised Mexico a chance to take back former territory in New Mexico, Texas, and Arizona if that nation would declare war on the United States. A stunned, angry American public now eagerly followed where Wilson reluctantly led. On April 2, 1917, the President asked Congress for a declaration of war. The resolution passed four days later.

THE ZIMMERMANN TELEGRAM

Berlin, January 19, 1917

On the first of February we intend to begin submarine warfare unrestricted. In spite of this, it is our intention to endeavor to keep neutral the United States of America.

If this attempt is not successful, we propose an alliance on the following basis with Mexico: That we shall make war together and together make peace. We shall give general financial support, and it is understood that Mexico is to reconquer the lost territory in New Mexico, Texas, and Arizona. The details are left to you for settlement.

You are instructed to inform the President of Mexico of the above in the greatest confidence as soon as it is certain that there will be an outbreak of war with the United States and suggest that the President of Mexico, on his own initiative, should communicate with Japan suggesting adherence at once to this plan; at the same time, offer to mediate between Germany and Japan.

Please call to the attention of the President of Mexico that the employment of ruthless submarine warfare now promises to compel England to make peace in a few months.

ZIMMERMANN

Source: Congressional Record, March 1, 1917, vol. LVI, pt. 1: 680–681.

PRESIDENT WILSON'S WAR MESSAGE, APRIL 2, 1917

ADDRESS DELIVERED AT JOINT SESSION OF
THE TWO HOUSES OF CONGRESS, APRIL 2, 1917

I have called the Congress into extraordinary session because there are serious, very serious, choices of policy to be made, and made immediately, which it was neither right nor constitutionally permissible that I should assume the responsibility of making.

On the third of February last I officially laid before you the extraordinary announcement of the Imperial German Government that on and after the first day of February it was its purpose to put aside all restraints of law or of humanity and use its submarines to sink every vessel that sought to approach either the ports of Great Britain and Ireland or the western coasts of Europe or any of the ports controlled by the enemies of Germany within the Mediterranean. . . .

The new policy has swept every restriction aside. Vessels of every kind, whatever their flag, their character, their cargo, their destination, their errand, have been ruthlessly sent to the bottom without warning and without thought of help or mercy for those on board, the vessels of friendly neutrals along with those of belligerents. Even hospital ships and ships carrying relief to the sorely bereaved and stricken people of Belgium, though the latter were provided with safe conduct through the proscribed areas by the German Government itself and were distinguished by unmistakable marks of identity, have been sunk with the same reckless lack of compassion or of principle. . . .

It is a war against all nations. American ships have been sunk, American lives taken, in ways which it has stirred us very deeply to learn of, but the ships and people of other neutral and friendly nations have been sunk and overwhelmed in the waters in the same way. There has been no discrimination. The challenge is to all mankind. Each nation must decide for itself how it will meet it. The choice we make for ourselves must be made with a moderation of counsel and a temperateness of judgment befitting our character and our motives as a nation. We must put excited feeling away. Our motive will not be revenge or the victorious assertion of the physical might of the nation, but only the vindication of right, of human right, of which we are only a single champion.

When I addressed the Congress on the twenty-sixth of February last I thought that it would suffice to assert our neutral rights with arms, our right to use the seas against unlawful interference, our right to keep our people safe against unlawful violence. But armed neutrality, it now appears, is impracticable. Because submarines are in effect outlaws when used as the German submarines have been used against merchant shipping, it is impossible to defend ships against their attacks as the law of nations has assumed that merchantmen would defend themselves against privateers or cruisers, visible craft giving chase upon the open sea. . . .

There is one choice we cannot make, we are incapable of making: we will not choose the path of submission and suffer the most sacred rights of our Nation and our people to be ignored or violated. The wrongs against which we now array ourselves are no common wrongs; they cut to the very roots of human life.

With a profound sense of the solemn and even tragical character of the step I am taking and of the grave responsibilities which it involves, but in unhesitating obedience to what I deem my constitutional duty, I advise that the Congress declare the recent course of the Imperial German Government to be in fact nothing less than war against the government and people of the United States; that it formally accept the status of belligerent which has thus been thrust upon it; and that it take immediate steps not only to put the country in a more thorough state of defense but also to exert all its power and employ all its resources to bring the Government of the German Empire to terms and end the war. . . .

Neutrality is no longer feasible or desirable where the peace of the world is involved and the freedom of its peoples, and the menace to that peace and freedom lies in the existence of autocratic governments backed by organized force which is controlled wholly by their will, not by the will of their people. We have seen the last of neutrality in such circumstances. We are at the beginning of an age in which it will be insisted that the same standards of conduct and of responsibility for wrong done shall be observed among nations and their governments that are observed among the individual citizens of civilized states.

We have no quarrel with the German people. We have no feeling towards them but one of sympathy and friendship. It was not upon their impulse that their government acted in entering this war. It was not with their previous knowledge or approval. . . .

The world must be made safe for democracy. Its peace must be planted upon the tested foundations of political liberty. We have no selfish ends to serve. We desire no conquest, no dominion. We seek no indemnities for ourselves, no material compensation for the sacrifices we shall freely make. We are but one of the champions of the rights of mankind. We shall be satisfied when those rights have been made as secure as the faith and the freedom of nations can make them. . . .

It is a distressing and oppressive duty, Gentlemen of the Congress, which I have performed in thus addressing you. There are, it may be, many months of fiery trial and sacrifice ahead of us. It is a fearful thing to lead this great peaceful people into war, into the most terrible and disastrous of all wars, civilization itself seeming to be in the balance. But the right is more precious than peace, and we shall fight for the things which we have always carried nearest our hearts,—

for democracy, for the right of those who submit to authority to have a voice in their own Governments, for the rights and liberties of small nations, for a universal dominion of right by such a concert of free peoples as shall bring peace and safety to all nations and make the world itself at last free. To such a task we can dedicate our lives and our fortunes, everything that we are and everything that we have, with the pride of those who know that the day has come when America is privileged to spend her blood and her might for the principles that gave her birth and happiness and the peace which she has treasured. God helping her, she can do no other.

Source: Washington Post, April 3, 1917.

OPPOSITION AND REPRESSION

Among the various groups in American society opposed to entry into the war were many American socialists, such as Eugene V. Debs. Prosecuted under the Espionage Act of 1917, he was sentenced to ten years in the Atlanta Federal Penitentiary for delivering the speech printed here. In 1920 as prisoner #9653 he conducted his fifth campaign for President on the Socialist Party ticket, receiving nearly a million votes. In a famous decision written by Justice Oliver Wendell Holmes, Jr., the Supreme Court in 1919 upheld the constitutionality of the Espionage Act.

Eugene V. Debs, Speech, Canton, Ohio, June 16, 1918

[I]t is extremely dangerous to exercise the constitutional right of free speech in a country fighting to make democracy safe in the world.

I realize that, in speaking to you this afternoon, there are certain limitations placed upon the right of free speech. . . . I may not be able to say all I think; but I am not going to say anything that I do not think. I would rather a thousand times be a free soul in jail than to be a sycophant and a coward in the streets. . . .

Are we opposed to Prussian militarism? (Shouts from the crowd of "Yes, Yes!") . . . I hate, I loathe, I despise Junkers and junkerdom. I have no earthly use for the Junkers of Germany, and not one particle more for the Junkers in the United States.

They tell us that we live in a great republic; that our institutions are democratic; that we are a free and self-governing people. This is too much even for a joke. . . .

To whom do the Wall Street Junkers in our country marry their daughters? After they have wrung their countless millions from your sweat, your agony and your life's blood, in a time of war and in a time of peace, they invest these untold millions in the purchase of titles of broken-down aristocrats, such as princes, dukes, counts and other parasites and no-accounts. Would they be satisfied to wed their daughters to honest workingmen? To real democrats? Oh, no! They scour the markets of Europe for vampires who are titled and nothing else. . . .

These are the gentry who are today wrapped up in the American flag, who shout from the housetops that they are the only patriots, and who have their magnifying glasses in hand, scanning the country for evidence of disloyalty, eager to apply the brand of treason to the men who dare to even whisper their opposition to junker rule in the United States. No wonder Sam Johnson declared that "patriotism is the last refuge of the scoundrel." He must have had this Wall Street gentry in mind, or at least their prototypes, for in every age it has been the tyrant, the oppressor and the exploiter who has wrapped himself in the cloak of patriotism, or religion, or both to deceive and overawe the people. . . .

Wars throughout history have been waged for conquest and plunder. In the Middle Ages when the feudal lords who inhabited the castles whose towers may still be seen along the Rhine Valley concluded to enlarge their domains, to increase their power, their prestige, their wealth they declared war upon one another. But they themselves did not go to war any more than the modern feudal lords, the barons of Wall Street go to war. The feudal barons of the Middle Ages, the economic predecessors of the capitalists of our day, declared all wars. And their miserable serfs fought all the battles. The poor, ignorant serfs had been taught to revere their masters; to believe that when their masters declared war upon one another, it was their patriotic duty to fall upon one another and to cut one another's throats for the profit and glory of the lords and barons who held them in contempt. And that is war in a nutshell. The master class has always declared the wars; the subject class has always fought the battles, while the subject class has had nothing to gain and all to lose—especially their lives.

Source: Eugene V. Debs, *The Canton Speech, with Statements to the Jury and the Court* (New York: Oriole Chapbooks, ND), 3, 6–7, 11.

Associate Justice Oliver Wendell Holmes, Jr., for the Court, *Schenck v. United States*, 1919

The document in question upon its first printed side recited the first section of the Thirteenth Amendment, said that the idea embodied in it was violated by the Conscription Act and that a conscript is little better than a convict. In impassioned language it intimated that conscription was despotism in its worse form and a monstrous wrong against humanity in the interest of Wall Street's chosen few. It said, "Do not submit to intimidation," but in form at least confined itself to peaceful measures such as a petition for the repeal of the act. The other and later printed side of the sheet was headed "Assert Your Rights." It stated reasons for alleging that any one violated the Constitution when he refused to recognize "your right to assert your opposition to the draft," and went on "If you do not assert and support your rights, you are helping to deny or disparage rights which it is the solemn duty of all citizens and residents of the United States to retain." It described the arguments on the other side as coming from cunning politicians and a mercenary capitalist press, and even silent consent to the conscription law as helping to support an infamous conspiracy. It denied the power to send our citizens away to foreign shores to shoot up the people of other lands, and added that words could not express the condemnation such cold-blooded ruthlessness deserves, &c., &c., winding up "You must do your share to maintain, support and uphold the rights of the people of this country." Of course the document would not have been sent unless it had been intended to have some effect, and we do not see what effect it could be expected to have upon persons subject to the draft except to influence them to obstruct the carrying of it out. The defendants do not deny that the jury might find against them on this point.

But it is said, suppose that that was the tendency of this circular, it is protected by the First Amendment to the Constitution. . . . We admit that in many places and in ordinary times the defendants in saying all that was said in the circular would have been within their constitutional rights. But the character of every act depends upon the circumstances in which it is done. The most stringent protection of free speech would not protect a man in falsely shouting fire in a theatre and causing a panic. It does not even protect a man from an injunction against uttering words that may have all the effect of force. The question in every case is whether the words used are used in such circumstances and are of such a nature as to create a clear and present danger that they will bring about the substantive evils that Congress has a right to prevent. It is a question of proximity and degree. When a nation is at war many things that might be said in time of peace are such a hindrance to its effort that their utterance will not be endured so long as men fight and that no Court could regard them as protected by any constitutional right. It seems to be admitted that if an actual obstruction of the recruiting service were proved, liability for words that produced that effect might be enforced. The statute of 1917 in sec. 4 punishes conspiracies to obstruct as well as actual obstruction. If the act, (speaking, or circulating a paper,) its tendency and the intent with which it is done are the same, we perceive no ground for saying that success alone warrants making the act a crime. . . .

Judgements affirmed.

Source: Schenck v. United States, 249 U.S. 47.

Chapter 7

MARGARET SANGER BATTLES FOR BIRTH CONTROL

When Margaret Sanger was born in 1879, making artificial contraception available was against federal law as well as the law of many states. The Comstock Act of 1873, named for its chief lobbyist, Anthony Comstock, president of the influential Society for the Suppression of Vice, had made it a federal crime to provide information about "the prevention of conception." By the time Margaret Sanger died in 1966 the Supreme Court in *Griswold v. Connecticut,* decided a year earlier, had established birth control—a term she coined—as a legal right, the first effective birth control pill had been marketed, and the American government was beginning to incorporate family planning into the nation's public health and social welfare programs as well as its foreign policy. While her life does not provide the full story of securing the right of contraception, her activities and decisions during the first half of the twentieth century greatly influenced this most intimate precinct of life.

Born Margaret Louisa Higgins in Corning, New York, Margaret Sanger was the sixth of eleven children. In explaining her social activism, she always referred to her mother's travail in raising too many children on too little money. After attending college and nursing school, she married William Sanger, an artist and architect who supported and even went to jail for her cause. Eight years of suburban living, during which the Sangers had three children, left Margaret restless and dissatisfied. In 1910, they moved to Manhattan, where she began work as a visiting nurse and became active in radical politics. She soon concentrated her activities on birth control: learning about it, disseminating information to poor women, finally creating institutions that would make the prevention of unwanted pregnancies an accepted part of American life.

Margaret Sanger was a great publicist of her cause and herself. In this chapter, we follow through her several autobiographical writings the evolution of her reformist commitment.

FINDING A VOCATION, 1912

Margaret Sanger absorbed from radicals like the anarchist Emma Gold-man ideas about the need for women to control their sexual lives. Her experiences while she was a visiting nurse in the lower East Side of Manhattan, a neighborhood crowded with desperately poor immigrants, stirred her to act on these beliefs.

AWAKENING TO THE CAUSE

Early in the year 1912 I came to a sudden realization that my work as a nurse and my activities in social service were entirely palliative and consequently futile and useless to relieve the misery I saw all about me. . . .

When I look back upon that period it seems only a short time ago; yet in the brief interval conditions have changed enormously. At that time it was not the usual thing for a poor woman to go to a hospital to give birth to her baby. She preferred to stay at home. She was afraid of hospitals when any serious ailment was involved. That is not the case today. Women of all classes are more likely to have their babies in lying-in hospitals or in private sanatoriums than at home; but in those days a woman's own bedroom, no matter how inconveniently arranged, was the usual place for confinement. That was the day of home nursing, and it gave a trained nurse splendid opportunities to learn social conditions through actual contact with them.

Were it possible for me to depict the revolting conditions existing in the homes of some of the women I attended in that one year, one would find it hard to believe. There was at that time, and doubtless is still today, a sub-stratum of men and women whose lives are absolutely untouched by social agencies.

The way they live is almost beyond belief. They hate and fear any prying into their homes or into their lives. They resent being talked to. The women slink in and out of their homes on their way to market like rats from their holes. The men beat their wives sometimes black and blue, but no one interferes. The children are cuffed, kicked and chased about, but woe to the child who dares to tell tales out of the home! Crime or drink is often the source of this secret aloofness; usually there is something to hide, a skeleton in the closet somewhere. The men are sullen, unskilled workers, picking up odd jobs now and then, unemployed usually, sauntering in and out of the house at all hours of the day and night.

The women keep apart from other women in the neighborhood. Often they are suspected of picking a pocket or "lifting" an article when occasion arises. Pregnancy is an almost chronic condition amongst them. I knew one woman who had given birth to eight children with no professional care whatever. The last one was born in the kitchen, witnessed by a son of ten years who, under his mother's direction, cleaned the bed, wrapped the placenta and soiled articles in paper, and threw them out of the window into the court below.

They reject help of any kind and want you to "mind your own business." Birth and death they consider their own affairs. They survive as best they can, suspicious of everyone, deathly afraid of police and officials of every kind. . . .

In this atmosphere abortions and birth become the main theme of conversation. On Saturday nights I have seen groups of fifty to one hundred women going into questionable offices well known in the community for cheap abortions. I asked several women what took place there, and they all gave the same reply: a quick examination, a probe inserted into the uterus and turned a few times to disturb the fertilized ovum, and then the woman was sent home. Usually the flow began the next day and often continued four or five weeks. Sometimes an ambulance carried the victim to the hospital for a curetage, and if she returned home at all she was looked upon as a lucky woman.

This state of things became a nightmare with me. There seemed no sense to it all, no reason for such waste of mother life, no right to exhaust women's vitality and to throw them on the scrap-heap before the age of thirty-five.

Everywhere I looked, misery and fear stalked—men fearful of losing their jobs, women fearful that even worse conditions might come upon them. The menace of another pregnancy hung like a sword over the head of every poor woman I came in contact with that year. The question which met me was always the same: What can I do to keep from it? or, What can I do to get out of this? Sometimes they talked among themselves bitterly.

"It's the rich that know the tricks," they'd say, "while we have all the kids." Then, if the women were Roman Catholics, they talked about "Yankee tricks," and asked me if I knew what the Protestants did to keep their families down. When I said that I didn't believe that the rich knew much more than they did I was laughed at and suspected of holding back information for money. They would nudge each other and say something about paying me before I left the case if I would reveal the "secret.". . .

I heard over and over again of their desperate efforts at bringing themselves "around"—drinking various herb-teas, taking drops of turpentine on sugar, steaming over a chamber of boiling coffee or of turpentine water, rolling down stairs, and finally inserting slippery-elm sticks, or knitting needles, or shoe hooks into the uterus. I used to shudder with horror as I heard the details and, worse yet, learned of the conditions *behind the reason* for such desperate actions. Day after day these stories were poured into my ears. I knew hundreds of these women personally, and knew much of their hopeless, barren, dreary lives. . . .

They claimed my thoughts night and day. One by one these women, with their worried, sad, pensive and ageing faces would marshal themselves before me in my dreams, sometimes appealingly, sometimes accusingly. I could not escape from the facts of their misery, neither was I able to see the way out of their problems and their troubles. Like one walking in a sleep, I kept on.

Finally the thing began to shape itself, to become accumulative during the three weeks I spent in the home of a desperately sick woman living on Grand Street, a lower section of New York's East Side.

Mrs. Sacks was only twenty-eight years old; her husband, an unskilled worker, thirty-two. Three children, aged five, three and one, were none too strong nor sturdy, and it took all the earnings of the father and the ingenuity of the mother to keep them clean, provide them with air and proper food, and give them a chance to grow into decent manhood and womanhood.

Both parents were devoted to these children and to each other. The woman had become pregnant and had taken various drugs and purgatives, as advised by her neighbors. Then, in desperation, she had used some instrument lent to her by a friend. She was found prostrate on the floor amidst the crying children when her husband returned from work. Neighbors advised against the ambulance, and a friendly doctor was called. The husband would not hear of her going to a hospital, and as a little money had been saved in the bank a nurse was called and the battle for that precious life began.

It was in the middle of July. The three-room apartment was turned into a hospital for the dying patient. Never had I worked so fast, never so concentratedly as I did to keep alive that little mother. Neighbor women came and went during the day doing the odds and ends necessary for our comfort. The children were sent to friends and relatives and the doctor and I settled ourselves to outdo the force and power of an outraged nature.

Never had I known such conditions could exist. July's sultry days and nights were melted into a torpid inferno. Day after day, night after night, I slept only in brief snatches, ever too anxious about the condition of that feeble heart bravely carrying on, to stay long from the bedside of the patient. With but one toilet for the building and that on the floor below, everything had to be carried down for disposal, while ice, food, and other necessities had to be carried three flights up. It was one of those old airshaft buildings of which there were several thousands then standing in New York City.

At the end of two weeks recovery was in sight, and at the end of three weeks I was preparing to leave the fragile patient to take up the ordinary duties of her life, including those of wifehood and motherhood. Everyone was congratulating her on her recovery. All the kindness of sympathetic and understanding neighbors poured in upon her in the shape of convalescent dishes, soups, custards, and drinks. Still she appeared to be despondent and worried. She seemed to sit apart in her thoughts as if she had no part in these congratulatory messages and endearing welcomes. I thought at first that she still retained some of her unconscious memories and dwelt upon them in her silences.

But as the hour for my departure came nearer, her anxiety increased, and finally with trembling voice she said: "Another baby will finish me, I suppose."

"It's too early to talk about that," I said, and resolved that I would turn the question over to the doctor for his advice. When he came I said: "Mrs. Sacks is worried about having another baby."

"She well might be," replied the doctor, and then he stood before her and said: "Any more such capers, young woman, and there will be no need to call me."

"Yes, yes—I know, Doctor," said the patient with trembling voice, "but," and she hesitated as if it took all of her courage to say it, "*what* can I do to prevent getting that way again?"

"Oh ho!" laughed the doctor good naturedly, "You want your cake while you eat it too, do you? Well, it can't be done." Then, familiarly slapping her on the back and picking up his hat and bag to depart, he said: "I'll tell you the only sure thing to do. Tell Jake to sleep on the roof!"

With those words he closed the door and went down the stairs, leaving us both petrified and stunned.

Tears sprang to my eyes, and a lump came in my throat as I looked at that face before me. It was stamped with sheer horror. I thought for a moment she might have gone insane, but she conquered her feelings, whatever they may have been, and turning to me in desperation said: "He can't understand, can he?—he's a man after all—but you do, don't you? You're a woman and you'll tell me the secret and I'll never tell it to a soul."

She clasped her hands as if in prayer, she leaned over and looked straight into my eyes and beseechingly implored me to tell her something—something *I really did not know*. It was like being on a rack and tortured for a crime one had not committed. To plead guilty would stop the agony; otherwise the rack kept turning.

I had to turn away from that imploring face. I could not answer her then. I quieted her as best I could. She saw that I was moved by the tears in my eyes. I promised that I would come back in a few days and tell her what she wanted to know. The few simple means of limiting the family like *coitus interruptus* or the condom were laughed at by the neighboring women when told these were the means used by men in the well-to-do families. That was not believed, and I knew such an answer would be swept aside as useless were I to tell her this at such a time.

A little later when she slept I left the house, and made up my mind that I'd keep away from those cases in the future. I felt helpless to do anything at all. I seemed chained hand and foot, and longed for an earthquake or a volcano to shake the world out of its lethargy into facing these monstrous atrocities.

The intelligent reasoning of the young mother—how to *prevent* getting that way again—how sensible, how just she had been—yes, I promised myself I'd go back and have a long talk with her and tell her more, and perhaps she would not laugh but would believe that those methods were all that were really known.

But time flew past, and weeks rolled into months. That wistful, appealing face haunted me day and night. I could not banish from my mind memories of that trembling voice begging so humbly for knowledge she had a right to have. I was about to retire one night three months later when the telephone rang and an agitated man's voice begged me to come at once to help his wife who was sick again. It was the husband of Mrs. Sacks, and I intuitively knew before I left the telephone that it was almost useless to go.

I dreaded to face that woman. I was tempted to send someone else in my place. I longed for an accident on the subway, or on the street—anything to prevent my going into that home. But on I went just the same. I arrived a few minutes after the doctor, the same one who had given her such noble advice. The woman was dying. She was unconscious. She died within ten minutes after my arrival. It was the same result, the same story told a thousand times before—death from abortion. She had become pregnant, had used drugs, had then consulted a five-dollar professional abortionist, and death followed. . . .

The Revolution came—but not as it has been pictured nor as history relates that revolutions have come. It came in my own life. It began in my very being as I walked home that night after I had closed the eyes and covered with a sheet the body of that little helpless mother whose life had been sacrificed to ignorance.

After I left that desolate house I walked and walked and walked; for hours and hours I kept on, bag in hand, thinking, regretting, dreading to stop; fearful of my conscience, dreading to face my own accusing soul. At three in the morning I arrived home still clutching a heavy load the weight of which I was quite unconscious.

I entered the house quietly, as was my custom, and looked out of the window down upon the dimly lighted, sleeping city. . . .

For hours I stood, motionless and tense, expecting something to happen. I watched the lights go out, I saw the darkness gradually give way to the first shimmer of dawn, and then a colorful sky heralded the rise of the sun. I knew a new day had come for me and a new world as well.

It was like an illumination. I could now see clearly the various social strata of our life; all its mass problems seemed to be centered around uncontrolled breeding. There was only one thing to be done: call out, start the alarm, set the heather on fire! Awaken the womanhood of America to free the motherhood of the world! I released from my almost paralyzed hand the nursing bag which unconsciously I had clutched, threw it across the room, tore the uniform from my body, flung it into a corner, and renounced all palliative work forever.

I would never go back again to nurse women's ailing bodies while their miseries were as vast as the stars. I was now finished with superficial cures, with doctors and nurses and social workers who were brought face to face with this overwhelming truth of women's needs and yet turned to pass on the other side. They must be made to see these facts. I resolved that women should have knowledge of contraception. They have every right to know about their own bodies. I would strike out—I would scream from the housetops. I would tell the world what was going on in the lives of these poor women. I *would* be heard. No matter what it should cost. *I would be heard.*

I went to bed and slept.

That decision gave me the first undisturbed sleep I had had in over a year. I slept soundly and free from dreams, free from haunting faces.

I announced to my family the following day that I had finished nursing, that I would never go on another case—and I never have.

Source: My Fight for Birth Control (New York: Farrar and Rinehart, 1931), 46–57. Reprinted by permission.

THE WOMAN REBEL

Margaret Sanger found her first support among socialists and labor leaders. Censorship by the post office of her publications made her a heroine of the left, and in 1914 she fled to Europe to avoid arrest as well as to learn more about methods of birth control. She writes of being the woman rebel.

PUBLISHING *THE WOMAN REBEL*

In those years just before the war a new religion was spreading over our country. It had no definite name, and its adherents would have been the first vociferously to deny that they were religious. This new faith was made up of scoffers, rebels, revolutionists, anarchists, socialists of all shades, from the "pink tea" intellectual to the dark purple lawbreaker. The term "radical" was used to cover them all. But while all were freethinkers, agnostics or atheists, they were as fanatical in their faith in the coming revolution as ever any primitive Christian was for the immediate establishment of the Kingdom of God. . . .

Almost without realizing it, you became a "comrade" or "fellow worker"; like the primitive Christian, a member of a secret order. The martyr, it has been well said, creates the faith. Well, there were martyrs aplenty in those days—men and women who had served sentences in prison for their beliefs and who were honored accordingly. One had hardly any social standing at all in radical circles unless one had "worked for wages," or brushed up against the police, or had served at least a few days in jail. As in the early Church, most of the members of this order were of the working classes, though there were eccentric millionaires, editors, lawyers, and rich women who had experienced "conversion" and were active in the "movement." Some could even predict the exact date of the coming Revolution. . . .

It is not hard to laugh about it all now, but no one could have been more serious and determined than we were in those days.

When the Lawrence, Massachusetts, strike broke out in 1912, the Syndicalists tossed me into their ranks of action. The Italian leaders in New York City planned to invite the children of the strikers to visit the workers' homes of other cities. Help was needed for the job of transferring them, and I was requested to go to Lawrence to assist in bringing the 250 children to their foster parents in New York. I did this with enthusiasm, and made an examination of the children's throats and chests before putting them aboard to avoid the possible spread of contagion. Four or five children were remanded. I was again appalled at the faces of these mothers. As they parted with the children, they had the same secret dread, the worried countenance, the age-wrinkled skin of sixty on faces less than thirty. . . .

I went home more puzzled than ever over the social problem, and searching, still searching for the solution. For in the great industrial strikes, urged by the Industrial Workers of the World and the revolutionary Socialists, I saw that the greatest suffering fell upon the women and children. They were the starved, the shivering, during those long days and nights when the agitators were busy urging the factory workers to hold out against their employers. And in not a few cases these starving women were not only forced to hear the pitiful whining of the children for something to eat, but within their frail and enfeebled bodies an un-born child was making ever-increasing demands upon an under-nourished system.

It was at this time I began to realize that Anthony Comstock was alive and active. His stunted, neurotic nature and savage methods of attack had ruined thou-sands of women's lives. He had indirectly caused the death of untold thousands. He and a weak-kneed Congress, which, through a trick, in 1873 had given him the power of an autocrat, were directly responsible for the deplorable condition of a whole generation of women left physically damaged and spiritually crippled from the results of abortion. No group of women had yet locked horns with this public enemy. Women in far western states who had fought for the sacred privi-lege of the ballot and *won* it years earlier had never raised their voices against the Comstock laws. Their own shallow emotions had not grappled with so funda-mental a need as sex. . . .

I came at last to the realization that I must fight the battle against Comstock's obscenity laws utterly alone. No organization would support me. No group of women would stand beside me in this fight. On all sides, in fact, I was advised to let it alone or suffer the consequences. I decided to test out public opinion on the broad issues of economic and feministic principles.

I took what money I was able to subtract from my rapidly decreasing bank account and started the first lap of my work by the publication of a monthly mag-azine, *The Woman Rebel*.

Its message was a scathing denunciation of all organized conventionalities. It went as far as was necessary to arouse the Comstockians to bite. While the main reason for its publication was to feel out the authorities on the Federal law, it had another purpose, namely, that of gathering friends and supporters to this cause. It championed freedom of speech and press and lived up to its principles.

I have no apologies for the publication of *The Woman Rebel*. It expressed ex-actly what I felt and thought at that time. Some recent critics claim that it went too far afield and lent itself to theories beside the question of contraception, all of which is true, but this only strengthened its substance, nevertheless, and widened its appeal. . . .

The response to its call was immediate. Requests for information came from labor unions, friends of labor, radicals, dissatisfied men and women all over the United States. The majority of labor papers carried news of *The Woman Rebel*, and within six months I had received over 10,000 requests for contraceptive in-formation.

One morning after the children were washed and dressed and sent away to their school in the neighborhood I started my day's work by looking over my huge batch of mail. My attention was immediately caught by an unstamped envelope from the New York Post Office. I tore it open. "Dear Madam," I read: "You are hereby notified that the Solicitor of the Post Office Department has decided that *The Woman Rebel* for March 1914 is unmailable under Section 489, Postal Laws and Regulations." It was signed by E. M. Morgan, Postmaster.

I re-read the letter. At first the significance of its contents did not register on my brain. I read it again, and yet again; and then I *knew* the fight was on! . . .

There followed several months of the most trying ordeal any woman could experience in a country said to be for the brave and the free. For weeks I was followed about by detectives. My every move was spied and reported upon. I had to act quickly and make quick decisions in order to accomplish what I had set out to do.

The first thing necessary was to get a name for contraception which would convey to the public the social and personal significance of the idea. A few friends and supporters of the paper gathered together one evening in my apartment to discuss the selection of a distinctive name. We debated in turn: "Malthusianism," "conscious generation," "voluntary parenthood," "voluntary motherhood," "preventception," "the new motherhood," "constructive generation," etc., etc.

All of these names were cast aside as not meeting the demands. Then we got a little nearer when "family control" and "race control" and "birth-rate control" were suggested.

Finally it came to me out of the blue—"Birth Control!"

We all knew at once that we had found the perfect name for the cause. There was no further discussion. Our object was attained. The group disbanded to meet no more.

That was the first time the words were used together. The phrase has now gone round the world like a magic message to herald the coming of a new dawn. It has become part of the English language and is embodied in the encyclopedia as well as in practically every modern book on sociology. It is discussed in newspapers all over the world, in colleges, religious conventions, and medical and philosophical institutes,—everywhere. "Birth control," as conceived and defined, is "the conscious control of the birth rate by means that prevent the conception of human life."

Source: My Fight for Birth Control, 76–84.

OPENING A CLINIC

Margaret Sanger returned from Europe in 1915. Inspired by the birth control clinics in the Netherlands that she had observed and their role in preventing the spread of venereal diseases, she decided to violate the law by opening the first American birth control clinic.

THE FIRST BIRTH CONTROL CLINIC, 1916

The selection of a place for the first birth control clinic was of the greatest importance. No one could actually tell how it would be received in any neighborhood. I thought of all the possible difficulties: The indifference of women's organizations, the ignorance of the workers themselves, the resentment of social agencies, the opposition of the medical profession. Then there was the law—the law of New York State.

Section 1142 was definite. It stated that *no one* could give information to prevent conception to *anyone* for any reason. There was, however, Section 1145, which distinctly stated that physicians (*only*) could give advice to prevent conception for the cure or prevention of disease. I inquired about the section, and was told by two attorneys and several physicians that this clause was an exception to 1142 referring only to venereal disease. But anyway, as I was not a physician, it could not protect me. Dared I risk it?

I began to think of the doctors I knew. Several who had previously promised now refused. I wrote, telephoned, asked friends to ask other friends to help me find a woman doctor to help me demonstrate the need of a birth control clinic in New York. None could be found. No one wanted to go to jail. No one cared to test out the law. Perhaps it would have to be done without a doctor. But it had to be done; that I knew. . . .

Finally at 46 Amboy Street, in the Brownsville section of Brooklyn, we found a friendly landlord with a good place vacant at fifty dollars a month rental; and Brownsville was settled on. It was one of the most thickly populated sections. It had a large population of working class Jews, always interested in health measures, always tolerant of new ideas, willing to listen and to accept advice whenever the health of mother or children was involved. I knew that here there would at least be no breaking of windows, no hurling of insults into our teeth; but I was scarcely prepared for the popular support, the sympathy and friendly help given us in that neighborhood from that day to this. . . .

With a small bundle of handbills and a large amount of zeal, we fared forth each morning in a house-to-house canvass of the district in which the clinic was located. Every family in that great district received a "dodger" printed in English, Yiddish and Italian. . . .

It was on October 16, 1916, that the three of us—Fania Mindell, Ethel Byrne and myself—opened the doors of the first birth control clinic in America. I believed then and do today, that the opening of those doors to the mothers of Brownsville was an event of social significance in the lives of American womanhood.

News of our work spread like wildfire. Within a few days there was not a darkened tenement, hovel or flat but was brightened by the knowledge that motherhood could be voluntary; that children need not be born into the world unless they are wanted and have a place provided for them. For the first time, women talked openly of this terror of unwanted pregnancy which had haunted their lives since time immemorial. The newspapers, in glaring headlines, used the words "birth control," and carried the message that somewhere in Brooklyn there was a place where contraceptive information could be obtained by all overburdened mothers who wanted it.

Ethel Byrne, who is my sister and a trained nurse, assisted me in advising, explaining, and demonstrating to the women how to prevent conception. As all of our 488 records were confiscated by the detectives who later arrested us for violation of the New York State law, it is difficult to tell exactly how many more women came in those few days to seek advice; but we estimate that it was far more than five hundred. As in any new enterprise, false reports were maliciously spread about the clinic; weird stories without the slightest foundation of truth. We talked plain talk and gave plain facts to the women who came there. We kept a record of every applicant. All were mothers; most of them had large families.

It was whispered about that the police were to raid the place for abortions. We had no fear of that accusation. We were trying to spare mothers the necessity of that ordeal by giving them proper contraceptive information. It was well that so many of the women in the neighborhood knew the truth of our doings. Hundreds of them who had witnessed the facts came to the courtroom afterward, eager to testify in our behalf.

One day a woman by the name of Margaret Whitehurst came to us. She said that she was the mother of two children and that she had no money to support more. Her story was a pitiful one—all lies, of course, but the government acts that way. She asked for our literature and preventives, and received both. Then she triumphantly went to the District Attorney's office and secured a warrant for the arrest of my sister, Mrs. Ethel Byrne, our interpreter, Miss Fania Mindell, and myself.

Source: My Fight for Birth Control, 152–158.

PHYSICIANS AND BIRTH CONTROL

The medical profession, rapidly rising in prestige and power in the early twentieth century, Margaret Sanger saw as a more substantial ally in her struggle for birth control than her radical comrades who gave other issues priority. With medical support, she established the American Birth Control League in 1921, the predecessor of Planned Parenthood. Birth control won acceptance and recognition not as a woman's right but as an issue in the medical profession, an outcome that has made her a controversial figure in the history of American women.

ENLISTING THE MEDICAL PROFESSION

In view of subsequent developments, there could be no doubt in my mind that the battle of the Brownsville Clinic had resulted in a decisive, indeed an over-

whelming victory. While it is true that the clinic at 46 Amboy Street had been bru-
tally raided by the New York police, that I had been sentenced to thirty days in
the workhouse, that my sister had sacrificed her health and jeopardized her life,
and that for no less than five years thereafter I was hounded by detectives and in
constant danger of arrest and conviction, yet after all these were insignificant
prices to pay for the great victory won on the battlefield of public opinion. . . .

Now I realized that this new clinic I was planning to conduct, even though
assisted by a duly licensed physician, would become inevitably a storm center, a
target for the attacks of our various enemies. I must make haste slowly. I saw that
premature publicity would be fatal to its growth and progress. It would first be
necessary to demonstrate its value as a social need. It would prove itself to be a
health center. It was to be, I decided, an experimental bureau, designed to demonstrate the practicability of the birth control clinic in all cities and towns. Therefore we must carefully guard its progress; we must organize it as a nucleus for research, a laboratory, as it were, dealing with human beings instead of with white
mice, with every consideration for environment, personality, and background. We
would help them as they were to help us. Women at last could contribute to scientific research and become part of this human laboratory.

With these ideals in mind, I set out to find a suitable and competent physician, a physician with the moral courage to risk her liberty to enter this battle with
me. . . .

It was during the year 1923—a year that remains in my memory as one of
smiles and tears, of heart aches and anxieties, that finally I discovered a woman
physician, Dr. Dorothy Bocker, who agreed to act in the capacity of medical director. . . .

This was the first real attempt to establish permanently the movement and to
center its activities around a clinic. During the first year there was no publicity.
No news of our activities was given to any one. There was no advertising; there
was nothing to disturb the routine of gathering facts from such patients as applied
to us. . . .

The first annual report of the Clinical Research Bureau on 900 cases was presented at a public luncheon the following year. This insignificant news attracted
the attention of those interested in this type of work throughout the country, and
served at once as an example and as an inspiration for others to follow. We were
besieged with questions on organization. Clinics began to be opened in other
cities, and people who had formerly said, "Don't try to do it!" now expressed
their approbation with the conventional, "I told you so."

As a result of the first report of the Clinical Research Bureau on 900 patients,
I decided that it was an auspicious moment to organize a medical and scientific
advisory council and to secure as medical advisor a physician with greater gyne-
cological experience than Dr. Bocker had. Through the recommendation of Dr.
Benjamin Tilton, one of our medical advisors, Dr. Hannah M. Stone accepted this
post and has held it to the present time, constantly strengthening her position as
one of the gentlest, most beloved and loyal workers in this field that one could

hope for. Dr. Stone's sympathetic response to mothers in distress, her courageous stand in remaining at my side, carrying on at our clinic despite the offer of a more lucrative position in one of New York's maternity hospitals, indicate qualities of staunch friendship and disinterested selflessness that are essential qualities for the successful carrying on of the clinical work. In addition, she has had to withstand abuse and misrepresentation that emanates even from members of her own profession.

In 1925, I also succeeded in persuading another member of the medical profession, Dr. James F. Cooper, to join our ranks and to go into the field as lecturer to medical societies. I was convinced that we must go into the States to reach the hearts of the medical profession and that we must get them to assist us in the battle for a new humanity. Dr. Cooper was an able speaker. He had been trained in the Boston Medical School, and had specialized in gynecology. . . .

In January 1925, Dr. Cooper went out into the field. He covered nearly all of the states in the Union. Reports of his good work came from every place in which he spoke, and in 1926 I again sent him on tour to gather medical supporters to our cause. . . .

About the time Dr. Stone and Dr. Cooper came into the field, another group of medical men were organizing for research and collection of scientific facts on fertility and sterility. The Maternal Health Committee of New York City, with Dr. Robert L. Dickinson as executive secretary, has made great inroads into the profession by its staunch, courageous adherence to the principles of the subject and its acceptance of the responsibility that birth control instruction is primarily a doctor's job. With the expansion and growth of the Maternal Health Committee, we can safely feel that it is only a question of time until that vast body will include contraceptive instruction as a preventive measure in its public work.

Each year the number of patients at the clinic increased. Doctors from far and near came to be instructed in our methods. Humbly the great ones came to learn; younger members of the profession especially came to enquire. We have on our books today the names of several hundred who have visited the clinic and learned from our staff the technique of contraception. . . .

The lone battle had been won, now that reinforcement had come from indignant and distinguished individuals in the New York Academy of Medicine.

Source: My Fight for Birth Control, 311–326.

Chapter 8

SIT DOWN AND FIGHT: LABOR WARS OF THE 1930S

When Franklin D. Roosevelt took the presidency from Herbert Hoover in the winter of 1933, he inherited a country in deep crisis. Millions languished in unemployment or got by on scraps of jobs, and homeless families lived in filthy shanty towns derisively termed Hoovervilles. Roosevelt, the wealthy, confident, and genial Democratic ex-governor of New York State, provided the leadership and vision to begin the lengthy process of recovery. He introduced sweeping changes in the role of government in the economy. Such laws as the Banking Act, the Federal Emergency Relief Act, the Agricultural Adjustment Act, and the Social Security Act made government a direct and active partner in the management of the economy. Though stewardship over the economy never reached the levels it did in the industrial countries of Europe, Roosevelt's New Deal radically reconfigured the government. Nowhere was this more true than in the most important relationship of the economy: that between labor and capital.

In 1933 a part of the National Industrial Recovery Act (NIRA)—legislation that aimed at achieving a more cooperative system within the nation's economy—encouraged workers to form unions and bargain collectively. It met a favorable response from labor and fierce resistance from industry. Conflicts between workers and management over recognition of unions broke out in 1934, with strikes and bloody battles between workers and police in many parts of the country. Longshoremen in San Francisco and teamsters in Minneapolis led general strikes that turned violent when police and strikebreakers fought them for control of the two cities. A textile strike that began in the South spread widely, and nearly half a million workers walked picket lines and fought police and national guardsmen.

For technical reasons, the NIRA, clearly a failure, was declared unconstitutional in 1935. As war raged in the streets and factories, Roosevelt understood that decisive leadership was necessary to make the country function again. Frustrated by the stubbornness of businessmen, uprisings in the working class, and the slowness of recovery, he pushed through legislation to control and regulate both capitalists and workers. The National Labor Relations Act, or Wagner Act (1935),

108

provided broad guarantees of basic rights for workers along with increased government regulation. The Wagner Act established the National Labor Relations Board to adjudicate conflict between workers and management. Once again the managers resisted union organization and labor rebelled. This time, the sit-down strike became the workers' strategy.

Early in 1936, the Firestone Rubber Company of Akron, Ohio, fired several unionists for organizing against a proposed wage cut. In defense of their sacked union brothers, workers sat down in the factory. Within two days Firestone gave in. When a similar situation occurred across town at Goodyear, the police deputized 150 strikebreakers to help them clear the factory. There they were met by ten thousand angry workers from all over Akron. Goodyear surrendered and the sit-down strike captured the imagination of millions. Over five hundred sit-downs occurred between 1936 and 1937.

The most famous sit-down started in December 1936 at General Motors' Fisher Body plant in Flint, Michigan, in response to the firing of two union members. Outside the plant, police tried to remove strikers with tear gas and bullets, but were no match for the five thousand workers who encircled the factory. Inside the plant, workers' committees organized food distribution and sanitation services, a postal system, a strike newspaper, recreation facilities, and classes in creative writing, public speaking, and labor history. The strike lasted forty days, forcing the most powerful company in the world to concede to the power of organized labor. General Motors accepted unionization and negotiated a contract with the United Auto Workers (UAW).

The year 1937 was the most bitter in American labor history. Through the winter and spring, police and private armies fought striking workers. The labor war of 1937 culminated in the Chicago Memorial Day Massacre, in which ten picketers were shot to death as they attempted to flee police who indiscriminately fired into a crowd of men, women, and children.

The labor wars of 1936 and 1937 along with Roosevelt's attempt to reduce federal spending in 1938 contributed to ending the fragile economic recovery. Unemployment soared to 10.4 million. The economy would not fully recover until the nation's entrance into World War II forced capitalists to invest, workers to take a pledge against strikes, and the government to engage in unprecedented deficit spending. Immediately after the war, there was a widespread but brief wave of strikes. But the labor militancy of the thirties had receded; the United States had uncontested control of world markets; and the economy was booming. In 1947 Congress as a political preemptive action against another period of labor wars passed over the veto of President Harry Truman the sweeping Labor Management Relations Act, better known as the Taft-Hartley Act.

THE WAGNER ACT

Passed in 1935, after the strike wave of 1934, the National Labor Relations Act sought to regulate collective bargaining between management and labor. Since the authority of Congress to do so derived from its constitutional power to regulate commerce among the states and with foreign nations, the opening section carefully explains that labor trouble has effects on commerce.

THE NATIONAL LABOR RELATIONS ACT, JULY 5, 1935

SECTION 1. The denial by employers of the right of employees to organize and the refusal by employers to accept the procedure of collective bargaining lead to strikes and other forms of industrial strife or unrest, which have the intent or the necessary effect of burdening or obstructing commerce by (a) impairing the efficiency, safety, or operation of the instrumentalities of commerce; (b) occurring in the current of commerce; (c) materially affecting, restraining, or controlling the flow of raw materials or manufactured or processed goods from or into the channels of commerce, or the prices of such materials or goods in commerce; or (d) causing diminution of employment and wages in such volume as substantially to impair or disrupt the market for goods flowing from or into the channels of commerce.

The inequality of bargaining power between employees who do not possess full freedom of association or actual liberty of contract, and employers who are organized in the corporate or other forms of ownership association substantially burdens and affects the flow of commerce, and tends to aggravate recurrent business depressions, by depressing wage rates and the purchasing power of wage earners in industry and by preventing the stabilization of competitive wage rates and working conditions within and between industries.

Experience has proved that protection by law of the right of employees to organize and bargain collectively safeguards commerce from injury, impairment, or interruption, and promotes the flow of commerce by removing certain recognized sources of industrial strife and unrest, by encouraging practices fundamental to the friendly adjustment of industrial disputes arising out of differences as to wages, hours, or other working conditions, and by restoring equality of bargaining power between employers and employees.

It is hereby declared to be the policy of the United States to eliminate the causes of certain substantial obstructions to the free flow of commerce and to mitigate and eliminate these obstructions when they have occurred by encouraging the practice and procedure of collective bargaining and by protecting the exercise by workers of full freedom of association, self-organization, and designation of representatives of their own choosing, for the purpose of negotiating the terms and conditions of their employment or other mutual aid or protection.

RIGHTS OF EMPLOYEES

SEC. 7. Employees shall have the right to self-organization, to form, join, or assist labor organizations, to bargain collectively through representatives of their own choosing, and to engage in concerted activities, for the purpose of collective bargaining or other mutual aid or protection.

SEC. 8. It shall be an unfair labor practice for an employer—

(1) To interfere with, restrain, or coerce employees in the exercise of the rights guaranteed in section 7.

(2) To dominate or interfere with the formation or administration of any labor organization or contribute financial or other support to it: *Provided,* That subject to rules and regulations made and published by the Board pursuant to section 6 (a), an employer shall not be prohibited from permitting employees to confer with him during working hours without loss of time or pay.

(3) By discrimination in regard to [hiring] or tenure of employment or any term or condition of employment to encourage or discourage membership in any labor organization: *Provided,* That nothing in this Act, or in the National Industrial Recovery Act (U.S.C., Supp. VII, title 15, secs. 701–712), as amended from time to time, or in any code or agreement approved or prescribed thereunder, or in any other statute of the United States, shall preclude an employer from making an agreement with a labor organization (not established, maintained, or assisted by any action defined in this Act as an unfair labor practice) to require as a condition of employment membership therein, if such labor organization is the representative of the employees as provided in section 9 (a), in the appropriate collective bargaining unit covered by such agreement when made.

(4) To discharge or otherwise discriminate against an employee because he has filed charges or given testimony under this Act.

(5) To refuse to bargain collectively with the representatives of his employees, subject to the provisions of Section 9 (a).

Source: Congressional Record, 74th Congress, 1st Session, 449–453.

SIT DOWN

The labor historian Sydney Fine sifted through thousands of documents to create his compelling description of "The Battle of the Running Bulls," the name given by UAW militants inside Fisher Body to the clash of January 11, 1937, with Flint police. ("Bull" was a term for a policeman.) As sit-down strikes spread across the country, business magazines like Forbes *protested against them while liberal and radical publications like* The Nation *supported labor. The business press viewed seizing factories as a criminal abridgement of private property and demanded changes in the National Labor Relations Act that would prevent such forms of union organizing. A decade later their demands were largely met by the Taft-Hartley Act of 1947.*

THE BATTLE OF THE RUNNING BULLS

The temperature in Flint, Michigan, fell to 16 degrees above zero on January 11, 1937. Strikers had been sitting in the massive Fisher Body Plant No. 1 and the smaller Fisher Body Plant No. 2 since December 30 of the old year. No effort had been made to dislodge them by the General Motors Corporation (GM), the police of the city of Flint, the sheriff of Genesee County, or the governor of the state of Michigan.

The more weakly held of the two plants was the Fisher Body No. 2 factory. Located in a valley about fifty yards north of the Flint River, the small No. 2 plant looked across Chevrolet Avenue to the sprawling Chevrolet complex on the western side of the street. The plant employed about one thousand workers and had a daily capacity of 450 bodies, which were delivered to the Chevrolet No. 2 plant on the other side of the street across an overpass that connected the two plants.

The strikers occupied only the second floor of the No. 2 factory while company police controlled the main gate. The food for the men inside the plant was prepared at a nearby restaurant and then delivered to the main gate, where it was inspected by the plant police—presumably to check against the presence of liquor—and then taken to the sit-downers. Not more than one hundred strikers occupied the plant on January 11, and their morale was not high. Robert C. Travis, the director of organization for the United Automobile Workers of America (UAW) in Flint, wondered if the union could continue to hold the factory.

Shortly after noon on January 11 the heat in Fisher Body No. 2, which the company, at the request of state authorities, had kept on since the beginning of the strike, was turned off without warning. During the course of the afternoon twenty-two plant policemen, armed with clubs and headed by Edgar T. Adams, the chief of the Fisher Body plant police in Flint, came through the main gate of the factory and joined the force of eight company guards already in the plant. The purpose of the visit was to remove the twenty-four foot ladder outside the plant that reached to the second floor and gave the strikers access to the street. Their mission accomplished, the company police departed, leaving two or three of their number behind to supplement the regular force of company guards inside the plant.

Alarmed at the course of events, the sit-downers sent couriers to union headquarters in the Pengelly Building to request the dispatch of additional pickets to augment the union picket force outside the plant. At least two of the unionists who came to the plant that afternoon reported that they had observed city police about two blocks from the plant, diverting traffic from Chevrolet Avenue. The exact time when the Flint police arrived in the vicinity of Fisher Body No. 2 on January 11 remains a matter of uncertainty to this day, but it was the judgment of an investigator for the United States Senate's La Follette Civil Liberties Committee, and this was corroborated by an Associated Press reporter, that there was a police presence in the area in advance of the dramatic events that were soon to occur.

About 6:00 P.M., as was customary, the union sought to take the evening meal for the strikers through the main gate, but entry to the plant was barred for the first time by the company police. The men inside then sought to hoist the food containers into the plant by rope, but it is not clear how successful they were, and there are conflicting accounts as to whether the company police attempted to interfere with this operation.

At about 8:15 or 8:30 P.M. union organizer Victor Reuther, entering Chevrolet Avenue from a small side street, arrived in front of the plant in the union sound car, which was convoyed to the scene by a five-car escort. The strikers by this time, denied heat and their regular evening meal, were "in no pleasant mood." Outside the plant Reuther found a group of about 150 pickets—not all of them strikers, not all of them Flint residents—and also a number of spectators. Seeking to cheer up the strikers, Reuther told them that the union would provide for them and asked if they wished to hear some music. No, replied the men. It was heat and food that they wanted, not music. Reuther then advised them to elect a committee to descend to the main gate and to request the company guards, of whom two shifts of eighteen to twenty men were by then present, to open the gate and to turn on the heat.

Roscoe Rich thereupon assembled a force of about thirty men, went down to the gate, and asked Captain Peterson, in charge of the No. 2 guards, for the key. When Peterson reported that he did not have the key, Rich or one of the others said that he would count to ten and, if the gate remained closed at that time, the men would have to force it open. The company police made no move either to open the gate or to deter the unionists, with the result that when the count ended the men broke the snap lock and forced the gate open. The pickets outside and the remainder of the sit-downers observing the scene from the inside cheered as some of the strikers rushed through the gate and mingled briefly with the people outside the plant. The captain of the company guards phoned the Flint police that he and his men had been "captured" and that the strikers were "crowding the door and were threatening," and then the guards ingloriously took refuge in the ladies' rest room, from where they did not emerge until the next morning, after the fighting had ended.

Reuther, who had left the sound car to observe the proceedings at the main gate, instructed the sit-downers to return to the plant and to post a guard at the door. Peace prevailed for a few minutes as sit-downers and pickets began singing a chorus of "Solidarity Forever." Suddenly, someone outside yelled, "For God's sake, fellows, here's a tear gas squad." The "Battle of the Running Bulls," as the union was later to name it, had begun, and Chevrolet Avenue was soon to take on the character of a battlefield.

Squad cars carrying about thirty policemen had come across the bridge spanning the Flint River south of Fisher No. 2. The officers, perhaps fifteen of whom were equipped with gas masks and armed with tear-gas guns, left their cars and moved toward the plant. Captain Edwin H. Hughes, in command, approached the main gate and demanded that it be opened. There was no response from inside. The captain then broke the panels of glass above the double doors of the gate and twice fired his gas gun into the plant. The pickets pressed closer to the gate but were forced to retreat and disperse when the police exploded tear-gas bombs in their midst. The police also fired their gas into the plant as they advanced upon it, but the strikers, with Reuther giving the orders from the sound car, directed fire hoses, two-pound steel automobile door hinges, bottles, stones, and assorted missiles at the police and drove them back.

The tide of battle ebbed and flowed outside the plant. After their initial repulse, the police regrouped on the bridge and drove down once again on the plant, firing their gas guns and hurling gas grenades toward the factory and into the pickets in front of the establishment. The sit-downers, many of whom had rushed to the roof of the plant, and the pickets, who had received a supply of "popular ammunition" from the men in the plant during the brief lull in the battle, responded with a water and missile barrage; and as the wind blew the gas back into their faces the police had to fall back. Hurling cans, frozen snow, milk bottles, door hinges, pieces of pavement, and assorted other weapons of this type, the pickets pressed at the heels of the retreating police. Undoubtedly enraged at the humiliation of defeat at the hands of so motley and amateur an army, the police drew pistols and riot guns and fired into the ranks of their pursuers. The strikers claimed that the police also fired into the pickets from the Chevrolet No. 2 plant directly across the street from Fisher No. 2, but this allegation appears to lack substantiation.

Fourteen strikers and strike sympathizers, some of whom were from out of town, and two spectators were wounded in the attack on the plant, thirteen of them by gunshot. Nine policemen, Thomas Wolcott, sheriff of Genesee County, and a deputy sheriff were also injured in the affray. The deputy sheriff was shot in the knee, apparently by an errant police bullet, one policeman was gassed, and the remaining injured suffered mainly head wounds from flying missiles.

Ambulances soon clanged up to the battlefield to remove the more seriously wounded to Hurley Hospital. The police in the meantime retreated to the bridge, continuing their shooting for a time, while their opponents outside the plant, according to one account, "limped away, vomiting, tears streaming down their faces, and with torn clothes." The first phase of the Battle of the Running Bulls was over, and the strikers and their allies were in command of the battlefield.

The fury of the battle had, for a dangerous moment, engulfed Sheriff Wolcott, who had arrived on the scene with four deputies after the tear-gas assault had begun and who soon became a battle casualty. His car was turned over while he was still inside it, and as he emerged from the vehicle he was struck on the head by a flying door hinge. The gasoline spilled from his car, and one of the strikers or strike sympathizers, apparently overwrought from the excitement of combat, had to be prevented from setting the car on fire. It was during this most violent phase of the battle that a Detroit *Times* reporter was slashed on the hand, and two reporters for the Flint *Journal,* which the strikers looked upon as a GM house organ, were beaten. One policeman during the melee was surrounded by strikers, knocked to the ground, and separated from his gas equipment.

Source: Sydney Fine, *Sit-Down: The General Motors Strike of 1936–1937* (Ann Arbor: University of Michigan Press, 1969), 1, 3–5. Reprinted by permission.

WHY LABOR LIKES THE SIT-DOWN

The sit-down strike, labor's newest weapon, will be its biggest gun in 1937. And, from striking labor's point of view, justifiably so. For in its short life, the sit-down has proved to be more than a match for employers. . . . Sit-downs work best in plants like that of Fisher Body in Cleveland—unfenced, facing on a street, with windows which can be reached from the ground. Through these windows is passed the food which strike sympathizers bring. . . . By staging a sit-down on a single production line, a few well-organized strikers can tie up entire plants in mass-production industries which depend on split-second timing and feeding of materials. That's one reason for the sit-down's effectiveness; a small group of workers on the Fisher Body assembly line in Flint prove[d] it by blocking production . . . Everyone (except employers and non-strikers) [had] a good time during a sit-down in another auto plant in Flint. Which is Point Two in the sit-down's strength: Strikers find it easy to maintain morale. . . . Point Three involves public opinion, which finally decides most big strikes. Public opinion swings against the side which first uses force; yet, in a sit-down, the employer must make the first move to use force if he is to assert his legal rights and eject sit-down strikers from his plant. In a walk-out, labor, instead, is jockeyed out of position; pickets must block entrance to the plant.

Source: "Why Labor Likes the Sit-Down," *Forbes*, February 1, 1937: 17.

SHALL LAW AND ORDER BE MAINTAINED?

It used to be popularly said: "There is one law for the rich, another for the poor."

To-day it can be said truthfully, "There is one law for workers, another for employers."

The New York *Times* editorially points out: "The Wagner Labor Act can only be violated by employers. Nothing whatever in this act restricts labor unions from any action or demand. . . . While the employer is compelled to bargain by the act, the employees are not."

The Government having passed such flagrantly one-sided legislation, is it astonishing that labor leaders have encouraged their followers to resort to lawlessness?

Is it astonishing that the authorities in many instances have made no determined attempt to suppress lawlessness?

But can thoughtful citizens contemplate such conditions with equanimity?

The nation has been treated repeatedly to the spectacle of strikers usurping plants and refusing to allow the owners to take possession.

When the sheriff read a court order to "sit-down" strikers in a Flint factory, demanding that they vacate the premises on which they were trespassing, they showed their contempt for the law and the courts by loudly laughing at him.

Did their union leaders command the law-breakers to obey the court? They did not.

What would these same labor leaders think or do if representatives of employers took possession of their offices or meeting halls and refused to allow anyone else to enter?

The arbitrary, high-handed, illegal acts of John L. Lewis's henchmen should cause citizens to think very seriously.

But will they cause Congress to alter the law, to embody in it even-handed justice?

Will they cause the Federal Administration, State and local authorities to enforce law and order?

Once law and order are violated with impunity by one class, how could the authorities consistently seek to enforce law and order if violated by another class?

And have we not always been taught that the maintenance of law and order is the first duty of the Government, that when law and order are widely defied, national disruption and decay are the ultimate, inevitable outcome?

Responsibility for these recent un-American happenings cannot legitimately be laid solely at the door of John L. Lewis or his followers.

The blame must be shared by the sponsors and enactors of the lop-sided Wagner Labor Act. Unionists were entitled to regard themselves as having been placed above the law, as having been accorded special privileges and immunity.

President Roosevelt three years ago, when intervening in another automobile labor dispute, laid down the principle that "if there be more than one group, each bargaining committee shall have a total membership *pro rata* to the number of men each member represents."

But John L. Lewis now proclaims that automotive managements must deal *only* with him and his union, the United Automobile Workers of America.

Has this fiery laborist become obsessed by such a Napoleonic sense of power that he feels he can successfully challenge and flout the President of the United States, that he can become a law unto himself, that he can dictate alike to the Government and the whole automotive industry, that he can compel every automobile worker to render obedience and financial tribute to him?

No authoritative figures have been issued to show that the vast majority—or even any large percentage—of auto wage earners have enrolled under the Lewis union banner.

The fundamental issue raised by Lewis does not cover wages, hours or working conditions. The fundamental issue is clear-cut: the closed *versus* the open shop, the right of employers to hire men regardless of union or non-union affiliations, the right of workers to earn a livelihood without handing over part of their pay to Lewis or any other person living off the levies imposed on workers.

Surely, automotive workmen and all other workmen should be free to join or not join a union, entirely as they wish.

Should it develop that an overwhelming percentage of the workers in any plant or industry elect to be represented in their dealings with employers by the officials of the American Federation of Labor or the Committee for Industrial Organization, then clearly they should be permitted to exercise this right.

But bullying, coercion, illegal usurpation of plants, unlawful picketing and other forms of lawlessness, should not be condoned by constituted authorities, from the President of the United States down, who, on taking their oath of office, swore to enforce law and order.

This is what should deeply concern every law-abiding citizen.

_____

Source: "Shall Law and Order Be Maintained?" editorial, *Forbes*, January 15, 1937: 9.

A GENERAL MOTORS STOCKHOLDER VISITS FLINT

As the owner of a few shares of the General Motors Corporation, I became somewhat alarmed when I learned that the workers were sitting down in my plants at Flint, Fisher Body No. 1 and Fisher Body No. 2, preventing the company from finishing and shipping cars and threatening to interrupt the orderly flow of dividends. Accordingly I took Sunday for a visit of investigation. Arriving at Flint I went to Fisher 2, and on introducing myself as their employer was cordially received by some 400 men occupying the plant. I must admit that I was fortunate in having as my companion Adolf Germer, who is on the board of strategy directing the strike.

My first anxiety was for the condition of my property, and I was relieved to find it well cared for. Springs and cushions were being used for beds, it is true, sometimes laid side by side as in a dormitory, sometimes isolated in cubicles between bales of goods. I was glad to see certain marks of domesticity—a clothes tree, an alarm clock, a whisk broom. The boys had made themselves pretty comfortable. I asked who was responsible for cleanliness, order, and protection of property, and learned that the government was what might be described, except for its unfortunate connotation, as a soviet. Mass assemblies were called at frequent intervals at which everything of importance was discussed. Court was held every morning. I asked what crimes were committed and was told that bringing in liquor and circulating rumors were the usual offenses. Those found guilty of the charges against them were put out.

After a hearty Sunday dinner of roast chicken and ice cream, I was preparing to go over to Fisher 1 when I noticed several round holes in the great glass windows, and inspecting more closely some of the foetus-like bodies of cars on the tracks, awaiting their delayed birth, I saw similar holes in the glass and dents in the metal sides. I thought these indicated wanton violence against my property, and asked how it occurred. Gun fire by the police, was the answer. I knew that there had been fighting on the Monday before in the street outside, but these disasters were on the second floor. It was obvious that there had been firing from a distance into the plant, endangering the lives of my employees, whom I was beginning to like though they were on strike, and damaging my property. Accordingly I asked for particulars, and as I have seen no clear account of the affair in any newspaper, despite the columns of newsprint that have been given to the strike, I will set down the facts as they were related to me by at least eight participants and eyewitnesses.

The sitdown strike involving 1,500 to 2,000 workers started at Fisher 1, when it appeared that the management was loading dies and special machinery into box cars to be shifted to other cities. Our company is fortunate in having factories scattered over the country; so that by transferring equipment a strike in Flint, Michigan, can be broken by workers in Atlanta, Georgia. Incidentally, that is why the workers demand the industrial form of organization and insist on dealing with General Motors as a whole instead of with the component companies.

The sitdown strike spread to Fisher Body 2, where from 400 to 600 men were involved. Relations were harmonious with the company police, who agreed to let the outer door stand open for food to be brought in. Attempts were made from time to time to shut off heat, light, and water, but workers with a mechanical turn of mind turned them on again.

On Monday afternoon the city police under Chief James Wills undertook to block both ends of the street in front of Fisher 2, to prevent food from being brought in. Later the police made an attack in force with tear gas and gun fire, to enter the plant. The strikers from inside countered the tear gas with streams of water, and the bullets with heavy hinges and other missiles. Some twenty-eight persons were injured, fourteen so seriously as to be taken to the hospital, which, I was told, had received warning beforehand to have an emergency ward ready. The defeat of the forces of law and order is referred to as Bulls' Run. The company police of Fisher 2 apparently took no part in the battle, and were found next morning in a ladies' rest room, where they had stood all night at attention, lacking room to sit down. They were released without acrimony by the workers in the factory.

Leaving Fisher 2, I went over to Fisher 1. After the battle, through Governor Murphy's efforts, the strikers and the management of General Motors had been brought to an agreement to go into conference on Monday, January 18, the workers to evacuate the Fisher plants on the promise that the company would not move machinery or dies. They were to march out of Fisher 1 at one-thirty, and a big crowd was collecting outside to see the evacuation. In the long facade of Fisher 1, which stretched away, it seemed, for half a mile into the foggy distance, no door was open, and I had to go in by a window; but once inside I found the boys very good-natured and, when they realized that I was their employer, flatteringly eager for my autograph. Suddenly a loud-speaker blared forth. It seemed that the General Motors management had agreed to negotiate also with the Flint Alliance, and this was regarded as a breach of faith by the board of strategy of the United Automobile Workers of America, since the question whether the U.A.W.A. should be the sole bargaining agency was one of the points to be negotiated. Accordingly orders were given to hold the plant, the sitdown strike to continue until negotiations were finally complete. The crowd surged back to Fisher 1, where an impromptu outdoor meeting was held to protest against the action of the company.

The agreement of the company officials to admit the Flint Alliance to the discussion was a highly provocative action and was deprecated as such by Governor Murphy. It looked like an attempt of the company to get out of the negotiation into which it had been persuaded. The Flint Alliance is an anti-strike organization mainly of white-collar workers and their families and various beneficiaries of General Motors, directed by George Boysen, ex-mayor of Flint and a former paymaster of the Buick Company. It is in no sense a labor union and is detested by the workers. It represents rather the political forces of Flint, which are aligned with General Motors—mayor, police, courts. On that Sunday in Flint there was meeting the Michigan Conference for the Protection of Civil Rights, at which it was forcibly pointed out to the workers that they had only to use their ballots to turn out the whole nest of unclean birds at the next election—defeat the mayor, move the impeachment of Judge Black for his action in granting a sweeping injunction against the union and in favor of a corporation, General Motors, in which he has substantial holdings, and force the removal of Chief of Police Wills for invoking violence both savage and futile.

The General Motors strike of 1937 may prove to be historic inasmuch as it has acclimated the sitdown strike in this country as a weapon of industrial conflict. The right of non-working employees to occupy the plant can hardly be classed among civil liberties. It is rather one of the industrial liberties which are on the way to becoming legally recognized. A little over a century ago it was illegal for workers to combine to refuse work for less than a certain sum. Quite recently it was against the law to picket a struck plant. Today picketing is among the civil rights. Already intelligent governors are applying the rule of reason and common sense to situations which law has not reached in its majestic progress. Governor Earle of Pennsylvania has refused to order the state troops to dispossess the bootleg miners, who are taking coal from seams which are their natural source of livelihood, which the legal owners refuse to work. Governor Murphy has refused to use his militia to throw out the sitdown strikers in the General Motors plants, and has ordered the company to cease the effort to cut off heat, light, and water.

The sitdown is the most effective form of strike. It permits the strikers to remain in comfort, even if somewhat bored, instead of tramping about on the picket line in heat, cold, wind, and wet. It obviates the most unpleasant and demoralizing feature of a strike, the use of strike-breakers. It eliminates violence, or at least places responsibility for it squarely on the police. It promotes the morale of the strikers. Above all it is a forcible reminder to workers, to management, to shareholders, and to the public that legal title is not the final answer to the question of *possession*. Who has the better human and natural right to call the Fisher plant his—I, whose connection with General Motors is determined by the price recorded on the New York Stock Exchange, or the worker whose life and livelihood are bound up in the operation of making cars? I bought my shares at long odds and probably have already collected the purchase price in dividends. When I place a winning bet in a horse race I do not claim a share in ownership of the horse. I know from my political economy that my position is the result of labor and sacrifice. Whose? Not mine. Obviously the enormous mass of wealth represented by the capitalization of General Motors, repeatedly enlarged by split-ups and stock dividends, is the surplus resulting from the toil of millions of workers over many years. Obviously they have not shared fairly in the wealth they have produced.

Source: Robert Morss Lovett, "A G.M. Stockholder Visits Flint," *The Nation,* January 30, 1937: 123–124.

VOICES FROM INSIDE THE FACTORY

The Punch Press *was the official newspaper of the Flint strikers. Workers inside the Fisher body plant joined the debates about the legality and morality of sit-down strikes, argued against the company's attempts to turn public opinion in Flint against the strike, and denied claims that only a minority of workers sought union recognition. Some of the strikers were woman workers, among the lowest paid employees at General Motors.*

THE *PUNCH PRESS*

"Is Sit-Down Illegal?" January 1937

LET US LOOK THIS QUESTION SQUARELY IN THE FACE. THERE IS NO STATUTE IN THE LAW BOOKS WHICH COVERS THE SIT-DOWN STRIKE. *THEREFORE IT IS OUR JOB TO SEE THAT THE SIT-DOWN IS LEGAL WHEN IT IS PUT IN THE STATUTES,* IF EVER.

AS FAR AS WE, THE WORKERS ARE CONCERNED, THE SIT-DOWN REMAINS THE MOST POWERFUL FACTOR IN BRINGING GM TO TIME.

TO ASSUME THAT SIT-DOWN IS ILLEGAL, AS GM WOULD HAVE US BELIEVE, MEANS TO GIVE UP THE STRIKE, TO GIVE UP THE FIGHT FOR HUMAN CONDITIONS IN GENERAL MOTORS.

IT MAY BE OLD FASHIONED, BUT IT IS A MORAL TRUTH THAT MEN HAVE A RIGHT TO LIVE AS HUMAN BEINGS WITH SOME SHARE OF HAPPINESS. THIS IS A RIGHT MORE BASIC AND COMPELLING THAN ANY LEGAL RIGHT CAN BE. LEGAL RIGHTS, ESPECIALLY WHEN MACHINERY THROUGH WHICH THEY WORK BELONG TO CORPORATIONS, MUST GIVE WAY BEFORE THE RIGHT OF MEN, WOMEN AND CHILDREN TO PARTICIPATE IN A FULL AND HAPPY EXISTENCE.

WE BELIEVE THE GOVERNMENT RECOGNIZES THIS TO THE EMBARRASSMENT OF GENERAL MOTORS.

Source: "Is Sit-Down Illegal?" *Punch Press,* January 1937.

"Travis Says Today that Democracy Is the Real Issue in Flint," February 8, 1937

In a statement issued to Flint Workers through the Punch Press Bob Travis [one of the strike leaders] made the following comments:

Twenty years ago the workers of America enrolled in the nation's fighting forces in an attempt to bring democracy to a war torn world. The attempt was not as successful as it might have been. As we look at the map of Europe, where the war for democracy was principally fought out, we find instead of democracy a new type of autocracy and tyranny right down the centre of Europe from the Baltic to the Mediterranean.

In all that vast territory with its crowded populations there are no such institutions as free trade unions. The workers have to hang their heads and join the company union whether they want to or not.

In America, too, among certain corporations, we have tyranny and autocracy. In America, too, the workers must fight against oppression to win industrial democracy.

But in America the free trade unions are still legal organizations. And the workers intend to keep them so.

General Motors is one of the corporations that prefer tyranny and autocracy over its workers in place of American democracy.

That is why the workers of America have enrolled in the present crusade to bring democracy to the motor industry.

This time, instead of carrying [it] into Europe, our boys are carrying it into the auto plants. With a new technique, cleverly and courageously developed, the sitters in Fisher One and Fisher Two and Chevrolet Four are steadfastly and patriotically fighting to establish once and for all time the principle that the organized workers have a legitimate voice in helping to determine the wages, the hours and the conditions under which they and their fellow workers shall be employed.

That is the big new issue here and now in Flint, twenty years after the big crusade against tyranny and autocracy in Europe.

Source: "Travis Says Today that Democracy Is the Real Issue in Flint," *Punch Press,* February 8, 1937.

"Alliance Leaders Unmasked," January 1937

THE BIGGEST ARROW IN GM'S QUIVER IS THEIR SOB STORY ABOUT "SATISFIED WORKERS WHO WANT TO GO BACK TO WORK."

THIS IS THE BIGGEST POINT OF THEIR PROPAGANDA CAMPAIGN.

IN ORDER TO GIVE THE IMPRESSION THAT MOST WORKERS IN FLINT ARE "SATISFIED WORKERS" THEY ORGANIZED THE FLINT ALLIANCE.

THE FLINT ALLIANCE IS COMPOSED LARGELY OF BUSINESS MEN WHO HAVE SOLD OUT TO GM.

NOW, A *COMMITTEE OF 14 "WORKERS"* WHO HAVE MET TO PLAN STRIKE BREAKING ACTIVITIES FOR THE ALLIANCE MASS MEETING TUESDAY, ARE SUPPOSED TO REPRESENT THE MAJORITY OF WORKERS IN FLINT.

WHO ARE THESE "REPRESENTATIVES" OF FLINT WORKERS?

F. E. BURSIDE OF FISHER NO. 1 IS A *FOREMAN*.

JOHN E. RICHARDSON, FISHER BODY VOLUNTEER, IS A *FOREMAN*.

E. E. SMITH OF CHEVROLET IS A "DRIVER" AND A *COMPANY UNION* OFFICIAL.

HARRY H. SMITH, FISHER BODY VOLUNTEER, IS NOT LISTED IN [THE] 1936 CITY DIRECTORY.

PAUL J. LOISELL IS A *COMPANY UNION OFFICIAL*.

WESLEY PERRY IS A *FOREMAN*.

SANFOR A. RASBACK IS AN *OFFICIAL* IN BUICK PAY DEPARTMENT.

THESE MEN, FOREMEN, COMPANY UNION OFFICIALS AND UNKNOWNS DO NOT REPRESENT THE WORKING MEN OF FLINT. WHAT GENERAL MOTORS SAYS WILL NOT CHANGE THIS FACT. THIS TIME GM BIT OFF MORE THAN IT [CAN] SWALLOW. NOW THE LAST VESTIGE OF SHAM IS STRIPPED FROM ITS OBEDIENT ALLIANCE OF "SATISFIED WORKERS."

Source: "Alliance Leaders Unmasked," *Punch Press,* January 1937.

"Union Sizes Up City Fathers," February 10, 1937

In Flint as in any other city the local government is supposed to be run democratically by the citizens for their own welfare.

It seldom happens that a situation occurs in which city government officials must show their sympathies so clearly as in the present strike situation.

In Flint the majority of citizens are striking auto workers who have suffered severely from the labor policies of General Motors. When a strike issue comes up the city manager, the mayor, the commission and the police chief have only the choice of siding with GM or the striking auto workers.

Chief Wills made his choice when he received tear gas and guns for GM and turned them over to company officials.

He emphasized the choice when he cooperated with Pugemier, Pinkerton Thug Organizer, and mobilized 200 thugs with the order "to shoot it out with strikers at Fisher 1 and 2 and Chevrolet 4.

Wills licks the boots of GM—yet he is supposed to serve Flint citizens.

Wills might be typical of all City officials. That will be learned as auto workers watch the actions of the manager, the mayor, and the commission.

Now the slogan is, "Keep an eye out for dirty work in the city government."

Source: "Union Sizes Up City Fathers," *Punch Press,* February 10, 1937.

"Attention AC Girls," February 11, 1937

If you like to be a goat; if you enjoy working at killing speed; if you are just tickled to get sweat shop wages; if you think it's fun to be bullied, herded around and treated like an animal, if you just *love* your boss, if you think that you can stand up to the company all by yourself, then STOP READING THIS ARTICLE AND DON'T JOIN THE UNION.

But if you are one of the majority of girls who would like to be treated like [a] decent human being; if you would like to be able to go home at night and have enough energy left to enjoy your evenings; if you think that girls doing the same work should get equal pay; if you don't enjoy getting the smallest GM pay checks in Flint, THEN GET ON THE BAND WAGON AND WIN BETTER WAGES, HOURS AND CONDITIONS BY JOINING THE UNION.

Without the union you are just another number, WITH THE UNION YOU HAVE THE STRENGTH OF THOUSANDS BEHIND YOU. The Kelsey-Hayes girls joined the union and won a *minimum* of 75 cents an hour. If the Kelsey-Hayes girls can do it, the AC girls certainly can. All over the country women have joined unions and won better wages and conditions. U-N-I-O-N spells strength.

GIRLS, ARE YOU GOING TO BE LEFT BEHIND WHEN VICTORY COMES????????

Source: "Attention AC Girls," *Punch Press,* February 11, 1937.

"Spark Plugs and Gals," February 1937 Extra

"They don't give us time enough to clean up our machines. We have to finish on our own time."

"The basic amount we have to produce is much too high."

"The foremen all have their favorites and always choose the tattle-tales."

Those are just a few of the dozens and dozens of grievances reported by the girls who work in the AC shops.

A survey shows that in spite of the increase in pay a couple of months ago, the average wage of the girls is 41 cents an hour. Starting at 35 cents, as soon as the girls become experienced after working two or three years and are earning 47 cents, the top rate, they are fired. Now girls are hired in their places at the low rate of 35 cents. That is the way the company saves money at the expense of its employees.

And why do one-third of the girls work five months a year, another third, nine months and the rest twelve months. In union shops work is divided equitably.

Everyone knows of the policy of the plant to hire high school graduates. The company wants girls whom it can easily mold—girls who haven't learned what a decent wage is.

In 1929 it took 30 girls and 8 men to produce the weekly schedule of speedometer cases. In 1936 the same amount was produced by two girls and one man with the aid of new machinery. Under union protection new machinery is used to lighten the work load.

The bonus system is still a mystery to the workers, who have no way of figuring for themselves how much bonus they are to receive. Some complicated formula, known only to the management, is used.

This is supposed to be a free country but the management of AC makes its own laws. Employees have been threatened with loss of job if they exercised their American right to join a union of their choosing.

Add all these facts together and the answer is that GM isn't doing right by the AC girls. And they won't do right by them as long as they remain unorganized. Only a strongly organized union will abolish these grievances.

TODAY—NOW—JOIN THE UNION.

Source: "Spark Plugs and Gals," *Punch Press,* February 1937 Extra.

Chapter 9

LEAVING HOME: AMERICAN WOMEN IN WORLD WAR II

World War II changed American life in fundamental ways. Events of the war immediately created the atomic age, the Cold War, and the crumbling of imperialism, all of them dominating the postwar relationship of the United States with the rest of the world. The culture of mass consumption, widespread prosperity, suburbanization, and minor civil rights agitation followed almost as directly. In particular, the war initiated far-reaching changes for American women. Despite powerful gender stereotypes as well as the difficulties of wartime shortages and restrictions, women moved about the country with an independence they had never been allowed before, assumed roles in the economy and sometimes in the armed forces not envisioned when the war began, and managed age-old responsibilities in new environments and ways. With the end of the war came a retreat to older patterns, but the war experience had lasting effects. Employment for married women, for example, grew rapidly even in the supposedly placid nineteen fifties. And so did divorce rates.

World War II was peculiarly a battle of production, to be won or lost on farms and in factories. The enemy's head start in producing war materials augmented by critical Allied losses early in the fighting meant that only vast increases in American productivity would defeat the Axis powers. The draining of ten million men into the military made critical the labor of women both in war industries and in what came to be called "essential civilian services." Were women available to fill these gaps, and would they be successful in doing the jobs that needed doing? Through the first years of the war, business publications worried about the "problem of womanpower." "If they do not come forward voluntarily," *Fortune* warned in February 1943, "they may have to be drafted."

"A PROBLEM IN WOMANPOWER"

Such is the way Business Week *described the nation's dilemma on September 25, 1943. Most single women and virtually all able men were em-*

125

ployed. Business and government were much concerned about getting married women into the labor force. Gas rationing interfered with transportation; household help had vanished into higher paying war jobs; housing shortages made it difficult to settle in crowded cities where war industries were concentrated; and prejudice against working wives remained. Some families feared that the mother's reception of a wage might make the father subject to conscription. To overcome these obstacles, government and industry cooperated to recruit woman workers. The possibility of using the selective service system to draft women into war jobs—as Great Britain was doing—was widely discussed.

RECRUITING WOMEN WORKERS

Draft for Women

Detroit plans to register women workers next month, but it will be on voluntary basis. First call for 80,000.

About a month from now, when the local supply of male employees is nearly exhausted, Detroit will try the nation's first voluntary selective service registration for women war workers.

• **Big Publicity Campaign**—As current plans shape up, 600,000 registration cards will be distributed to households in the Detroit economic area—Wayne County, plus communities as far away as Pontiac. Air raid wardens will visit homes to explain the need for women in Detroit's rapidly expanding munitions plants. Carefully planned newspaper and radio publicity will appeal to their patriotism.

Women will be urged to fill out the cards and return them to the U.S. Employment Service. This agency will act as a clearing house to dispatch qualified women to war plants on call, and to analyze the training needs of the balance.

• **Badly Needed**—"Women will be asked to leave their homes for factories because the employment emergency is real," says E. C. Kanzler, regional director of the War Production Board. "Their registration will be entirely voluntary. We are providing the machinery whereby the woman who wants war work can get it." "And we shall try to minimize transportation for her," he adds.

Participants in [the] program, which is still subject to changes in detail are the WPB, the Automotive Council for War Production, the Detroit Board of Commerce, the 25 largest manufacturers in the area, the U.S. Employment Service, the Women's Bureau of the U.S. Department of Labor, the Wayne County Defense Council, and C.I.O. and A.F.L. groups.

190,000 Workers

Registration of women in Detroit reveals big backlog of potential workers—and 54,000 with some experience.

Detroit women want to work in war plants. Hopes had been that some 80,000 would volunteer for factory jobs on availability registration cards distributed to all homes in the Michigan metropolis in mid-August . . . but the response, unlike the experience in Seattle . . . was far greater than that. Preliminary tabulations indicate that the number will finally be close to 200,000. And about one out of four of those registering have had factory experience.

• **Why They Want to Help**—The cards, mailed back to the United States Employment Service, bore enthusiastic reactions to the invitations to register for war work. Sample inscriptions, written on edges and around corners:

"My husband is in Australia, and I want to help make weapons for him and his buddies."

"I'll do anything my country wants to help lick the Japs and Nazis."

"I regard it as a duty to my country to do whatever will be helpful.". . .

• **Some Can't Be Relied Upon**—USES officials warned against undue optimistic interpretation of these figures. They pointed out that some of the 190,000 "willing" women probably would not be able to hold down factory jobs due to age or infirmity. Others might be expected to be talked out of working by their husbands. Still others would renege when they found their homes too far from the factories. Some would simply exercise the feminine prerogative of changing their minds.

But, on the other hand, it was pointed out that many women did not return cards, or perhaps filled them in as "not available" due to fears that if they qualified themselves for jobs their husbands would lose their dependency status in the draft and have to go to war.

• **Better Than Expected**—One official believes it entirely possible that, if the final tally shows 190,000 women declaring a willingness to do arms plant jobs, an actual showdown of job offers will find only about 125,000 or so really ready to start. This, however, is far in excess of early expectations of 80,000.

Source: Business Week, July 11, 1942: 72 and September 5, 1942: 33.

PRESIDENT FRANKLIN ROOSEVELT REPORTS ON THE HOME FRONT, FIRESIDE CHAT, OCTOBER 12, 1942

My fellow Americans:

As you know, I have recently come back from a trip of inspection of camps and training stations and war factories.

The main thing that I observed on this trip is not exactly news. It is the plain fact that the American people are united as never before in their determination to do a job and to do it well. . . .

There are now millions of Americans in army camps, in naval stations, in factories, and in shipyards.

Who are these millions upon whom the life of our country depends? What are they thinking? What are their doubts? What are their hopes? And how is the work progressing?

The Commander in Chief cannot learn all of the answers to these questions in Washington. And that is why I made the trip I did. . . .

As I told the three press association representatives who accompanied me, I was impressed by the large proportion of women employed—doing skilled manual labor running machines. As time goes on, and many more of our men enter the armed forces, this proportion of women will increase. Within less than a year from now there will probably be as many women as men working in our war production plants. . . .

In order to keep stepping up our production, we have had to add millions of workers to the total labor force of the Nation. And as new factories come into operation, we must find additional millions of workers.

This presents a formidable problem in the mobilization of manpower.

It is not that we do not have enough people in this country to do the job. The problem is to have the right numbers of the right people in the right places at the right time.

We are learning to ration materials; and we must now learn to ration manpower.

The major objectives of a sound manpower policy are:

First, to select and train men of the highest fighting efficiency needed for our armed forces in the achievement of victory over our enemies in combat.

Second, to man our war industries and farms with the workers needed to produce the arms and munitions and food required by ourselves and by our fighting allies to win this war.

In order to do this, we shall be compelled to stop workers from moving from one war job to another as a matter of personal preference; to stop employers from stealing labor from each other; to use older men, and handicapped people, and more women, and even grown boys and girls, wherever possible and reasonable, to replace men of military age and fitness; to train new personnel for essential war work; and to stop the wastage of labor in all non-essential activities.

There are many other things that we can do, and do immediately, to help meet this manpower problem.

The school authorities in all the States should work out plans to enable our high school students to take some time from their school year, and to use their summer vacations, to help farmers raise and harvest their crops, or to work somewhere in the war industries. This does not mean closing schools and stopping education. It does mean giving older students a better opportunity to contribute their bit to the war effort. Such work will do no harm to the students.

People should do their work as near their homes as possible. We cannot afford to transport a single worker into an area where there is already a worker available to do the job.

In some communities, employers dislike to employ women. In others they are reluctant to hire Negroes. In still others, older men are not wanted. We can no longer afford to indulge such prejudices or practices.

Every citizen wants to know what essential war work he can do the best. He can get the answer by applying to the nearest United States Employment Service office. There are 4,500 of these offices throughout the Nation. They form the corner grocery stores of our manpower system. This network of employment offices is prepared to advise every citizen where his skills and labors are needed most, and to refer him to an employer who can utilize them to best advantage in the war effort.

It may be that all of our volunteer effort—however well intentioned and well administered—will not suffice wholly to solve this problem. In that case, we shall have to adopt new legislation [i.e. draft women for war jobs]. And if this is necessary, I do not believe that the American people will shrink from it.

In a sense, every American, because of the privilege of his citizenship, is a part of the Selective Service.

The Nation owes a debt of gratitude to the Selective Service boards. The successful operation of the Selective Service System and the way it has been accepted by the great mass of our citizens give us confidence that, if necessary, the same principle could be used to solve any manpower problem.

Source: Samuel I. Rosenman, ed., *The Public Papers and Addresses of Franklin D. Roosevelt* (New York: Harper and Bros., 1950), 416–423.

"ROSIE THE RIVETER"

American women responded without a draft. In 1940, twelve million American women worked outside the home; five years later nineteen million did. Many of the new workers labored at traditionally male jobs in factories and on farms. These were the women referred to collectively as "Rosie the Riveter." However much the war disrupted their lives, at work they were stunningly successful. The Chairman of the War Production Board, Donald Nelson, summarized this achievement: "For nine years before Pearl Harbor, Germany, Italy and Japan prepared intensively for war, while as late as 1940 the war production of peaceful America was virtually nothing. Yet two years later the output of our war factories equaled that of the three Axis nations combined. In 1943 our war production was one and one half times, and in 1944, more than doubled Axis war production. . . ." The stories of a few women cannot sum the experience of millions, but the documents here suggest some of the motives women had for choosing war work and indicate some of the many new experiences they encountered when they did.

BEATRICE MORALES CLIFTON BECOMES
ROSIE THE RIVETER

My father's family was born in Mexico. They were from Durango. And my mother used to mention Paral and all them places in Mexico, so I guess that was the area, Chihuahua, that my grandmother and grandfather were from. My parents married in Mexico. My dad was a factory worker. He used to weave material for the textile mills. Supposedly he was a very good worker. The companies were always asking him to work for them. My mother was one of those workers, too, and that's how I think that they met. They had three children in Mexico, two girls and a boy. Later, on the change of life, I came.

They came here in 1912 or '13, right around the time of the Revolution. My mother used to say that it was so hectic. They would come around and say, "Who lives?"—Madero or whatever. If they didn't answer the right word, they'd shoot them. She was afraid that they would take my father into the army, 'cause there— it's not like over here—they make you. So that's how they more or less escaped. . . .

Julio was a good provider. We'd buy groceries and whatever it was supposed to be. But with the children, he never interfered. He would tell me alone, "You're being too hard with them." But we got along perfect. He never beat up on my children or anything like that. I was the one that tightened the rein. I used to be real strict. . . .

After Pearl Harbor, we moved to 214 Pasadena Avenue. They took a lot of Japanese away, and they left a lot of houses. But I had a lot of trouble because they wouldn't rent to me because I was a Mexican. They'd tell it to my face. That used to make me feel kind of bitter. One time, one of them told me, "Why don't you say you're Italian? You could pass." But finally I got this house, that was a pretty good size. There was blacks and there was white, Mexicans, and I guess over there on Pasadena Avenue there must have been quite a few Japanese people. All these people owned their house, but I didn't own mine.

I'd never thought about working. My brother at that time had separated from his wife, and he had an adopted girl. . . . He brought that girl to me and says, "I'll have her stay with you and I'll give you some money every week." She was sixteen or fifteen and she wanted a job.

They had these offices everywhere in Pasadena, of aircraft. I went in there to try and get her something, but they said, "We've got aircraft work right now for everybody, except she's too young." He says, "Why don't you get it?" I said, "Me?" He said, "Yeah, why don't you get the job?" I said, "Well, I don't know." But the more I kept thinking about it, the more I said, "That's a good idea." So I took the forms and when I got home and told my husband, oh! he hit the roof. He was one of those men that didn't believe in the wife ever working; they want to be the supporter. I said, "Well, I've made up my mind. I'm going to go to work regardless of whether you like it or not." I was determined.

My family and everybody was surprised—his family. I said, "Well, yeah, I'm going to work." "And how does Julio feel?" "He doesn't want me to, but I'm going anyway." When he saw that, he just kept quiet; he didn't say no more. My mother didn't say nothing because I always told her, "Mother, you live your life and I live mine." We had that understanding. When I decided to go to work, I told her, "I'm going to go to work and maybe you can take care of the children." She said, "Yeah.". . .

I filled out the papers and everything and I got the job. Why I took Lockheed, I don't know, but I just liked that name. Then they asked me, "Do you want to go to Burbank, to Los Angeles?" I said, "I don't know where Burbank is." I didn't know my way around. The only way that I got up to Los Angeles was with Julio driving me there. I said, "Well, Los Angeles. The streetcar passes by Fair Oaks, close to where I live, and that drops me off in front."

To me, everything was new. They were doing the P-38s at that time. I was at Plant 2, on Seventh and Santa Fe. It was on the fifth floor. I went up there and saw the place, and I said, "Gee——." See, so many parts and things that you've never seen. Me, I'd never seen anything in my whole life. It was exciting and scary at the same time.

They put me way up in the back, putting little plate nuts and drilling holes. They put me with some guy—he was kind of a stinker, real mean. A lot of them guys at the time resented women coming into jobs, and they let you know about it. He says, "Well, have you ever done any work like this?" I said, "No." I was feeling just horrible. Horrible. Because I never worked with men, to be with men alone other than my husband. So then he says "You know what you've got in your hand? That's a rivet gun." I said, "Oh." What could I answer? I was terrified. So then time went on and I made a mistake. I messed up something, made a ding. He got so irritable with me, he says, "You're not worth the money Lockheed pays you."

He couldn't have hurt me more if he would have slapped me. When he said that, I dropped the gun and I went running downstairs to the restroom, with tears coming down. This girl from Texas saw me and she followed me. She was real good. She was one of these "toughies"; dressed up and walked like she was kind of tough. She asked me what was wrong. I told her what I had done and I was crying. She says, "Don't worry." She started cussing him. We came back up and she told them all off.

I was very scared because, like I say, I had never been away like that and I had never been among a lot of men. Actually, I had never been out on my own. Whenever I had gone anyplace, it was with my husband. It was all building up inside of me, so when that guy told me that I wasn't worth the money Lockheed paid me, it just came out in tears.

At the end of that first day, I was so tired. I was riding the streetcar and I had to stand all the way from Los Angeles clear to Pasadena. When I got home, the kids just said, "Oh, Mom is here." My husband, he didn't have very much to say, 'cause he didn't approve from the beginning. As time went on, his attitude changed a little, but I don't think he ever really, really got used to the idea of me working. But he was a very reserved man. He wasn't the type of guy that you'd sit down and you'd chatter on. Like me, I'm a chatterbox. You had to pull the words out of him. . . .

They had a union, but it wasn't very strong then. It wasn't like it is now. But I joined. I joined everything that they told me. . . . And they gave me a list of the stuff that I would be needing. At that time they used to sell you your tools and your toolboxes through Lockheed. So I bought a box. I bought the clothing at Sears. It was just a pair of pants and a blouse. To tell you the truth, I felt kind of funny wearing pants. Then at the same time, I said, "Oh, what the heck." And those shoes! I wasn't used to low shoes. Even in the house, I always wore high heels. That's how I started.

As time went on, I started getting a little bit better. I just made up my mind that I was going to do it. I learned my job so well that then they put me to the next operation. At the very first, I just began putting little plate nuts and stuff like that. Then afterwards I learned how to drill the skins and burr them. Later, as I got going, I learned to rivet and buck. I got to the point where I was very good. . . .

I was just a mother of four kids, that's all. But I felt proud of myself and felt good being that I had never done anything like that. I felt good that I could do something, and being that it was war, I felt that I was doing my part.

I went from 65 cents to $1.05. That was top pay. It felt good and, besides, it was my own money. I could do whatever I wanted with it because my husband, whatever he was giving to the house, he kept on paying it. I used to buy clothes for the kids; buy little things that they needed. I had a bank account and I had a little saving at home where I could get ahold of the money right away if I needed it. Julio never asked about it. He knew how much I made; I showed him. If there was something that had to be paid and I had the money and he didn't, well, I used some of my money. But he never said, "Well, you have to pay because you're earning money." My money, I did what I wanted.

I started feeling a little more independent. Just a little, not too much, because I was still not on my own that I could do this and do that. I didn't until after. Then I got really independent. . . .

[When her son comes down with pneumonia, she quits her job.]

My husband, right away, he jumped: "You see, the kids are like this because you're not here." My mother was there, but he blamed everything on me. We got into a little bit of an argument on account of that, and then I said, "Okay, I'll quit." I didn't want to, but I said my boy comes first. Afterwards, I realized I could have gone on a leave of absence. But I wasn't too familiar with all that, so I just panicked and quit.

When I quit, I just took over the same as I was before—taking care of my kids. Well, it was kind of quiet and I wasn't too satisfied. That's why I started looking to go to work. . . .

I was already thinking of Lockheed. I wasn't satisfied. I felt myself alone and I said, "Oh, I can't do this: I can't stay here." In 1950 I wrote to Lockheed asking them if they had a job for me because I knew that they were still taking people. They wrote and told me that they weren't taking any women, but that they would the following year. The next year, the minute I received that telegram, I headed for Lockheed.

I went to the office all ready. This was in Burbank. They give you a list of rides and stuff and that's how I started—riding with people from Pasadena. I think they started me at $1.65, or something like that. Riveting. We were working on the side panels of the T-33.

It wasn't like it was before because I already knew a little of it, so it wasn't as hard. I was working two months when they told me, being that I was new I had to either go on nights or I'd be laid off. So I told them, "I'll go on nights!"

Then, you see, if you knew blueprints, it would help in your job. I figured sooner or later I might need this. This friend of mine—she lived around where I lived in Pasadena and she was a black lady—she was going to Frank Wiggins School, and she told me, "How about it, do you want to go?" We were working nights, so we'd go to school in the morning and we'd get out of there about 1:00 or 1:30, and we'd go have lunch and then we'd go to work.

Source: Sherna Berger Gluck, *Rosie the Riveter Revisited* (Boston: Twayne, 1987), 203–213. Reprinted by permission.

THE GIRLS OF ELKTON, MARYLAND

The little town [of Elkton, Maryland] was crammed to bursting with girls. Houses were full, restaurants were full, stores were full of war workers. The population of 3,800 has doubled. The conversion of a local factory to a munitions plant was followed by further expansions and additions until the plant now employs many thousands. Another munitions company nearby added nearly 2,000 more; 80 per cent of both are women. Girls between eighteen and twenty-five are what both companies prefer.

These girls are part of the vast migration that's going on all over the country. They are the pioneers in the mobilization of the great army of women workers. Many of them are on their first jobs.

Ask a group of girls why they came and you get answers like this: "I wanted to help." "My husband's in the Navy. I felt nearer to him, working like this." "My brother enlisted. I wanted to enlist too."

They have come for service but they have come for adventure also. Their one discipline is that of the munitions plant. They are accountable to no one. They are the recruits of industry and like the boys in the armed forces they are eager for life, eager for fun. They want to dance. There is a massed vitality in these girls that is formidable, and their coming has changed the life, not only of Elkton, but of the whole country. . . .

The draft and the munitions plants between them took the workers from every other enterprise. People sold their dairy farms because there was no one left to milk the cows. By June, 1941, half the stores and all the restaurants displayed "Help Wanted" signs. Household help had practically vanished.

The local children felt the stir of change. Families were upset and family life disrupted because parents in war jobs worked on different schedules. Delicate as a seismograph, the Office of Child Welfare recorded the upset state of Cecil County. Little girls ran away in unprecedented numbers. Boys took to pilfering and "borrowing" cars. The load of juvenile delinquency bounced up. This occurred even in families where parents had not gone away. The less stable of the children felt the impact of war. . . .

Married couples coming to work could not find a place to stay, and they doubled in with other people. Quickly there was overcrowding. Promising little slums sprang up here and there. Three families lived where one had been before. . . .

The presence of many Negro workers made another problem. Elkton has a Negro population of five hundred. Their houses are small, their families are large. There was no place to put the more than doubled colored population which flowed into town. Colored workers sat up all night in kitchens and sitting rooms, since their hosts had no beds for them; girls who came in jitneys and jalopies in the first rush sometimes worked by day and slept cramped in the cars. . . .

The company does not assume any responsibility for the Negro girls that come looking for work, nor for finding them places to live, as it does for the white girls. The theory is that the Negroes employed shall all commute, and if they come to Elkton they come at their own risk. There is one small Negro restaurant, and unless the girls have kitchen privileges they eat bakery stuff and sardines in their rooms. In the plant they mostly work in separate departments from the white girls, though there are some white foremen who direct the Negroes. Of course numerous local people expected "trouble," but there hasn't been any. The only ripple has been caused by some Northern white girls who twit the Southern girls about their attitude toward the Negroes.

In the end one problem piled on another created a situation too difficult for a small community to meet. There wasn't enough of anything—rooms, food, or restaurants. There was no place for sick people and not a single place of amusement, except a couple of small movie houses, for the crowds of boys and girls adrift on the streets. Even the water system was overtaxed. Moreover the town sulked at what were euphemistically referred to as "certain elements" in the plant, and certain elements in the plant feuded with the town. . . .

[Federal manpower officials arrive to expedite construction of dormitories.]

Now there are several more dormitories almost finished, and they are going to open progressively. There are to be eleven dormitories for white occupants, complete with a community house which will have a grill, a sandwich bar, and an infirmary. Ground will soon be broken for the four much-needed Negro dormitories, which are also to have a community house. A seventy-five-room addition to the hospital has had its specifications signed, and Elkton is to have a new sewer system. . . .

For the first time the girls have a place of their own besides a beer parlor or juke joint where they can dance, play games, write a letter, or receive friends. The clubhouse is theirs. It was made over from a fine old three-storey house and has assembly rooms, game rooms, a writing room, and spare bedrooms for stranded girls.

The girls and the town have been brought together through the U.S.O. There was plenty of good will in Elkton but no channel through which it could flow. Now a gradual welding is going on between the war production workers and townspeople. . . .

It is in the dormitories that one gets to know the girls. A feeling of adventure streams through them. Take the case of Ellen Dearson. One Sunday morning she was a solitary girl standing near the bus station. There was never anyone as lonely and forsaken-looking as she. Her skirt flapped about her ankles, her hair fell lank about her ears. Everything about her spoke of some remote Southern hill town.

She had started on her journey from West Virginia in a company bus full of newly recruited girls, and had got separated from them and had been sent on by the regular bus, but her suitcase hadn't come with her. She didn't know what company she was working for. She didn't remember the name of the man who had hired her and she hadn't a penny in her pocket. She had had nothing to eat since the day before, but would accept only a cup of coffee. "I don't feel hungry—you mustn't spend all this money on me," she protested. She was frightened but she was self-contained and kept her fierce reticence. She was going to let no "foreigner" see her disturbance, but you could feel her all aquiver like a taut violin string.

Two months later she had on a wine-colored corduroy skirt, a pretty shirt-waist, and some costume jewelry, little red flowers that went with her dress. Her dark hair was swept back from her eyes, which had been so guarded and lackluster before, but now shone with pride as though to say, "You wouldn't know me." There was a discreet touch of rouge on her thin face. I'd see her running in and out of the dormitory, always with a group of girls, her face alight. She was rich. She made more money than she had ever thought possible. The dormitory was luxury. The clothes were something she had not even dreamed of. Here all at once was companionship, adventure, a different status. . . .

Over in the old dormitory there is the feeling of an established community. Around six the lobby fills up. The girls iron and press their clothes. One of the girls, who was formerly in a beauty shop, is doing some handsome hairdressing. The girls are waiting in their coats for their beaus to pick them up. . . .

Uncle Sam gives orders that strict morality is to be observed on his premises. But what the girls do after they leave government-owned territory is none of anyone's business. The girls come and go at their will. There are no hours to be kept. The doors of the dormitories are always open, and they must be to the three shifts. . . .

It's amazing how the girls stand up to the danger of their occupation. "Those who can take it stay, and those who can't take it clear out, and the sooner the better for the rest of us. If the boys can take what they do I guess we can," the girls say. The danger of the work identifies them with the men of their family who are overseas.

They never talk about the war and seem to have no curiosity about it. . . .

There is a feeling among them that is electric and vital. They have shown such a pioneering and adventurous spirit in coming at all that one feels they are waiting for something, perhaps for a way to be found to fill their minds and to bring them closer to the great currents of thought sweeping through the world. They are so near to the war, and are playing so important a part, and their clever fingers are so necessary—yet there is lacking here, as elsewhere, a final urgency which war demands. These girls are waiting for some voice to speak a message which will release all their energy for total war.

Source: Mary Heaton Vorse, "The Girls of Elkton, Maryland," *Harper's Magazine*, March 1943: 347–354. Reprinted by permission.

NEW LIVES VS. OLD ROLES

Traditional roles changed as well. Wartime marriages, many of which led to peacetime divorces, could project women into unexpected lives with as many challenges as Rosie the Riveter faced. Here is one example.

DELLIE HAHNE'S MARRIAGE

There was this tremendous romance and glamour to the men in the service. And at the very top were the flyboys—"Off we go, into the wild blue yonder." Anybody who flew was absolute tops in the social scale, and my brother was a pilot, so it gave me a great deal of importance. I would drive out to the air base in Santa Ana to visit him on weekends. That's how I met my husband. . . .

Six weeks later we were married. I saw him six weekends and then married him.

The social pressure for young women to marry soldiers was incredibly strong. It was in everything we did, everything we read, the songs we listened to on the radio, in movies like *The Clock,* where Judy Garland meets a soldier and, in a matter of hours, decides to marry him. The disapproval of refusing to marry a soldier is laughable now, but it existed. I felt the pressure. I told my brother after my husband proposed—this was after the fifth time I'd seen him—I said, "You know, I don't think I want to marry Glenn." And he said, "Oh, Dellie, don't say that. Not marry Glenn?" And his wife, my sister-in-law, said, "But you have to." And I didn't have the sense to fight it. Besides, I wanted to marry anyway. I had absorbed all these attitudes.

The serviceman was giving everything to his country—arms, legs, his eyesight, his blood, his life. The least you could do was give yourself to this man. And since sex outside of marriage was frowned upon, the only thing left was to marry him. It was almost your duty. . . .

It was expected of you to follow your husband, even pregnant women and women with small children. That was the least you could do. You belonged to a select group—the war brides. You were giving your all to the guys who were giving their all to us.

The conditions on the railroad were horrendous. The trains were packed with women following their husbands. What broke my heart was the sight of pregnant women. They weren't women; they were girls, really, seventeen-, eighteen-, twenty-year-olds who had married soldiers and gone to say good-bye to them, or were on their way home, and they were five, six months pregnant. I would think, What in hell are they going to do? The guy is going overseas—do they go home and live with their families? How are they going to support themselves on an allotment of fifty dollars a month?

Following your husband was really very difficult. The trains were a mess. We were allowed into the dining car twice a day, morning and night. We weren't given lunch. Only the servicemen were allowed to eat lunch. In some trains we could sit in the aisles on our suitcases or in the vestibules. We never had a guarantee that we would remain on the train. There were several times when I was put off the train. I remember being put off in a place called El Reno, Oklahoma, which to me was nowhere, and I had to fend for myself. I had to find a hotel, find a way to get out the next day or whenever I could. It was a tremendous lesson in growing up.

I had led a very sheltered life. My mother was the type of woman who liked to run the show; she made all my decisions for me, and I never questioned it. The first decision I ever made on my own was on my first day in college when I had to decide whether to eat lunch at the hot-dog stand down the road or in the cafeteria. It was the first decision I'd ever had to make in my life, and I couldn't do it. I just stood in the hall, frozen.

Just shortly after that I became a war wife, knocking around the country, trying to figure out how to feed myself without ration points, coming into a strange town, finding out where to rent a room, how much to pay. I never had a checking account in my life. I opened one in my first town and didn't sign my name on the check the way I had signed it on the application card; I didn't think it meant anything. So my first check bounced. I learned very quickly how to take care of myself. I think a great number of us did, because we were forced on our own traveling from one town to another. The war produced some good things, and self-reliance was one of them for me.

Source: Mark J. Hanna et al., *The Homefront: America During World War II* (New York: G. P. Putnam's Sons, 1984), 179–181.

WOMEN IN UNIFORM

Millions of women donned uniforms in World War II. About 350,000 served formally in the armed forces: Army WAC, Navy WAVE, Coast Guard SPAR, Marine Corps Women's Reserve, Army Nurse Corps and

Navy Nurse Corps. Uniformed women ferried airplanes from base to base as quasi-military Air Force WASPs. Many woman civilian employees on military bases wore uniforms, as did Red Cross workers, air-raid wardens, the Women's Land Army (volunteer agricultural workers), members of the Cadet Nurse Corps, many USO workers, and about a hundred women war correspondents accredited by the War Department. Motives that Clarice F. Pollard cites for joining the Women's Auxiliary Army Corps (WAAC)—which later in the war became the Women's Army Corps (WAC)—were common.

CLARICE F. POLLARD: A G.I. LADY

What was I doing posing there uncertainly in that stark, cheerless room wrapped in a white bed sheet and clutching a urine specimen in a container?

I, and several other similarly draped women, looked quizzically and hesitatingly at one another, until rescued by a lady in the uniform of the Women's Army Auxiliary Corps who directed us to the proper section of the medical department where we completed our physical examinations. We then dressed, were finger-printed and completed the pages of questions on the enlistment applications for the Corps that had to do with our personal histories and individual preferences. For instance two examples of the latter were: "Do you mind standing in line for food or other services?" I did, but answered "No." "Does it make you uncomfortable to live and move in groups such as under military circumstances?" to which I again answered "No," although I loved my privacy. I replied in the negative because I felt that I could tolerate these conditions provided they were not to be forever.

Afterward, the Army General Classification Test (AGCT) was administered to be used as a guide for job placement and qualification for leadership. Following the lengthy registration process, we were assigned Army serial numbers and escorted back to the reception area where we were asked to stand as a group and raise our right hands and I raised mine with the other inductees. We then all faced a WAAC officer who led the declaration of loyalty to the United States, which we intoned together:

> I, Clarice Fortgang, do solemnly swear that I will support and defend the Constitution of the United States against all enemies foreign and domestic; that I will bear true faith and allegiance to the same, and that I will obey the orders of the President of the United States and the orders of the officers appointed over me according to regulations and uniform code of Military Justice. So help me God. . . .

When our world was transformed with the Japanese attack at Pearl Harbor, Hawaii, on the morning of December 7, 1941, and the United States declared war on Japan, it became necessary to add Civilian Defense activities to the work of the day, whereon I became an Air Raid Warden in my immediate neighborhood. With my neighbors I patrolled our streets during the nationally ordered after-dark blackouts of cities and in addition, volunteered as a hostess for the United Service Organization (USO) at Fort Hamilton in Brooklyn, New York. A chance remark on the radio led me to search for the camouflage division of the Army which employed artists to design and construct models in miniature for that department. Numerous inquiries as to their location proved fruitless, but did bring me in contact with information about the newly created Women's Auxiliary Army Corps and subsequently led to the idea of enlisting in the WAAC where the Military could reap larger benefits from my efforts than if I chose to remain within the confines of greater New York. In that case there would not be restrictions on my donation to the war effort, and perhaps even an assignment to the camouflage section.

Life was changing the core of my family, for it was a question of when my brother Leonard was going to be called into the Service. Male friends, neighbors and relatives were in the Armed Forces, and dates began to appear more often in uniform. The tempo of urgency picked up each time I said goodbye to intimates and neighbors with disrupted lives while I prayed that my brother would not have to leave his environs as they had, and I felt a compulsion to stand between him and the enemy. For myself, the thought of dictators who condemned the helpless and abolished the privileges of national and self determination was abhorrent to me, therefore I hoped to contribute to an effort that would deliver the enslaved and keep my world free of the same.

Now that I was on my way to war, what else would I part company with other than work, family, friends and Saturday night dates?

I would forsake the full-fashioned silk hosiery with seams down the back, saucy pillbox hats with nose veils and my array of hand-sewn gloves. I would say adieu to the ankle-strapped shoes, the fur coat and muff, the spring suits with nipped-in waists and padded shoulders—but not all of them—because one blue suit with white cotton blouses would accompany me to Basic Training.

* * *

When traditionally only men left their homes to make the world safe for democracy, I was fortunate to be among those who believed that the pursuit of freedom was likewise a female mission. It was a privilege to be present during the transformation of the male outlook that brought the Women's Army Corps side by side with, and marching to, the same beat as those time-honored soldiers.

What changes had taken place in the area of opportunities offered to females in the Military during the period of my association with the WAC in the Second World War?

We early volunteers, restricted to three choices of assignment: the kitchen, office or motor transport, saw in a short span of time, a century of evolution in the employment of our talents. Through demonstrations of our competence, we found entry into every task the Armed Forces had to offer, short of the battlefield.

For example: my colleagues who worked on the piers soon expanded to sending civilians, nurses, other WACs and male soldiers in and out of the country. They subsequently handled all needed inventory that included guns and ammunition for the men, and saw to it that returning soldiery, enlisted and commissioned, were properly equipped and on the right trains to various camps for return to action, medical care or discharge.

Our ladies were occupied in the Postal Battalions where all "V" mail letters were censored and sent to their destinations. Other jobs included work in water, rail, motor vehicle and mechanical maintenance, salvage, photo labs, mess and supply depots. They scrutinized tons of manifests, cargo reports and convoy lists and were Multigraph operators, supply technicians, tailors and movie projectionists.

The ones stationed aboard hospital ships acted as guides, medical admitting staff and finance assistants for the wounded and some were radio operators, medical technicians and nurses aides. WACs who attended the School for Personnel Services as I did conducted discussions about veterans benefits, discharge procedures and wrote and distributed news sheets; in addition, they were responsible for morale and so supplied music and variety shows. Overseas, women of the Transportation Corps routed war supplies, while others of the Ground Forces checked in and even delivered the stores to their destinations when necessary, and our Army Air Forces (Air WACs) performed many of the forementioned duties as well as those peculiar to their branch of the service—and the list goes on.

I came into the Service with two primary goals which never abated in intensity. One was to insure the continued freedom for everyone to make their own decisions in the matter of life and liberties, and to contribute to that end, so that the men and women involved could be restored safely and soon to their nearest and dearest. I could not return home until these targets were within reason of my efforts.

Could I save them all? No one person could. I could be thankful that my closest and most beloved were returned alive. I had given my best and hoped never to look at war again.

Source: Clarice F. Pollard, *Laugh, Cry and Remember: The Journal of a G. I. Lady* (Phoenix: Journeys Press, 1991), 23–24, 25–27, 216–217.

Chapter 10

THE ATOMIC BOMB AND
THE ERA OF TOTAL WAR

The decision to drop atomic bombs on the Japanese cities of Hiroshima and Nagasaki in August 1945 is one of the most famous and controversial in American history. In the summer of 1995, the Smithsonian Institution in Washington, D.C., displayed a restored version of *Enola Gay*, the airplane that had carried the first atomic bomb to Hiroshima. This exhibit, which probed the morality of the decision, stirred almost as much controversy as the O. J. Simpson trial of the same summer. Fifty years later, although public opinion polls showed a solid majority in favor of the decision, many Americans, especially intellectuals and academicians, still questioned the need to use the atomic bomb on a largely civilian target. The Internet is filled with web sites posting competing interpretations and collections of original documents defending these interpretations; high school teachers around the country teach it as one of the most important decisions in our past; and there are hundreds of books on the subject in dozens of languages.

Few decisions in the history of the United States have involved less democratic debate and less of a sense that other choices were possible. Harry S Truman, a President who had not been elected to that office but assumed it after Franklin Roosevelt's death, made a decision to use a secret weapon. The United States had already spent two billion dollars to develop the bomb in the Manhattan Project and hired over a hundred thousand people to build it. If successful, the bomb could accomplish the central national goal for the last days of World War II: total victory over the Japanese. Americans were tired of war, fired up against the Japanese who had bombed Pearl Harbor and mistreated prisoners of war, and feared massive casualties in an invasion of Japan.

Much of the historical controversy surrounding this decision revolves around two of the documents contained in this chapter, both written by leading scientists of the Manhattan Project after the successful exploding of an atomic device but before the bombing of Japanese cities: the *Report of the Committee on Political and Social Problems* (also known as the Franck report, after its lead author, James Franck) and the petition circulated by another atomic scientist, Leo Szilard. Both documents questioned using the bomb against military targets without prior arrangements to safeguard civilian populations. The secrecy of the project ensured that their petitions circulated only among politicians and generals with high security clearances, men who were concerned more with practical considerations like targeting, the weather over Japan, and how to inflict the maximum psychological damage on the Japanese than with the ethical questions raised by scientists, most of whom were European refugees. These two documents notwithstanding, the authorities could reasonably presume that these scientists had made their choice when they signed on to the Manhattan Project.

If there was a critical decision that led to use of atomic weapons on civilians, it had been made years earlier by the political leaders of the United States, Britain, Germany, Japan, and other major powers when they concluded that aerial bombardment of civilians was an acceptable part of war. This decision violated long-standing traditions of warfare that mostly separated combatants from noncombatants. Modern war, however, was no longer a limited contest waged by elites, their employees, and some badly armed conscripts for the right to collect rent or taxes. The era of total war had arrived and the fate of the victims of the atomic bomb had been sealed earlier in the war by decisions to use terror bombing on civilians in cities like Dresden, London, and Tokyo.

[A NOTE ON THE USE OF THE INTERNET
TO STUDY HISTORY]

This chapter, as well as the final chapter on Social Security, draws many documents from web sites. Historians apply the same critical standards to such materials as they do to more traditional sources. Just as they usually judge information from the *New York Times* as more reliable than that from *National Enquirer* or depend on articles from the *New England Journal of Medicine* over pamphlets sold in health food stores, so they take seriously one web site while rejecting another. Their criteria include the knowledge and reputation of the webmaster, the care taken in preparing the site, and the footnoting of the origin or archival location of documents. And they cross-check references for documents before they accept them as valid. The web sites used here meet the evolving standards historians are applying to material on the internet, and students are invited to examine them or use them for further research. All documents were located and printed on July 15, 1998, as indicated in the citations.

THE ERA OF TOTAL WAR ARRIVES

The leading nations of the world had long attempted to establish rules of conduct for modern warfare. Yet even before World War II, in conflicts in Spain and Ethiopia, civilian populations were bombed from the air. As the war approached, President Franklin D. Roosevelt made efforts to protect civilians in wartime. But once the United States entered the war, these old restraints vanished.

CONVENTION RESPECTING THE LAWS AND CUSTOMS OF WAR ON LAND

The Hague, Netherlands, October 18, 1907:
Ratified by the United States Senate, March 10, 1908

ARTICLE XXII
The right of belligerents to adopt means of injuring the enemy is not unlimited.

ARTICLE XXIII
In addition to the prohibitions provided by special Conventions, it is especially forbidden:
(a) To employ poison or poisoned weapons;
(b) To kill or wound treacherously individuals belonging to the hostile nation or army;
(c) To kill or wound an enemy who, having laid down his arms, or having no longer means of defense, has surrendered at discretion;
(d) To declare that no quarter will be given;
(e) To employ arms, projectiles, or material calculated to cause unnecessary suffering;

ARTICLE XXV
The attack or bombardment, by whatever means, of towns, villages, dwellings, or buildings which are undefended is prohibited.

ARTICLE XXVI
The officer in command of an attacking force must, before commencing a bombardment, except in cases of assault, do all in his power to warn the authorities.

ARTICLE XXVII
In sieges and bombardments all necessary steps must be taken to spare, as far as possible, buildings dedicated to religion, art, science, or charitable purposes, historic monuments, hospitals, and places where the sick and wounded are collected, provided that they are not being used at the time for military purposes.
It is the duty of the besieged to indicate the presence of such buildings or places by distinctive and visible signs, which shall be notified to the enemy beforehand.

Source: http://www.dannen.com/decision/index.html (July 15, 1998).

PROTECTION OF CIVILIAN POPULATIONS AGAINST BOMBING FROM THE AIR IN CASE OF WAR

Unanimous resolution of the League of Nations Assembly,
September 30, 1938

Considering that on numerous occasions public opinion has expressed through the most authoritative channels its horror of the bombing of civilian populations;

Considering that this practice, for which there is no military necessity and which, as experience shows, only causes needless suffering, is condemned under the recognised principles of international law;

Considering further that, though this principle ought to be respected by all States and does not require further reaffirmation, it urgently needs to be made the subject of regulations specially adapted to air warfare and taking account of the lessons of experience;

I. Recognizing the following principles as a necessary basis for any subsequent regulations:

1) The intentional bombing of civilian populations is illegal;

2) Objectives aimed at from the air must be legitimate military objectives and must be identifiable;

3) Any attack on legitimate military objectives must be carried out in such a way that civilian populations in the neighbourhood are not bombed through negligence.

Source: http://www.dannen.com/decision/index.html (July 15, 1998).

APPEAL OF PRESIDENT FRANKLIN D. ROOSEVELT ON AERIAL BOMBARDMENT OF CIVILIANS, SEPTEMBER 1, 1939

The President of the United States to the Governments of France, Germany, Italy, Poland and His Britannic Majesty:

The ruthless bombing from the air of civilians in unfortified centers of population during the course of hostilities which have raged in various quarters of the earth during the past few years, which has resulted in the maiming and in the death of thousands of defenseless men, women, and children, has sickened the hearts of every civilized man and woman, and has profoundly shocked the conscience of humanity.

If resort is had to this form of inhuman barbarism during the period of the tragic conflagration with which the world is now confronted, hundreds of thousands of innocent human beings who have no responsibility for, and who are not even remotely participating in, the hostilities which have now broken out, will lose their lives. I am therefore addressing this urgent appeal to every government which may be engaged in hostilities publicly to affirm its determination that its armed forces shall in no event, and under no circumstances, undertake the bombardment from the air of civilian populations or of unfortified cities, upon the understanding that these same rules of warfare will be scrupulously observed by all of their opponents. I request an immediate reply.

FRANKLIN D. ROOSEVELT

Source: http://www.dannen.com/decision/index.html (July 15, 1998).

EFFECTS OF BOMBING ON THE JAPANESE PEOPLE

The United States Strategic Bombing Survey was established by the Secretary of War on 3 November 1944, pursuant to a directive from the late President Roosevelt. It was established for the purpose of conducting an impartial and expert study of the effects of our aerial attack. . . .

THE HEALTH AND MORALE OF THE JAPANESE CIVILIAN POPULATION UNDER ASSAULT

Total civilian casualties in Japan, as a result of 9 months of air attack, including those from the atomic bombs, were approximately 806,000. Of these, approximately 330,000 were fatalities. These casualties probably exceeded Japan's combat casualties which the Japanese estimate as having totaled approximately 780,000 during the entire war. The principal cause of civilian death or injury was burns. Of the total casualties approximately 185,000 were suffered in the initial attack on Tokyo of 9 March 1945. Casualties in many extremely destructive attacks were comparatively low. Yokahoma, a city of 900,000 population, was 47 percent destroyed in a single attack lasting less than an hour. The fatalities suffered were less than 5,000.

The Japanese had constructed extensive firebreaks by tearing down all houses along selected streets or natural barriers. The total number of buildings torn down in this program, as reported by the Japanese, amounted to 615,000 as against 2,510,000 destroyed by the air attacks themselves. These firebreaks did not effectively stop the spread of fire, as incendiaries were dropped on both sides of the breaks. They did, however, constitute avenues of escape for the civilian population.

The Japanese instituted a civilian-defense organization prior to the war. It was not until the summer of 1944, however, that effective steps were taken to reduce the vulnerability of Japan's civilian population to air attacks. By that time, the shortage of steel, concrete and other construction materials was such that adequate air-raid shelters could no longer be built. Each family was given the obligation of providing itself with some kind of an excavation covered with bamboo and a little dirt. In addition, tunnels were dug into the sides of hills wherever the topography permitted.

Japanese planning and the means for carrying out the plans were thus deficient for a first-class civilian defense program. In spite of these limitations, such civilian defense measures as they were able to put through contributed substantially in minimizing casualties. School children and other nonessential urban dwellers were evacuated to the country. Those who remained were organized to combat fires and to provide mutual assistance. The air raid warning system was generally efficient. The weight of the individual attacks was, however, far heavier than the Japanese had envisaged or were able to cope with. In the major fire attacks, the civilian defense organizations were simply overwhelmed.

Sixty-four percent of the population stated that they had reached a point prior to surrender where they felt personally unable to go on with the war. Of these, less than one-tenth attributed the cause to military defeats, one-quarter attributed the cause to shortages of food and civilian supplies, the largest part to air attack.

A striking aspect of the air attack was the pervasiveness with which its impact on morale blanketed Japan. Roughly one-quarter of all people in cities fled or were evacuated, and these evacuees, who themselves were of singularly low morale, helped spread discouragement and disaffection for the war throughout the islands. This mass migration from the cities included an estimated 8,500,000 persons. Throughout the Japanese islands, whose people had always thought themselves remote from attack, United States planes crisscrossed the skies with no effective Japanese air or antiaircraft opposition. That this was an indication of impending defeat became as obvious to the rural as to the urban population.

Progressively lowered morale was characterized by loss of faith in both military and civilian leaders, loss of confidence in Japan's military might and increasing distrust of government news releases and propaganda. People became short-tempered and more outspoken in their criticism of the government, the war and affairs in general.

Source: "Summary Report (Pacific War)," *United States Strategic Bombing Survey*, Washington, D.C., July 1, 1946. http://www.anesi.com/ussbs01.htm (July 15, 1998).

BUILDING THE ULTIMATE WEAPON

Extreme secrecy surrounded the atomic bomb. Most of the workers on the Manhattan Project had little knowledge of what the product of their labors would be. So very few were in a position even to express an opinion on the uses to which it should be put. Even President Harry S Truman had not known of the bomb project when he took office in April 1945. His decision to use the weapon was based on recommendations developed in a very short time by a few high-level scientists, military men, and political leaders. Albert Einstein's letter of 1939 is an important early document.

USHERING IN THE ATOMIC AGE: ALBERT EINSTEIN TO PRESIDENT FRANKLIN D. ROOSEVELT, AUGUST 2, 1939

Sir:

Some recent work by E. Fermi and L. Szilard, which has been communicated to me in manuscript, leads me to expect that the element uranium may be turned into a new and important source of energy in the immediate future. Certain aspects of the situation which has arisen seem to call for watchfulness and, if necessary, quick action on the part of the Administration. I believe therefore that it is my duty to bring to your attention the following facts and recommendations:

In the course of the last four months it has been made probable—through the work of Jolist in France as well as Fermi and Szilard in America—that it may become possible to set up a nuclear chain reaction in a large mass of uranium, by which vast amounts of power and large quantities of new radium-like elements would be generated. Now it appears almost certain that this could be achieved in the immediate future.

This new phenomenon would also lead to the construction of bombs, and it is conceivable—though much less certain—that extremely powerful bombs of a new type may thus be constructed. A single bomb of this type, carried by boat and exploded in a port, might very well destroy the whole port together with some of the surrounding territory. However, such bombs might very well prove to be too heavy for transportation by air.

The United States has only very poor ores of uranium in moderate quantities. There is some good ore in Canada and the former Czechoslovakia, while the most important source of uranium is Belgian Congo.

In view of this situation you may think it desirable to have some permanent contact maintained between the Administration and the group of physicists working on chain reactions in America. One possible way of achieving this might be for you to entrust with this task a person who has your confidence and who could perhaps serve in an unofficial capacity. His task might comprise the following:

a) to approach Government Departments, keep them informed of the further development, and put forward recommendations for Government action, giving particular attention to the problem of securing a supply of uranium ore for the United States;

b) to speed up the experimental work, which is at present being carried on within the limits of the budgets of University laboratories, by providing funds, if such funds be required, through his contacts with private persons who are willing to make contributions for this cause, and perhaps also by obtaining the co-operation of industrial laboratories which have the necessary equipment.

I understand that Germany has actually stopped the sale of uranium from the Czechoslovakian mines which she has taken over. That she should have taken such early action might perhaps be understood on the ground that the son of the German Under-Secretary of State, von Weizäcker, is attached to the Kaiser-Wilhelm-Institute in Berlin where some of the American work on uranium is now being reported.

Yours very truly,

(Albert Einstein)

Source: http://www.dannen.com/szilard.html and http://www.atomicarchive.com/Docs/Einstein.html (July 15, 1998).

TARGETING THE WEAPON: MINUTES OF THE TARGET COMMITTEE, LOS ALAMOS, NM, MAY 12, 1945

The agenda for meetings of May 1945 presented by Dr. J. Robert Oppenheimer consisted of the following:

A: Height of Detonation
B: Report on Weather and Operations
C: Gadget Jettisoning and Landing
D: Status of Targets
E: Psychological Factors in Target Selection
F: Use Against Military Objectives
G: Radiological Effects
H: Coordinated Air Operations
I: Rehearsals
J: Operating Requirements for Safety of Airplanes . . .

* * *

Status of Targets

Dr. Stearns described the work he had done on target selection. He has surveyed possible targets possessing the following qualification: (1) they be important targets in a large urban area of more than three miles in diameter, (2) they be capable of being damaged effectively by a blast, and (3) they are unlikely to be attacked by next August. Dr. Stearns had a list of five targets which the Air Force would be willing to reserve for our use unless unforeseen circumstances arise. These targets are:

(1) Kyoto—This target is an urban industrial area with a population of 1,000,000. It is the former capital of Japan and many people and industries are now being moved there as other areas are being destroyed. From the psychological point of view there is the advantage that Kyoto is an intellectual center for Japan and the people there are more apt to appreciate the significance of such a weapon as the gadget. (Classified as an AA Target)

(2) Hiroshima—This is an important army depot and port of embarkation in the middle of an urban industrial area. It is a good radar target and it is such a size that a large part of the city could be extensively damaged. There are adjacent hills which are likely to produce a focussing effect which would considerably increase the blast damage. Due to rivers it is not a good incendiary target. (Classified as an AA Target)

(3) Yokohama—This target is an important urban industrial area which has so far been untouched. Industrial activities include aircraft manufacture, machine tools, docks, electrical equipment and oil refineries. As the damage to Tokyo has increased, additional industries have moved to Yokohama. It has the disadvantage of the most important target areas being separated by a large body of water and of being in the heaviest anti-aircraft concentration in Japan. For us it has the advantage as an alternate target for use in case of bad weather of being rather far removed from the other targets considered. (Classified as an A Target)

(4) Kokura Arsenal—This is one of the largest arsenals in Japan and is sur-

rounded by urban industrial structures. The arsenal is important for light ordnance, anti-aircraft and beach head defense materials. The dimensions of the arsenal are 4100′×2000′. The dimensions are such that if the bomb were properly placed full advantage could be taken of the higher pressures immediately underneath the bomb for destroying the more solid structures and at the same time considerable blast damage could be done to more feeble structures further away. (Classified as an A Target)

(5) Niigata—This is a port of embarkation on the N.W. coast of Honshu. Its importance is increasing as other ports are damaged. Machine tool industries are located there and it is a potential center for industrial dispersion. It has oil refineries and storage. (Classified as a B Target)

(6) The possibility of bombing the Emperor's palace was discussed. It was agreed that we should not recommend it, but that any action for this bombing should come from authorities on military policy. It was agreed that we should obtain information from which we could determine the effectiveness of our weapon against this target.

It was the recommendation of those present at the meeting that the first four choices of targets for our weapon should be the following:

a. Kyoto
b. Hiroshima
c. Yokohama
d. Kokura Arsenal

Psychological Factors in Target Selection
A. It was agreed that psychological factors in the target selection were of great importance. Two aspects of this are (1) obtaining the psychological effect against Japan and (2) making the initial use sufficiently spectacular for the importance of the weapon to be internationally recognized when publicity on it is released.

B. In this respect Kyoto has the advantage of the people being more highly intelligent and hence better able to appreciate the significance of the weapon. Hiroshima has the advantage of being such a size and with possible focussing from nearby mountains that a large fraction of the city may be destroyed. The Emperor's palace in Tokyo has a greater fame than any other target but is of least strategic value.

Use Against "Military" Objectives
A. It was agreed that for the initial use of the weapon any small and strictly military objective should be located in a much larger area subject to blast damage in order to avoid undue risks of the weapon being lost due to bad placing of the bomb.

Source: http://www.dannen.com/decision/index.html and http://www.whistlestop.org/study_collections/bomb/large/bomb.htm (July 15, 1998).

THE SCIENTISTS' HESITATIONS:
THE FRANCK REPORT, JUNE 11, 1945

Members of the Committee:

James Franck (Chairman)

Donald J. Hughes

J. J. Nickson

Eugene Rabinowitch

Glenn T. Seaborg

J. C. Stearns

Leo Szilard

Political and Social Problems

Scientists have often before been accused of providing new weapons for the mutual destruction of nations, instead of improving their well-being. It is undoubtedly true that the discovery of flying, for example, has so far brought much more misery than enjoyment or profit to humanity. However, in the past, scientists could disclaim direct responsibility for the use to which mankind had put their disinterested discoveries. We cannot take the same attitude now because the success which we have achieved in the development of nuclear power is fraught with infinitely greater dangers than were all the inventions of the past. All of us, familiar with the present state of nucleonics, live with the vision before our eyes of sudden destruction visited on our own country, of Pearl Harbor disaster, repeated in thousandfold magnification, in every one of our major cities.

In the past, science has often been able to provide adequate protection against new weapons it has given into the hands of an aggressor, but it cannot promise such efficient protection against the destructive use of nuclear power. This protection can only come from the political organization of the world. Among all arguments calling for an efficient international organization for peace, the existence of nuclear weapons is the most compelling one. In the absence of an international authority which would make all resort to force in international conflicts impossible, nations could still be diverted from a path which must lead to total mutual destruction, by a specific international agreement barring a nuclear armaments race.

The development of nuclear power not only constitutes an important addition to the technological and military power of the United States, but also creates grave political and economic problems for the future of this country.

Nuclear bombs cannot possibly remain a "secret weapon" at the exclusive disposal of this country, for more than a few years. The scientific facts on which their construction is based are well known to scientists of other countries. Unless an effective international control of nuclear explosives is instituted, a race of nuclear armaments is certain to ensue following the first revelation of our possession of nuclear weapons to the world. Within ten years other countries may have nuclear bombs, each of which, weighing less than a ton, could destroy an urban area of more than five square miles. In the war to which such an armaments race is likely to lead, the United States, with its agglomeration of population and industry in comparatively few metropolitan districts, will be at a disadvantage compared to the nations whose population and industry are scattered over large areas.

We believe that these considerations make the use of nuclear bombs for an early, unannounced attack against Japan inadvisable. If the United States would be the first to release this new means of indiscriminate destruction upon mankind, she would sacrifice public support throughout the world, precipitate the race of armaments, and prejudice the possibility of reaching an international agreement on the future control of such weapons.

Much more favorable conditions for the eventual achievement of such an agreement could be created if nuclear bombs were first revealed to the world by a demonstration in an appropriately selected uninhabited area.

If chances for the establishment of an effective international control of nuclear weapons will have to be considered slight at the present time, then not only the use of these weapons against Japan, but even their early demonstration may be contrary to the interests of this country. A postponement of such a demonstration will have in this case the advantage of delaying the beginning of the nuclear armaments race as long as possible. If, during the time gained, ample support could be made available for further development of the field in this country, the postponement would substantially increase the lead which we have established during the present war, and our position in an armament race or in any later attempt at international agreement will thus be strengthened.

On the other hand, if no adequate public support for the development of nucleonics will be available without a demonstration, the postponement of the latter may be deemed inadvisable, because enough information might leak out to cause other nations to start the armament race, in which we will then be at a disadvantage. At the same time, the distrust of other nations may be aroused by a confirmed development under cover of secrecy, making it more difficult eventually to reach an agreement with them.

If the government should decide in favor of an early demonstration of nuclear weapons it will then have the possibility to take into account the public opinion of this country and of the other nations before deciding whether these weapons should be used in the war against Japan. In this way, other nations may assume a share of the responsibility for such a fateful decision.

To sum up, we urge that the use of nuclear bombs in this war be considered as a problem of long-range national policy rather than military expediency, and that this policy be directed primarily to the achievement of an agreement permitting an effective international control of the means of nuclear warfare.

The vital importance of such a control for our country is obvious from the fact that the only effective alternative method of protecting this country, of which we are aware, would be a dispersal of our major cities and essential industries.

Source: Report of the Committee on Political and Social Problems, Manhattan Project "Metallurgical Laboratory," University of Chicago, June 11, 1945. http://www.dannen.com/decision/index.html (July 15, 1998).

SCIENTISTS RECOMMEND MILITARY USE

Recommendations on the Immediate Use of Nuclear Weapons, by the Scientific Panel of the Interim Committee on Nuclear Power, June 16, 1945.

Arthur H. Compton
E. O. Lawrence
J. Robert Oppenheimer
Enrico Fermi

You have asked us to comment on the initial use of the new weapon. This use, in our opinion, should be such as to promote a satisfactory adjustment of our international relations. At the same time, we recognize our obligation to our nation to use the weapons to help save American lives in the Japanese war.

(1) To accomplish these ends we recommend that before the weapons are used not only Britain, but also Russia, France, and China be advised that we have made considerable progress in our work on atomic weapons, that these may be ready to use during the present war, and that we would welcome suggestions as to how we can cooperate in making this development contribute to improved international relations.

(2) The opinions of our scientific colleagues on the initial use of these weapons are not unanimous: they range from the proposal of a purely technical demonstration to that of the military application best designed to induce surrender. Those who advocate a purely technical demonstration would wish to outlaw the use of atomic weapons, and have feared that if we use the weapons now our position in future negotiations will be prejudiced. Others emphasize the opportunity of saving American lives by immediate military use, and believe that such use will improve the international prospects, in that they are more concerned with the prevention of war than with the elimination of this specific weapon. We find ourselves closer to these latter views; we can propose no technical demonstration likely to bring an end to the war; we see no acceptable alternative to direct military use.

(3) With regard to these general aspects of the use of atomic energy, it is clear that we, as scientific men, have no proprietary rights. It is true that we are among the few citizens who have had occasion to give thoughtful consideration to these problems during the past few years. We have, however, no claim to special competence in solving the political, social, and military problems which are presented by the advent of atomic power.

Source: Recommendations on the Immediate Use of Nuclear Weapons, June, 16, 1945. http://www.atomicarchive.com/Docs/Franck.html and http://www.dannen.com/decision/index.html (July 15, 1998).

THE SZILARD PETITION, JULY 3, 1945

A PETITION TO THE PRESIDENT OF THE UNITED STATES

Discoveries of which the people of the United States are not aware may affect the welfare of this nation in the near future. The liberation of atomic power which has been achieved places atomic bombs in the hands of the Army. It places in your hands, as Commander-in-Chief, the fateful decision whether or not to sanction the use of such bombs in the present phase of the war against Japan.

We, the undersigned scientists, have been working in the field of atomic power for a number of years. Until recently we have had to reckon with the possibility that the United States might be attacked by atomic bombs during this war and that her only defense might lie in a counterattack by the same means. Today with this danger averted we feel impelled to say what follows:

The war has to be brought speedily to a successful conclusion and the destruction of Japanese cities by means of atomic bombs may very well be an effective method of warfare. We feel, however, that such an attack on Japan could not be justified in the present circumstances. We believe that the United States ought not to resort to the use of atomic bombs in the present phase of the war, at least not unless the terms which will be imposed upon Japan after the war are publicly announced and subsequently Japan is given an opportunity to surrender.

If such public announcement gave assurance to the Japanese that they could look forward to a life devoted to peaceful pursuits in their homeland and if Japan still refused to surrender, our nation would then be faced with a situation which might require a re-examination of her position with respect to the use of atomic bombs in the war.

Atomic bombs are primarily a means for the ruthless annihilation of cities. Once they were introduced as an instrument of war it would be difficult to resist for long the temptation of putting them to such use.

The last few years show a marked tendency toward increasing ruthlessness. At present our Air Forces, striking at the Japanese cities, are using the same methods of warfare which were condemned by American public opinion only a few years ago when applied by the Germans to the cities of England. Our use of atomic bombs in this war would carry the world a long way further on this path of ruthlessness.

Atomic power will provide the nations with new means of destruction. The atomic bombs at our disposal represent only the first step in this direction and there is almost no limit to the destructive power which will become available in the course of this development.

Source: A Petition to the President of the United States (First Version, July 3, 1945). http://www.dannen.com/decision/index.html (July 15, 1998).

HARRY S TRUMAN: DIARY ENTRY, JULY 25, 1945

We have discovered the most terrible bomb in the history of the world. It may be the fire destruction prophesied in the Euphrates Valley Era, after Noah and his fabulous Ark.

Anyway we "think" we have found the way to cause a disintegration of the atom. An experiment in the New Mexico desert was startling—to put it mildly. Thirteen pounds of the explosive caused the complete disintegration of a steel tower 60 feet high, created a crater 6 feet deep and 1,200 feet in diameter, knocked over a steel tower ½ mile away and knocked men down 10,000 yards away. The explosion was visible for more than 200 miles and audible for 40 miles and more.

This weapon is to be used against Japan between now and August 10th. I have told the Sec. of War, Mr. Stimson, to use it so that military objectives and soldiers and sailors are the target and not women and children. Even if the Japs are savages, ruthless, merciless and fanatic, we as the leader of the world for the common welfare cannot drop that terrible bomb on the old capital or the new.

He and I are in accord. The target will be a purely military one and we will issue a warning statement asking the Japs to surrender and save lives. I'm sure they will not do that, but we will have given them the chance. It is certainly a good thing for the world that Hitler's crowd or Stalin's did not discover this atomic bomb. It seems to be the most terrible thing ever discovered, but it can be made the most useful. . . .

Source: http://www.dannen.com/decision/index.html (July 15, 1998).

TRUMAN TELLS THE NATION, AUGUST 9, 1945

The world will note that the first atomic bomb was dropped on Hiroshima, a military base. That was because we wished in this first attack to avoid, insofar as possible, the killing of civilians. But that attack is only a warning of things to come. If Japan does not surrender, bombs will have to be dropped on her war industries and, unfortunately, thousands of civilian lives will be lost. I urge Japanese civilians to leave industrial cities immediately, and save themselves from destruction.

Source: http://www.dannen.com/decision/index.html (July 15, 1998).

A JAPANESE RESPONSE, AUGUST 10, 1945

TOKYO. *The Nippon Times,* August 10, 1945.

In the air attack on Hiroshima Monday morning, the enemy used a new type of bomb of unprecedented power. Not only has the greater part of the city been wiped out, but an extraordinary proportion of the inhabitants have been either killed or injured. The use of a weapon of such terrifying destructiveness not only commands attention as a matter of a new technique in the conduct of war. More fundamentally and vitally it opens up a most grave and profound moral problem in which the very future of humanity is put at stake.

Whether the enemy fully realizes the moral implications of the use of such an instrument of destruction or not, he cannot escape the awful responsibility for his action. For there is no doubt that he has carried out this deed with cold-hearted calculation. This was no mere excess committed in the heat of battle. It was an act of premeditated wholesale murder, the deliberate snuffing out of the lives of tens of thousands of innocent civilians who had no chance of protecting themselves in the slightest degree. How deliberate and callous the enemy is in his unprincipled action is proved by the infamous threat of President Truman to use this diabolic weapon on an increasing scale. . . .

It goes without saying that such action flagrantly contravenes the basic principle of international law as expressed in Article XXII of The Hague Convention in Regard to the Laws of War which definitely proclaims that belligerent nations can have no claim to a right to exercise unlimited power. For, what is it but a presumptuous abuse of unlimited and unprincipled power when the United States resorts to the use of such a weapon as this bomb which spreads indiscriminate and wanton destruction upon an extensive civilian population?

But it is not primarily a matter of legal justifiability or even of the principles of international conduct. It is a matter which goes to the very heart of the fundamental concept of human morality. How can a human being with any claim to a sense of moral responsibility deliberately let loose an instrument of destruction which can at one stroke annihilate an appalling segment of mankind? This is not war; this is not even murder; this is pure nihilism. This is a crime against God and humanity which strikes at the very basis of moral existence. . . .

[The] hypocritical character of the Americans had already been amply demonstrated in the previous bombings of Japanese cities. Strewing explosives and fire bombs indiscriminately over an extensive area, hitting large cities and small towns without distinction, wiping out vast districts which could not be mistaken as being anything but strictly residential in character, burning or blasting to death countless thousands of helpless women and children, and machine-gunning fleeing refugees, the American raiders had already shown how completely they violate in their actual deeds the principles of humanity which they mouth in conspicuous pretense. . . .

The United States may claim, in a lame attempt to raise a pretext in justification of its latest action, that a policy of utter annihilation is necessitated by Japan's failure to heed the recent demand for unconditional surrender. But the question of surrendering or not surrendering certainly can have not the slightest relevance to the question of whether it is justifiable to use a method which under any circumstances is strictly condemned alike by the principles of international law and of morality.

Source: Nippon Times, August 10, 1945.

USING THE BOMB: END OF WORLD WAR II OR BEGINNING OF THE COLD WAR?

Another argument among historians over the decision to use the atomic bomb has been whether American policymakers saw it simply as a weapon to end the Pacific war quickly or whether it was intended as well to cow the Soviet Union into cooperation with American policy after the war. When President Truman met with the Soviet leader Joseph Stalin for the first time at the Potsdam Conference, which took place from July 17 to August 2, 1945, he mentioned with studied casualness a powerful "new weapon." American policymakers were already in conflict with the Russians over the future of Europe and had as well been negotiating with Moscow to enter the Pacific war after the defeat of Germany. If the bomb could induce Japanese surrender quickly enough, the Soviet Union might be kept from advances in Asia and possibly made more tractable in working out a settlement in Europe. But exactly what Truman meant to convey to his Soviet counterpart and what Stalin understood by it has long been a subject of debate.

J. Robert Oppenheimer Testifies on the Bomb, Potsdam, and the Soviet Union, April 1954

Lloyd Garrison: Wasn't there a particular effort to get it [the bomb] done before the Potsdam Conference?

Oppenheimer: Yes, that was of course quite late. After the collapse of Germany, we understood that it was important to get this ready for the war in Japan. We were told that it would be very important—I was told I guess by Mr. Stimson—that it would be very important to know the state of affairs before the meeting at Potsdam at which the future conduct of the war in the Far East would be discussed.

Garrison: Discussed with the Russians?

Oppenheimer: I don't want to overstate that. It was my understanding, and on the morning of July 16, I think Dr. Bush told me, that it was the intention of the United States statesmen who went to Potsdam to say something about this to the Russians, I never knew how much. Mr. Stimson explained later that he had planned to say a good deal more than what was said, but when they saw what the Russians looked like and how it felt, he didn't know whether it was a good idea. The historical record as it is published indicates that the President said no more than we had a new weapon which we planned to use in Japan, and it was very powerful. I believe we were under incredible pressure to get it done before the Potsdam meeting and Groves and I bickered for a couple of days. . . .

Source: http://www.dannen.com/decision/index.html (July 15, 1998).

Did the Soviet Union Know About the Bomb? Three Witnesses at Potsdam

Secretary of State James Byrnes:

I am just as convinced now as I was when I wrote that first book, "Speaking Frankly," in 1947, that Stalin did not appreciate the significance of the [bomb]. I have read stories by so-called historians who assert that he must have known, but they were not present. I was. I watched Stalin's face. He smiled and said only a few words, and Mr. Truman shook hands with him, left, coming back to where I was seated and the two of us went to our automobile.

I recall telling the President at the time, as we were driving back to our headquarters, that, after Stalin left the room and got back to his own headquarters, it would dawn on him, and the following day the President would have a lot of questions to answer. President Truman thought that most probable. He devoted some time in talking to me that evening as to how far he could go—or should go.

Stalin never asked him a question about it. I am satisfied that Stalin did not appreciate the significance of President Truman's statement. I'm pretty certain that they knew we were working on the bomb, but we had kept secret how far that development had gone.

Charles Bohlen, Truman's Interpreter:

Three days after the successful test blast, after consulting his advisers and Churchill (the British had cooperated in the project), Truman decided it would be wise to tell Stalin the news. Explaining that he wanted to be as informal and casual as possible, Truman said during a break in the proceedings that he would stroll over to Stalin and nonchalantly inform him. He instructed me not to accompany him, as I ordinarily did, because he did not want to indicate that there was anything particularly momentous about the development. So it was Pavlov, the Russian interpreter, who translated Truman's words to Stalin. I did not hear the conversation, although Truman and Byrnes both reported that I was there.

In his memoirs, Truman wrote that he told Stalin that the United States had "a new weapon of unusual destructive force." Apparently, the President did not tell Stalin the new weapon was an atomic bomb, and the Soviet leader did not ask or show any special interest. He merely nodded and said something. "All he said was that he was glad to hear it and hoped we would make good use of it against the Japanese," Truman wrote. Across the room, I watched Stalin's face carefully as the President broke the news. So offhand was Stalin's response that there was some question in my mind whether the President's message had got through. I should have known better than to underrate the dictator. Years later, Marshal Georgi K. Zhukov, in his memoirs, disclosed that that night Stalin ordered a telegram sent to those working on the atomic bomb in Russia to hurry with the job.

Georgii Zhukov, Soviet Marshal:

I do not recall the exact date, but after the close of one of the formal meetings Truman informed Stalin that the United States now possessed a bomb of exceptional power, without, however, naming it the atomic bomb.

As was later written abroad, at that moment Churchill fixed his gaze on Stalin's face, closely observing his reaction. However, Stalin did not betray his feelings and pretended that he saw nothing special in what Truman had imparted to him. Both Churchill and many other Anglo-American authors subsequently assumed that Stalin had really failed to fathom the significance of what he had heard.

In actual fact, on returning to his quarters after this meeting Stalin, in my presence, told Molotov about his conversation with Truman. The latter reacted almost immediately. "Let them. We'll have to talk it over with Kurchatov and get him to speed things up."

I realized that they were talking about research on the atomic bomb.

It was clear already then that the US Government intended to use the atomic weapon for the purpose of achieving its Imperialist goals from a position of strength in "the cold war." This was amply corroborated on August 6 and 8. Without any military need whatsoever, the Americans dropped to atomic bombs on the peaceful and densely-populated Japanese cities of Hiroshima and Nagasaki.

Source: http://www.dannen.com/decision/index.html (July 15, 1998).

Chapter 11

MOVING IN:
THE FLIGHT TO
THE SUBURBS

"Suburbanization," writes Kenneth T. Jackson in his study *The Crabgrass Frontier*, "has been as much a governmental as a natural process." While Americans have long preferred detached houses with space around them to city apartments, the mass movement to the suburbs after World War II depended heavily on government policy. Governments on all levels built the roads that put inexpensive land within reach of commuters. A set of federal programs made possible the financing of houses for millions of demobilized veterans after the war. The Federal Housing Administration (FHA) and the Veterans Administration (VA) subsidized home buyers and the banks that served them by guaranteeing the repayment of mortgages in the event of default. Purchasers could secure an FHA mortgage with only a five percent down payment, while with scarcely any initial investment veterans under GI loan programs could buy houses. The income tax deduction on mortgage payments made most suburban housing cheaper than city apartments. And a series of complex transactions under which government might front virtually all the money for builders to put up houses enabled developers like Levitt & Sons to operate on a scale never before possible in the housing industry. Even the technological expertise to streamline the construction process for which Levitt became famous had been acquired at government expense when during World War II the firm produced military barracks under advantageous federal contracts.

The long rows of almost identical houses these builders created were more than shelters; they became a new way of life centered on the increasing number of children that Americans had in the baby-boom era between the end of the war and the late 1950s. Scout troops multiplied, and Little League sport teams engaged children; local politics preoccupied many adults; church membership increased sharply; PTAs brought parents into school activities; groups devoted to specific hobbies increased; leisure activities such as bowling and camping became popular. Soon enough, strip zoning created massive corridors of storefronts, drive-in eateries, and used-car lots. Then came the malls. Critics complained of the suburbs' intellectual sterility, their conformity, their materialism. Yet millions of workers escaped city tenements, education improved, and entertainment appeared in unparalleled varieties. The old problems of depression and war seemed far away.

GOVERNMENT POLICIES ENCOURAGE MOVING TO THE SUBURBS

Paul H. Douglas, a retired Democratic Illinois senator, headed a National Commission on Urban Problems appointed by President Lyndon Johnson early in 1967. Federal housing policy was one subject examined in its extensive hearings. While the commission criticized the effect of FHA policies on inner cities and noted that the "white middle class" derived its principal benefits, the report's assessment of the role of federal programs on the growth of suburbs is otherwise favorable. Here is the report's summary of the FHA's role; its assessment of Veterans Administration programs elsewhere in the report is similar.

REPORT OF THE NATIONAL COMMISSION ON URBAN PROBLEMS, DECEMBER 12, 1968

A GENERAL APPRAISAL OF FHA

Within its limits, FHA has performed well. By insuring a large portion of the appraised value, it greatly diminished the amount of down payment required. Recourse to costly second mortgages in this field was reduced. It made first mortgages more attractive and increased the amount of capital invested in them.

As the proportion of the appraised value which is insured has risen to well over 90 percent, the amount of the down payment has, of course, been correspondingly reduced. With risks reduced and payments lower, millions of young families have enjoyed homeownership at a much earlier age, and have been able to bring their children up in what we like to think of as the conventional American manner.

An increasing proportion of home purchase money was being financed on credit. Financial institutions in effect were possessing a larger share of the value of the house. Homeownership was expanded by letting the "owner" become more of a renter.

FHA has also been a vital factor in financing and promoting the exodus from the central cities and in helping to build up the suburbs. That is where the vast majority of FHA-insured homes have been built. The suburbs could not have expanded as they have during the postwar years without FHA. Superhighways constructed at Government expense have also opened up the areas outside the cities and supported the exodus of a large proportion of the white middle class.

By prescribing minimum standards of construction, including toilet and hot water facilities, and by discouraging the use of shoddy building materials, FHA has lessened the possibility that the new suburbs would soon turn into slums. At the same time, while it did not enthusiastically embrace new methods of construction and materials, it has been more receptive to them than have most of the building code writers and officials of the central cities. For example, FHA permitted Romex and plastic pipe when these new products were effectively forbidden by most codes. FHA actions in this respect have been beneficial.

Taking all factors into consideration, it is difficult to see how any institution could have served the emerging middle class more effectively than has the FHA and its counterpart, the Federal home loan bank systems. Most important, FHA helped to end the practice of letting the big final payment of principal come due at the end of the mortgage term, supplanting this with amortization of this amount over the life of the mortgage. It has brought consumer protection into the entire mortgage field, with conventional lenders following FHA's lead. For example, interest is only computed on the amounts actually owed. Many investors and lenders have been influenced by FHA to moderate their terms as regards interest, down payments and length of mortgages. All of these steps have brought in more purchasers among the lower and middle sections of the middle class.

Source: Building the American City: Report of the National Commission on Urban Problems to the Congress and to the President of the United States, Paul H. Douglas, Chairman (Washington: Government Printing Office, 1969), 99–100.

VETERANS AND THEIR FAMILIES
MOVE TO THE SUBURBS

The hero—or villain—of the postwar growth of the suburbs was William J. Levitt, whose firm, Levitt & Sons, eventually built 140,000 houses. Applying mass production methods to reduce costs, the company understandably achieved a mass production look. An article in Coronet *magazine stresses Levitt's success at alleviating the extreme housing shortage resulting from a decade and a half of depression and war.*

LEVITT LICKS THE HOUSING SHORTAGE

Undaunted by high costs and other barriers, a resourceful young builder is putting up thousands of homes for vets.

Less than an hour's commuting distance from the heart of bustling Manhattan, a young Long Island builder, late of the U.S. Navy's Seabees, is showing how to go about solving America's critical housing shortage.

Builders around the nation scream about barriers that stand in the way of putting up homes for veterans at a reasonable price. Local code restrictions, union featherbedding and exorbitant material prices, they say, make home construction a next-to-impossible task.

Forty-one-year-old Bill Levitt of Manhasset, Long Island, has found ways to climb over these barriers. Today, he is "the nation's biggest home builder."

Most contractors think of home construction in groups of four or five dwellings. Levitt thinks in terms of thousands. "At peak operating speed," he says, "I can complete one house every 20 minutes."

These are one-family dwellings priced to sell at $7,990. But veterans don't have to buy them. If they prefer, they can rent one of the four-room houses for $65 a month. Already 3,900 of the homes have been built; another 2,100 will be completed before the end of this year.

Levitt likes to talk about the community which he has unblushingly named Levittown: "Two years ago, it was rolling farm-land in the heart of the potato country. Before Christmas, it will be a community of 25,000 people—complete with free swimming pools and ultramodern shopping centers."

How good are the houses? "I challenge any builder in the New York area to duplicate them for less than $9,500," says Levitt.

How does he do it? The story begins on a spring morning in 1947, when 1,200 veterans jammed the town hall at Hempstead, Long Island. They were in a grim mood. The community had banned basementless houses—and this ban stood between the men and the chance for shelter at a price they could pay. Shouting down the opposition of local property owners, the vets steam-rollered the town fathers into lifting the ban.

Reminiscing about the meeting in his oak-paneled office at Levitt & Sons, Bill Levitt says: "You don't think that protest meeting evolved out of thin air, do you? We told the boys that if they really wanted homes they would have to get out and fight. We spread the news by ads and word-of-mouth among veterans' groups. The boys did the rest at Town Hall."

Building homes without basements helps Levitt save about $1,000 per dwelling. And he insists that the three-inch concrete base which he installs under homes provides as much insulation from cold and dampness as any cellar.

During the most critical phase of the lumber shortage in 1947, Levitt, like other builders, was faced with the problem of paying gray-market prices if he wanted to keep going. But to do this, he would have had to increase the price of his homes. Characteristically, he found an unorthodox Levitt solution. Buying a 40 per cent interest in a Seattle lumber mill, he got 40 per cent of the output—at regular prices.

Costly? "Not at all," says Levitt, swinging in great arcs in his swivel chair and tapping cigarette ashes over the Oriental rug in his plushy office. "Including the money I paid for the interest in the mill, the lumber still cost me less than I would have had to pay in the gray market. A lot of other builders could have done the same thing."

Builders complain that union featherbedding runs up costs and that unions tend to prohibit such cost savers as paint spray guns. Many lathers, who used to nail 55 bundles a day, now knock off after finishing 35. Bricklayers lay only half the number of bricks they did before the war, builders assert.

Levitt is one builder who has no trouble with union regulations. His 3,000 construction employees belong to no union. How does he get away with it?

"For one thing," he says, "we pay our men the regular union scale or more. How much a worker gets depends on how hard he works under our incentive system. But the average mechanic makes about $90 a week. And we offer him what few other builders can—steady, year-round employment." . . .

"Everybody was talking about housing for the vets," he relates. "We decided to do something about it. But don't misunderstand me. We're not philanthropists. We're in business to make a profit, like everyone else—and we're doing it."

The first postwar houses were priced at $10,000. Some 1,000 of these attractive two-story, six-room dwellings were put up for veterans, sited on landscaped plots along winding roads.

Veterans stampeded to buy the houses but, recalls Levitt: "There were many who turned away feeling glum. They just couldn't afford the $80 monthly payments required to carry the houses."

So was born Levittown—a new community of basementless houses. Within a few months after announcing plans, the Levitt firm was swamped with 50,000 applications from veterans. Thus, the more than 6,000 homes which will be completed by the end of this year will only dent the potential demand.

The basementless houses have radiant heating, four good-sized rooms and space for two additional rooms and a bath in the attic. They sit on 60-by-100-foot plots, completely landscaped.

Like all Levitt dwellings, they come equipped with refrigerator, washing machine, electric range and Venetian blinds. With understandable pride, Levitt declares: "I'm a kind of General Motors of the building industry.". . .

On the building site, Levitt's operation resembles industry's assembly line. But there is one essential difference: the product doesn't move. Instead, the men move from job to job. At the site, trucks drop the complete "package" for each house—not a nail more or less. Assembly crews move from site to site and erect the houses from the "packages."

Watching the hundreds of his field staff in operation is like trying to follow a dozen three-ring circuses. As many as 600 houses are under construction at one time. Here a crew is running up walls; another group is installing staircases; still another is putting in window casements.

Normal building procedure consists of 26 operations. Under the Levitt method, these are broken down still further—to 100. A carpenter, for example, doesn't hammer staircases into place and then move to hanging doors. He does just the one job; another carpenter does the other.

Bricklayers are assigned to finishing the identical section of masonry in each house. Plumbers are delegated to fit the same connections in house after house.

A couple of men do nothing but caulk windows. But there are enough dwellings under construction to keep both hopping all day. Everything is done on a split-second basis. Completion of the houses follows a timetable. . . .

Source: Joseph M. Guilfoyle and J. Howard Rutledge, "Levitt Licks the Housing Shortage," *Coronet*, September 1948: 112–115.

John Keats, in a widely read critique of the emerging suburban life, takes a different view from that of Levitt.

No One's Dream House

Let's step back in time to consider the history of today's housing developments:

The first good intentions which pave our modern Via Dolorosa [Road of Sorrows] were laid at war's end. Conscious of the fact that some 13,000,000 young men risked disfigurement, dismemberment and death in circumstances not of their choosing, a grateful nation decided to show its appreciation to the survivors. The GI Bill of Rights was enacted, and one of the articles provided an incentive for bankers to assume low-interest mortgages on houses purchased by veterans. The deal was, the bankers could recover a certain guaranteed sum from the government in event of the veteran's default. The real-estate boys read the Bill, looked at one another in happy amazement, and the dry, rasping noise they made rubbing their hands together could have been heard as far away as Tawi Tawi. Immediately, thanks to modern advertising, movable type, radio, television and other marvels, the absurdity was spread—and is still spread—that the veteran should own his home.

There was never the slightest justification for this nonsense. Never in the last 180 years of United States history was there an indication that a young man entering civil life from childhood or war should thereupon buy a house.

It is and has always been the nature of young people to be mobile. Rare indeed is the man whose life is a straight arrow's flight from the classroom to the job he'll hold until he dies. Many a retiring corporate officer put in his early years driving a bread truck, then had a fling at a little unsuccessful business of his own, then wandered into the door-to-door sale of cemetery lots before catching on at the buttonworks he was one day to direct. Owning property implies a certain permanence—precisely that quality a bright young man should, and does, lack. A young man should be mobile until he finds his proper path. A man with a house is nailed to its floor.

The housing article in the GI Bill, however, opened vast vistas. Not only was there a government guarantee to be had, but there was also land to be sold, and since the veteran had been led both by private and government propaganda to believe he should own his home, the remaining consideration in the hard, practical minds of the real-estate men was how much house could be offered for how little money. Or, to put it in the more usual way, how little house could be offered for how much money. Cost became the sole criterion of the first postwar house, and the first economy was in space.

The typical postwar development operator was a man who figured how many houses he could possibly cram onto a piece of land and have the local zoning board hold still for it. Then he whistled up the bulldozers to knock down all the trees, bat the lumps off the terrain, and level the ensuing desolation. Then up went the houses, one after another, all alike, and none of those built immediately after the war had any more floor space than a moderately priced, two-bedroom apartment. The dining room, the porch, the basement, and in many cases the attic, were dispensed with and disappeared from the American scene. The result was a little box on a cold concrete slab containing two bedrooms, bath, and an eating space the size of a broom closet tucked between the living room and the tiny kitchen. A nine-by-twelve rug spread across the largest room wall to wall, and there was a sheet of plate glass in the living-room wall. That, the builder said, was the picture window. The picture it framed was of the box across the treeless street. The young Americans who moved into these cubicles were not, and are not, to know the gracious dignity of living that their parents knew in the big two- and three-story family houses set well back on grassy lawns off the shady streets of, say, Watertown, New York. For them and their children, there would be only the box on its slab. The Cape Code Rambler had arrived.

It was inevitable that the development house was looked upon as an expedient by the young purchasers. It was most certainly not the house of their dreams, nor was the ready-made neighborhood a thing to make the soul sing. It was, simply, the only thing available. They had no choice—they couldn't afford to build their house, nor were they given a choice of architecture. Instead, they were offered a choice between a house they didn't much want and the fantastic rents that bobbed to the surface as soon as the real-estate lobby torpedoed rent control. The development house was the only living space on the market priced just within the means of the young veterans.

Source: John Keats, *The Crack in the Picture Window* (Boston: Houghton Mifflin Co., 1956), xiii–xv.

This excerpt from the Levittown homeowners' guide suggests what a novel experience suburban life was for many of the ex–city dwellers moving twenty-five miles east on Long Island to the first Levittown.

TEACHING CITY FOLK TO BE SUBURBANITES

WELCOME TO LEVITTOWN!

You have just purchased what we believe to be the finest house of its size in America. We wish you health and happiness in Levittown for many years to come.

In order that you may enjoy your house, and derive the utmost pleasure from it, we have undertaken to prepare this handbook so that you may better understand our position and your responsibilities. . . .

ELECTRICAL

Now let us start at the front door and walk through your new home. The two electrical switches as you enter control the foyer light and the light over the front door in the Country Clubber. In the Jubilee the two switches control the outside light and a receptacle on the front wall of the living room. In your kitchen you will find the oil burner emergency switch, clearly identified by a red plate.

Your circuit breaker is located in the #2 bedroom closet of the Jubilee, and in the garage of the Country Clubber. No fuses are required. Upon any lighting failure check your circuit breaker first. Simply reset the switch by returning it to its normal position. Repeated tripping of the breaker indicates a short circuit.

You will find ample receptacles conveniently located throughout the house. In rooms not provided with a lighting fixture the wall switch controls the nearest receptacle. Do not use any greater than 60 watt bulbs or 75 watt spot type bulbs in your ceiling recessed fixtures. You must supply a 40 watt 48 inch "rapid" starting fluorescent bulb for the bathroom of the Jubilee. In the Country Clubber you must supply four standard light bulbs for each bathroom. You will find that 40 watt bulbs will supply ample illumination.

Your dining room light fixture was designed for a standard 100 watt bulb.

CONDENSATION

Condensation is the formation of water, usually on a very smooth surface. It takes place when warm, moist air comes in contact with a cold surface. Your new home has been tightly constructed and well insulated. Moisture created by your living activities in the house and the operation of your modern home appliances can therefore only be expelled by adequate ventilation. The normal living habits of a family of four people, using shower, washing dishes, cooking, and the use of automatic appliances, create 18 gallons of moisture each week. Be sure to air out your home for at least a few minutes each day. The use of your exhaust fan and adequate window ventilation are the simple, practical steps that can be taken by you to allow moisture to escape. . . .

THE LAWN AND ITS UPKEEP

No single feature of a suburban residential community contributes so much to the charm and beauty of the individual home and locality as well-kept lawns. Stabilization of values, yes, increase in values, will most often be found in those neighborhoods where lawns show as green carpets, and trees and shrubbery join to impart the sense of residential elegance. Where lawns and landscape material are neglected the neighborhood soon assumes a sub-standard or blighted appearance and is naturally shunned by the public. Your investment in your garden is large at the beginning, but will grow larger and larger as the years go by. For while furniture, houses and most material things tend to depreciate with the years, your lawn, trees and shrubs become more valuable both esthetically and monetarily.

We grade your premises, fertilize the soil, then seed and roll the lawn. After that we turn the newly made lawn over to you for your care. The first thing to do is to water for many hours a day. The grass seed will not germinate otherwise; most of the seed will dry up. There is one way and only one way to water a lawn. Use an *OVERHEAD SPRINKLER* on one spot for a short time then shift the sprinkler to another spot. If you use it too long on any one place on a lawn, it will create puddles and will wash out the seed. *DON'T USE THE HOSE WITH NOZZLE ATTACHED; THE SEED WILL BE WASHED AWAY.* Don't step on a soft lawn especially with high heeled shoes; use a board or several of them. Try to keep children from running over the new soil, though we admit that is no easy task.

THE CARE OF TREES, SHRUBS AND EVERGREENS

Now the first thing to do to newly transplanted material is to water it. We have given this advice again and again and to see the neglect of many owners in this respect is extremely disheartening. Many who attempt to water do more harm than good. There is but one way to water a newly transplanted tree, shrub or evergreen. Place the hose *(WITHOUT NOZZLE)* at the root of the plant and give it a good soaking. For a large tree proceed from several positions. The hole or holes made by rushing water should be plugged up when through watering.

IMPORTANT

Never use a hose to water your lawn. Always use an overhead sprinkler. You cannot grow a lawn if you water it with a hose, especially with a nozzle attached. Don't even keep a nozzle on your premises; it will only do harm!

Source: "Homeowners' Guide: Some Information for Residents of Levittown to Help Them Enjoy Their New Homes," 1, 2–3, 4, 12–13, 16, 20.

SEGREGATED HOUSING AS NATIONAL POLICY

Federal housing policy was tightly, if not quite deliberately, structured to create segregated housing. The FHA absorbed and then nationalized the standards of real estate professionals who assumed that mixed neighborhoods would always decline in value. In the interest of fiscal soundness, the FHA encouraged restrictive covenants, channeled loans away from most urban areas, denied credit even to solidly middle-class nonwhites if they sought housing in white neighborhoods, and refused mortgages in mixed neighborhoods, called "red-lining" for the color ink used on maps to indicate such areas. Until the 1960s all those Levitt houses were mortgaged only to whites. Laws creating public housing achieved the same purposes. Local groups could usually veto public housing in their neighborhoods, so only areas that already had large minority populations would accept public housing. Because land in these almost exclusively inner-city sites was expensive, high rises became common—while in Great Britain most public housing construction was of single family homes.

Supporters of more liberal housing policies, like Democratic Senator Paul H. Douglas of Illinois, acquiesced in such discrimination as the cost of getting through congressional committees controlled by southerners the legislation that would provide badly needed housing. In the 1960s all these policies came under criticism and were modified, but the direction of American housing policy, the demographics of cities and suburbs, and the assumptions of tens of millions of Americans had been set in a dangerous channel.

The impact of FHA loan guarantee policies are assessed adversely as early as 1955 by Charles Abrams, a housing expert of the era, and the difficulty of securing FHA mortgages in urban areas is illustrated by a story from Paterson, New Jersey.

FORBIDDEN NEIGHBORS

The Federal Housing Administration
The Federal Housing Administration, created under the National Housing Act of 1934, was launched in an effort to encourage home-building and mortgage-lending during the depression. Lending institutions which make loans to builders and homeowners are now unconditionally insured by the government, while builders who obtain these insured mortgages are able to borrow far more than their costs on the strength of the federal guarantee. The homeowner or borrower pays a small premium to the government for insurance given not to him but to the mortgagee.

A government offering such bounty to builders and lenders could have required compliance with a nondiscrimination policy. Or the agency could at least have pursued a course of evasion, or hidden behind the screen of local autonomy. Instead, FHA adopted a racial policy that could well have been culled from the Nuremberg laws. From its inception FHA set itself up as the protector of the all-white neighborhood. It sent its agents into the field to keep Negroes and other minorities from buying homes in white neighborhoods. It exerted pressure against builders who dared to build for minorities, and against lenders willing to lend on mortgages. This official agency not only kept Negroes in their place but pointed at Chinese, Mexicans, American Indians, and other minorities as well. It not only insisted on social and racial "homogeneity" in all of its projects as the price of insurance but became the vanguard of white supremacy and racial purity—in the North as well as the South. Racism was bluntly written into FHA's official manual: "If a neighborhood is to retain stability, it is necessary that properties shall continue to be occupied by the same social and racial classes." [*Underwriting Manual*. Washington, Federal Housing Administration, 1938, §937.]

One of FHA's responsibilities was recorded as the "prevention of infiltration." The agency warned against "adverse influences" which included "unharmonious racial groups." It even exhorted the use of a model covenant, providing that "no persons of any race other than____[race to be inserted] shall use or occupy any building or any lot, except that this covenant shall not prevent occupancy by domestic servants of a different race domiciled with an owner or tenant."

The 1935 manual listed the important influences which the government considered "adverse." Among the most important was "infiltration of inharmonious racial or nationality groups" (§310). "Rapid transition to use by a lower class of inhabitants, is to be considered positive instability" (§307). The appeal of a residential neighborhood results from "the kind and social status of the inhabitants" (§315).

FHA then described methods to enforce "homogeneity" and exclusion of the "undesirable." It said:

> . . . when fullest advantage has been taken of available means to protect the area against adverse influence and to insure that it will develop into a homogeneous residential district, possessing strong appeal to the class of persons expected to desire accommodations in it, a high neighborhood rating will be warranted (§330).

The 1936 manual perfected and expanded the racial and social doctrine of 1935. The "valuator must determine whether or not the coming generation will regard locations in such neighborhoods as desirable." It warned that "the mixed neighborhood" in competition with the "homogeneous" neighborhood will suffer, and that "the chances are that within a comparatively short period of time a lower grade of social occupancy will exist" (§210d).

FHA included "racial occupancy" among the adverse influences (§228), and affirmed that "usually the protection against adverse influences afforded by these means includes prevention of lower class occupancy, and inharmonious racial groups" (§229).

> The Valuator should investigate areas surrounding the location to determine whether or not incompatible racial and social groups are present, to the end that an intelligent prediction may be made regarding the possibility or probability of the location being invaded by such groups. . . . A change in social or racial occupancy generally leads to in-

stability and a reduction in values. The protection offered against adverse changes should be found adequate before a high rating is given to the future (1936, §233; 1938, §937).

Of prime consideration to the Valuator is the presence or lack of homogeneity regarding . . . classes of people living in the neighborhood (1936, §252).

. . . FHA advocated not only deed restrictions but zoning to bar the wrong kind of people, and it classed the nuisances to be guarded against—"stables, pig pens," etc. In the same category was occupancy by the wrong kind of race (1936, §284 (3)f). . . .

Success and acceptance in the business world was no reason for letting a minority person enter the neighborhood, FHA said. The "type of people with whom the borrower associates socially, rather than those with whom he is associated in business activities" is the important thing, and it then concluded: "The highest rating could hardly be ascribed in cases where the borrower's chosen associates are other than substantial, law-abiding, sober-acting, sane-thinking people of acceptable ethical standards" (1938, §1014). The presumption, of course, is evident that all candidates eligible for an FHA subdivision would automatically qualify for the heavenly kingdom as well.

The revised 1940 manual made few changes. FHA was still asking, "Is the neighborhood homogeneous in population?" Nonhomogeneity was described as a "mixture of groups which tend to be socially antipathetic," including "inharmonious social groups" and races (1940, §207, 217). The wrong kind of people meant obsolescence. Important among adverse influences were infiltration of "smoke, odors, fog" and "inharmonious racial or nationality groups."

These were no slips of the pen nor the irresponsible utterances of a senseless clerk. They were part and parcel of FHA policy from its inception to 1948. After continued protests by the National Association for the Advancement of Colored People and other groups, FHA revised its underwriting manual. But it was not yet ready to yield on the issue. The changes simply made the language vague enough to take the heat off while still affirming the anti-racial policy. FHA continued to deny housing insurance to Negroes except in Negro neighborhoods and commitments in such areas were rare. It continued to insure properties subject to racial covenants and often insisted on the use of covenants. . . .

Even as late as November, 1948, months after modification of its written policy and after the Supreme Court had held racial covenants unenforceable, FHA was still the stronghold of officialized intolerance. Assistant Commissioner W. J. Lockwood, commenting on the York Center Community Cooperative, a proposed interracial housing project in Illinois, defined revised FHA policy:

> If it is therefore apparent, with respect to the particular neighborhood or property under analysis, that infiltration will be unacceptable to the local real estate market and desirability of properties will be reduced

in the market's mind, then this Administration has no alternative but to so recognize the conditions in its valuation of specific properties within that sphere of influence.

The commissioner's statement of policy on housing projects restricted against Negroes is plain:

> I find nothing in such [restrictive covenant] decisions to indicate that in the absence of statutory authority the government, or any agency thereof, is authorized to withdraw its normal protection and benefits from persons who have executed but do not seek judicial enforcement of such covenants.

On November 19, 1948, Lockwood said FHA "has never had a housing project of mixed occupancy," and ventured "the unofficial and informal statement that we believe that such projects would probably in a short period of time become all Negro. . . ." Referring to racial infiltration, Lockwood said FHA must have due regard "for the influence of such conditions not only upon a certain parcel of realty but also considers the reflection of those conditions upon properties owned by other citizens.". . .

When protests continued, FHA finally modified its manual to exclude references to inharmonious racial groups. The 1949 edition omitted references to mortgages in areas threatened by minority infiltrations. On December 2, 1949, FHA agreed not to insure mortgages on properties subject to racial restrictive covenants filed after February 15, 1950. The fight to bring FHA within the Constitution was beginning to show results.

But the damage had been done. It was more serious than most realize. It was the first time in our national history that a federal agency had openly exhorted segregation. Before FHA, a home-buyer's prejudices were personalized, his decisions were of his own making. Although private covenants were being enforced by the judicial arm, they were unsanctioned by public policy at the executive and administrative levels and the courts too would strike down the attempt of a village, community, or city to officialize bias. Even segregation in the southern states had its condition of presumed equality and federal morality remained above any such qualification.

FHA's declarations had gathered together all the humbug of half-informed pseudo-experts—realtor-sociologists, appraiser-psychologists, behaviorist-lobbyists—and codified them into official dogma. It made the forbidden fruit of bias the required fare of the market. . . .

FHA succeeded in modifying legal practice so that the common form of deed included the racial covenant. Builders everywhere became the conduits of bigotry. . . .

The evil that FHA did was of a peculiarly enduring character. Thousands of racially segregated neighborhoods were built, millions of people re-assorted on the basis of race, color, or class, the differences built in, in neighborhoods from coast to coast. . . .

Finally, FHA policy succeeded in depriving minorities of the housing they desperately needed. FHA developments would not have them. Land sold to Negroes or Mexican-Americans meant, under FHA's policy, that adjoining land would be classed as undesirable. . . .

The result was accentuation of housing shortages for the people who needed housing most, concentration of minorities into older deteriorated sections, pressure upon newer areas by minorities seeking space, chaotic competition for dwellings between majority and minority, and deepening of tensions between classes—one of the most sensitive aspects of American neighborhoods today.

Source: Charles Abrams, *Forbidden Neighbors: A Study of Prejudice in Housing* (New York: Harper and Bros., 1955), 229–237. Reprinted by permission.

In downtown Paterson, New Jersey, FHA mortgages were hard to get.

JULIUS THREET'S VISION

In Paterson there is a man named Julius Threet, a successful real-estate agent and local developer. Mr. Threet is a man of vision. "Look at this," he says, pointing out the expanse of Paterson. "A city like this, built on hills and with the river running through. It should be beautiful." Mr. Threet also has a slogan: "Pride Through Ownership." Having both a vision and a slogan has made him more determined than other men. He decided to renovate some of Paterson's worst tenements, turning them into nonprofit cooperative apartments. In 1968 he obtained a Federal Housing Administration mortgage for this purpose. On paper it looked like any one of the some eleven million mortgages, all but a handful of them for suburban homes, that the F.H.A. has guaranteed since it was established in 1934. It was, in fact, an extraordinary mortgage. As far as Threet has been able to determine, it marked the first time that the F.H.A. had guaranteed a private mortgage in any ghetto area of New Jersey. This means that for the four decades since the F.H.A. came into existence and started setting national mortgage policies, the federal government has, in effect, forbidden individual, private ownership of homes in the inner cities and left them with little choice for housing other than public housing, housing owned by slumlords, and the type of people who can procure loan-shark financing outside legal commercial channels. It had, moreover, taken Threet three years of cutting through the F.H.A.'s red tape to obtain the mortgage.

Source: Christopher Norwood, *About Paterson: The Making and Unmaking of an American City* (New York: Saturday Review Press/ E. P. Dutton & Co., 1974), 124.

Chapter 12

"I QUESTION AMERICA": FANNIE LOU HAMER OF RULEVILLE, MISSISSIPPI

In the 1950s and 1960s as the civil rights movement confronted its fiercest opposition and achieved its greatest victories, Ella Baker, Rosa Parks, Jo Ann Robinson, Gloria Richardson, Septima Clark, Daisy Bates, Ruby Doris Smith, Annell Ponder, Fannie Fullerwood, Victoria Gray, Prathia Hall, Pauli Murray, Ann Moody, Diane Bevel Nash, and innumerable other women organized, spoke, wrote, demonstrated, fought, and suffered. How they or any other of the movement activists in the South found their public voice and the courage to risk so much is a question that haunts anyone who studies this era. Fannie Lou Hamer, twentieth child of a Mississippi sharecropping family, ranks among the greatest and the bravest of these women. Her story is inextricably linked to that of the civil rights movement in Mississippi, the state where opposition was most brutal and movement tactics most creative.

GROWING UP BLACK IN MISSISSIPPI

The Mississippi Delta, the bottomland created by the Mississippi River, has been described as "the most Southern place on earth," a land of rich soil and poor people, most of them African-American. Born in Ruleville in the heart of the Delta, Mrs. Hamer had a remarkable life story to tell, and she never stopped telling it.

TO PRAISE OUR BRIDGES

I was born October sixth, nineteen and seventeen in Montgomery County, Mississippi. My parents moved to Sunflower County when I was two years old, to a plantation about four and a half miles from here, Mr. E. W. Brandon's plantation. I've been here now almost 47 years in Sunflower County. My parents were sharecroppers and they had a big family. Twenty children. Fourteen boys and six girls. I'm the twentieth child. All of us worked in the fields, of course, but we never did get anything out of sharecropping. We'd make fifty and sixty bales and end up with nothing.

I was about six years old when I first went to the fields to pick cotton. I can remember very well the landowner telling me one day that if I would pick thirty pounds he would give me something out of the commissary: some Cracker-Jacks, Daddy Wide-Legs, and some sardines. These were things that he knew I loved and never had a chance to have. So I picked thirty pounds that day. Well, the next week I had to pick sixty and by the time I was thirteen I was picking two and three hundred pounds.

We'd make fifty and sixty bales and wouldn't clear enough money to live on in the winter months. My father kept sharecropping until one year on this plantation he cleared some money. It must have been quite a little bit because he bought some wagons and cultivators, plow tools and mules in the hope that he could rent the next year. We were doing pretty well. He even started to fix up the house real nice and had bought a car.

Then one night this white man went to our lot and went to the trough where the mules had to eat and stirred up a gallon of Paris Green into the mules' food. It killed everything we had. When we got there, one mule was already dead. The other two mules and the cow had their stomachs all swelled up. It was too late to save them. That poisoning knocked us right back down flat. We never did get back up again. That white man did it just because we were getting somewhere. White people never like to see Negroes get a little success. All of this stuff is no secret in the state of Mississippi. . . .

Well, after the white man killed off our mules, my parents never did get a chance to get up again. We went back to sharecropping, halving, it's called. You split the cotton half and half with the plantation owner. But the seed, fertilizer, cost of hired hands, everything is paid out of the cropper's half. My parents tried so hard to do what they could to keep us in school, but school didn't last but four months out of the year and most of the time we didn't have clothes to wear. I dropped out of school and cut corn stalks to help the family.

My parents were getting up in age and weren't young when I was born. I used to watch my mother try and keep her family going after we didn't get enough money out of the cotton crop. To feed us during the winter months mama would go 'round from plantation to plantation and would ask the landowners if she could have the cotton that had been left, which was called scrappin' cotton. When they would tell her that we could have that cotton, we would walk for miles and miles and miles in the run of a week. We wouldn't have on shoes or anything because we didn't have them. She would always tie our feet up with rags because the ground would be froze real hard. We would walk from field to field until we had scrapped a bale of cotton. Then she'd take that bale of cotton and sell it and that would give us some of the food that we would need.

Then she would go from house to house and she would help kill hogs. They would give her the intestines and sometimes the feet and the head and things like that and that would help to keep us going. So many times for dinner we would have greens with no seasoning and flour gravy. My mother would mix flour with a little grease and try to make gravy out of it. Sometimes there'd be nothing but bread and onions.

My mother was a great woman. She went through a lot of suffering to bring the twenty of us up, but still she taught us to be decent and to respect ourselves, and that is one of the things that has kept me going.

In 1930 when she was out working, cleaning up the new ground (or we used to call it deadening) for a quarter, when something flew up and hit her in the eye. When she died she was totally blind because we weren't able to carry her to a good eye specialist. She was about 90 years old when she died with me in 1961.

My life has been almost like my mother's was, because I married a man who sharecropped. We didn't have it easy and the only way we could ever make it through the winter was because Pap had a little juke joint and we made liquor. That was the only way we made it. I married in 1944 and stayed on the plantation until 1962 when I went down to the courthouse in Indianola to register to vote. That happened because I went to a mass meeting one night.

Until then I'd never heard of no mass meeting and I didn't know that a Negro could register and vote. Bob Moses, Reggie Robinson, Jim Bevel and James Forman were some of the SNCC workers who ran that meeting. When they asked for those to raise their hands who'd go down to the courthouse the next day, I raised mine. Had it up high as I could get it. I guess if I'd had any sense I'd a-been a little scared, but what was the point of being scared. The only thing they could do to me was kill me and it seemed like they'd been trying to do that a little bit at a time ever since I could remember.

But I've found out some things since I've been trying to organize in Sunflower County. People ask me, "Mrs. Hamer, why haven't they tried to dynamite your house or tried to shoot you?" I'll tell you why. I keep a shotgun in every corner of my bedroom and the first cracker even look like he wants to throw some dynamite on my porch won't write his mama again. One night somebody come calling up, "We're coming by tonight." I told him, "Come on. I'll be waiting for you." Guess you know that cracker ain't showed up yet. White folks may act like they's crazy, but they ain't that crazy. Ain't no man going to bother you if he know you going to kill him.

Source: Fannie Lou Hamer, "To Praise Our Bridges," in Dorothy Abbott, ed., *Mississippi Writers: Reflections of Childhood and Youth,* Volume II: *Nonfiction* (Jackson: University Press of Mississippi, 1986), 321–325.

JOINING THE MOVEMENT

On August 22, 1964, Mrs. Hamer told her story to the Credentials Committee at the Democratic National Convention. This particular recounting of her history dominated the news for four days and deeply influenced American history.

FANNIE LOU HAMER, TESTIMONY BEFORE THE CREDENTIALS COMMITTEE, DEMOCRATIC NATIONAL CONVENTION, AUGUST 22, 1964

Mrs. Hamer sat at the witness table before the 110 credentials committee members, the press, and the television cameras, and started to speak. [The Mississippi Freedom Democratic Party lawyer] Joe Rauh said he already knew her story by heart. He was a lawyer, and he knew a good witness. Mrs. Hamer spoke with special directness that day: "Somebody just wound her up," Rauh recalled.

Mr. Chairman, and the Credentials Committee, my name is Mrs. Fannie Lou Hamer, and I live at 626 East Lafayette Street, Ruleville, Mississippi, Sunflower County, the home of Senator James O. Eastland, and Senator Stennis.

It was the 31st of August in 1962 that eighteen of us traveled twenty-six miles to the county courthouse in Indianola to try to register to try to become first-class citizens. We was met in Indianola by Mississippi men, highway patrolmens, and they only allowed two of us in to take the literacy test at the time. After we had taken this test and started back to Ruleville, we was held up by the City Police and the State Highway Patrolmen and carried back to Indianola, where the bus driver was charged that day with driving a bus the wrong color.

After we paid the fine among us, we continued on to Ruleville, and Reverend Jeff Sunny carried me four miles in the rural area where I had worked as a time-keeper and sharecropper for eighteen years. I was met there by my children, who told me the plantation owner was angry because I had gone down to try to register. After they told me, my husband came, and said the plantation owner was raising cain because I had tried to register, and before he quit talking the plantation owner came, and said, "Fannie Lou, do you know—did Pap tell you what I said?"

I said, "Yes, sir."

He said, "I mean that," he said. "If you don't go down and withdraw your registration, you will have to leave," said, "Then if you go down and withdraw," he said. "You will—you might have to go because we are not ready for that in Mississippi."

And I addressed him and told him and said, "I didn't try to register for you. I tried to register for myself." I had to leave that same night.

On the 10th of September, 1962, sixteen bullets was fired into the home of Mr. and Mrs. Robert Tucker for me. That same night two girls were shot in Ruleville, Mississippi. Also Mr. Joe McDonald's house was shot in.

And in June, the 9th, 1963, I had attended a voter-registration workshop, was returning back to Mississippi. Ten of us was traveling by the Continental Trailway bus. When we got to Winona, Mississippi, which is Montgomery County, four of the people got off to use the washroom, and two of the people—to use the restaurant—two of the people wanted to use the washroom. The four people that had gone in to use the restaurant was ordered out. During this time I was on the bus. But when I looked through the window and saw they had rushed out, I got off of the bus to see what had happened, and one of the ladies said, "It was a state highway patrolman and a chief of police ordered us out."

I got back on the bus and one of the persons had used the washroom got back on the bus, too. As soon as I was seated on the bus, I saw when they began to get the four people in a highway patrolman's car. I stepped off the bus to see what was happening and somebody screamed from the car that the four workers was in and said, "Get that one there," and when I went to get in the car, when the man told me I was under arrest, he kicked me.

I was carried to the county jail, and put in the booking room. They left some of the people in the booking room and began to place us in cells. I was placed in a cell with a young woman called Miss Euvester Simpson. After I was placed in the cell I began to hear sounds of licks and screams. I could hear the sounds of licks and horrible screams, and I could hear somebody say, "Can you say, yes sir, nigger? Can you say yes, sir?"

And they would say other horrible names. She would say, "Yes, I can say yes, sir."

"So say it."

She says, "I don't know you well enough."

They beat her, I don't know how long, and after a while she began to pray, and asked God to have mercy on those people.

And it wasn' too long before three white men came to my cell. One of these men was a State Highway Patrolman and he asked me where I was from, and I told him Ruleville. He said, "We are going to check this." And they left my cell and it wasn't too long before they came back. He said, "You are from Ruleville all right," and he used a curse word, and he said, "We are going to make you wish you was dead."

I was carried out of that cell into another cell where they had two Negro prisoners. The State Highway Patrolman ordered the first Negro to take the blackjack. The first Negro prisoner ordered me, by orders from the State Highway Patrolman for me, to lay down on a bunk bed on my face, and I laid on my face. The first Negro began to beat, and I was beat by the first Negro until he was exhausted, and I was holding my hands behind me at that time on my left side because I suffered from polio when I was six years old. After the first Negro had beat until he was exhausted, the State Highway Patrolman ordered the second Negro to take the blackjack.

The second Negro began to beat and I began to work my feet, and the State Highway Patrolman ordered the first Negro who had beat to set on my feet to keep me from working my feet. I began to scream and one white man got up and began to beat me in my head and tell me to hush. One white man—my dress had worked up high, he walked over and pulled my dress down—and he pulled my dress back, back up. . . .

There was a slight pause. Tears were welling in her eyes, but she went on. "All of this is on account we went to register, to become first-class citizens, and if the Freedom Democratic Party is not seated now, I question America, is this America, the land of the free and the home of the brave where we have to sleep with our telephones off the hooks because our lives be threatened daily because we want to live as decent human beings, in America?

"Thank you."

Someone took off her microphone. She dabbed at her eyes, picked up her purse, and left the witness table. Some of the seasoned politicians listening were in tears.

Source: Kay Mills, *This Little Light of Mine: The Life of Fannie Lou Hamer* (New York: Plume Book, 1994), 118–121.

MISSISSIPPI SUMMER

The most dramatic initiative of the Mississippi movement was the recruiting of a thousand white college students to spend the summer of 1964 teaching black children in freedom schools and working on voter registration campaigns. Mississippians found the campaign enormously provocative: northerners were invading their state; whites and blacks worked and lived together; young white women socialized with young black men; and the main intention was to register Mississippi blacks to vote, an activity that Mississippi society and government had bitterly opposed for three quarters of a century. Designed to seize the nation's attention and force the media to look at Mississippi, the daring summer project succeeded in the most painful way possible. Civil rights activists of both races were attacked, and the murder of three received national attention. Over a thousand were arrested, thirty-five churches were burned, and thirty buildings were bombed. Mrs. Hamer explains why she thinks it was worth the cost.

"MAKE DEMOCRACY A REALITY"

Ninety per cent of the Negro people in Mississippi have gone to church all their lives. They have lived with the hope that if they kept "standing up" in a Christian manner, things would change. After we found out that Christian love alone wouldn't cure the sickness in Mississippi, then we knew we had other things to do.

There was no real Civil Rights Movement in the Negro community in Mississippi before the 1964 Summer Project. There were people that wanted change, but they hadn't dared to come out and try to do something, to try to change the way things were. But after the 1964 project when all of the young people came down for the summer—an exciting and remarkable summer—Negro people in the Delta began moving. People who had never before tried, though they had always been anxious to do something, began moving. Now, in 1966, even Negroes who live on the plantations slip off the plantations and go to civil rights meetings.

"We wanted to do this so long," they say. When some of us get up and blast out at the meetings, these women go back home—these men go back home—and in the next day or two the kids come. They say, "My mother told us what you talked about last night." That's great! To see kids, to see these people—to see how far they've come since 1964! To me it's one of the greatest things that ever happened in Mississippi. And it's a direct result of the Summer Project in 1964.

I believe in Christianity. To me, the 1964 Summer Project was the beginning of a New Kingdom right here on earth. The kinds of people who came down from the North—from all over—who didn't know anything about us—were like the Good Samaritan. In that Bible story, the people had passed by the wounded man—like the church has passed the Negroes in Mississippi—and never taken the time to see what was going on. But these people who came to Mississippi that summer—although they were strangers—walked up to our door. They started something that no one could ever stop. These people were willing to move in a nonviolent way to bring a change in the South. Although they were strangers, they were the best friends we ever met. This was the beginning of the New Kingdom in Mississippi. To me, if I had to choose today between the church and these young people—and I was brought up in the church and I'm not against the church—I'd choose these young people. They did something in Mississippi that gave us the hope that we had prayed for for so many years. We had wondered if there was anybody human enough to see us as human beings instead of animals.

These young people were so Christlike! James Chaney, Andrew Goodman, and Michael Schwerner gave their lives that one day we would be free. If Christ were here today, He would be just like these young people who the southerners called radicals and beatniks. Christ was called a Beelzebub, called so many names. But He was Christ. I can hardly express what those students and that summer meant to me—what it meant to the people who didn't dare say anything. Because when they would get a chance, they would express how they felt. As a result of that summer, we Negroes are working—slow—but we're moving. Not only did it have an effect on the black people of Mississippi but it touched some of the white people who don't yet dare speak out. This is important.

My family was like thousands of other families in Mississippi. My grandmother was a slave. My mother passed way in 1961. She was ninety-eight years old. We were taught something in Mississippi I'm not ashamed of today. We were taught to love. We were taught to not hate. And we taught to stand on principle, stand on what we believe. I often remember my mother telling me, "If you respect yourself, one day somebody else will respect you."

The reason that we Negroes in Mississippi are not bitter is because most of us were brought up in church from an early age. A child has to be taught to hate. We were taught to love and to have faith. My father used to read a scripture from the Bible: "Faith is the substance of things hoped for and the evidence of things not seen." We Negroes had hoped and we had faith to hope, though we didn't know what we had hoped for. When the people came to Mississippi in 1964, to us it was the result of all our faith—all we had always hoped for. Our prayers and all we had lived for day after day hadn't been in vain. In 1964 the faith that we had hoped for started to be translated into action. Now we have action, and we're doing something that will not only free the black man in Mississippi but hopefully will free the white one as well. No man is an island to himself.

I used to say when I was working so hard in the fields, if I could go to Washington—to the Justice Department—to the F.B.I.—get close enough to let them know what was going on in Mississippi, I was sure that things would change in a week. Now that I have travelled across America, been to the Congress, to the Justice Department, to the F.B.I. I am faced with things I'm not too sure I wanted to find out. The sickness in Mississippi is not a Mississippi sickness. This is America's sickness. We talk about democracy, we talk about the land of the free, but it's not true. We talk about freedom of speech, but in every corner of this United States men who try to speak the truth are crushed. The crisis in Mississippi made young people who are going to the college campuses all across the United States start to question: "What is going on around here?" Now, because of these young people, we have a chance to make democracy a reality. We often talk about it. We often express it. But you can go to the slums in Harlem, the slums in Chicago, the slums in California, the slums in Pennsylvania, the slums in Washington, D.C., and you'll find the race problem no different in kind from the problem in Mississippi. We don't have democracy now. But the great part about the young people in this country is that they want to change things. They want to make democracy a reality in the whole country—if it is not already too late.

Mrs. Fannie Lou Hamer
Ruleville, Mississippi

Source: Fannie Lou Hamer, "Foreword," to Tracy Sugarman, *Stranger at the Gate: A Summer in Mississippi* (New York: Hill and Wang, 1966), vii–ix.

MISSISSIPPI FREEDOM DEMOCRATIC PARTY

For all its blood and anguish, Freedom Summer accomplished the registration of few Mississippi blacks within the state's official voting rosters. But the movement developed another ingenious strategy: unofficially registering citizens in the newly created Mississippi Freedom Democratic Party with the intention of running freedom candidates and challenging the regular Democratic Party delegation in August at the Democratic National Convention in Atlantic City, New Jersey. The comments here are from participants in Freedom Summer.

THE FREEDOM DEMOCRATIC PARTY

Dear friends,   Greenwood [Mississippi, August 1964]

To my way of thinking, the most exciting aspect of this summer is the politics of it, especially the grass roots elements of politics down here.

The Freedom Democratic Party, which accepts the political processes of America, including party politics, is something even newer than other forms of political action such as demonstrations, sit-ins, freedom rides, etc. A freedom ride or demonstration has short-term, usually symbolic goals. When a person sits in at a hamburger joint, he is protesting discrimination in all white public accommodations. But it is time now to go after the long-range goals of political power through direct participation—through the right to vote. This must be done by the FDP, because the Negro is denied these rights in the regular Mississippi Democratic Party.

Until court orders finally demand it, the registering of Negroes on the official books of the state seems a hopeless task: 94% of the eligible Negroes in Mississippi aren't registered. Old Martha Lamb, the official registrar of Leflore County, just won't give in to the waves of black faces which confront her every day. . . .

Because official registration is hopeless for the moment, we are concentrating our efforts on FDP registration. But this is tough too. The Negro community in the South, particularly Mississippi, has had absolutely no political education. And whenever he has tried to take the bold step into politics, he has been beaten back into submission and kept in ignorance. The closest thing to politics around here is church elections when they elect Deacons. . . . As for the expression of interests and needs through the political process, the Negroes are totally inexperienced. If nothing else is accomplished this summer, at least a good education in politics and political expression will have been achieved by the Negroes, paving the way for more effective action in the future. . . .

I still feel, and always will, that political power is the most powerful instrument of peaceful, legitimate change. And as the Negro gets the vote, he gets representation. With representation, the powers of the state must begin to look more to his interests, and as the whites adjust to this power change, then progress is made on all fronts. They don't have to love each other, but they do have to accept the realities of change.

The FDP meets the standards of a regular party. Its meetings are open, its meetings are documented. Legal proof, showing not only voter intimidation by the whites of the regular party, but also the qualifications of the FDP meetings and elected delegates, is being gathered and sent to the Credentials Committee of the Democratic Convention which starts at Atlantic City on August 24. But besides meeting basic requirements and being open, we have a larger claim to acceptance by the National Democratic Party. We support the national party and its platform and candidates. The regular Democratic Party does not. Senator Eastland of Mississippi has voted against most of the major bills proposed by this administration. This time, the regular Mississippi Democratic Party will probably not support Johnson. . . . When the FDP presents its legal and political credentials to the National Credentials Committee, these credentials should be accepted. If not, the Negro in the South is left with few other avenues of expression.

The FDP is a product of imaginative and responsible thinking. Hopefully, the American people are still imaginative enough to accept this move. . . .

Best regards,

Phil

Dear Mom, Dad and Vickie,   Rural Madison County, July 28 [1964]

Yesterday we canvassed. . . . One lady couldn't work because she had cut her leg badly with the hoe while chopping cotton, and her leg was full of stitches. She lived in a two-room unpainted shack (kindly provided by the management). You climbed on the porch by stepping on a bucket—there were huge holes in the porch for the unwary. The woman was sitting dejectedly on the bed as she couldn't walk very well. She was surrounded by shy children, some of them naked. . . . We tried to explain what Freedom Registration meant—it seemed like a rather abstract approach to her problems. . . .

Love,

Kay

Dear folks,   Columbus [Ohio]

The precinct meeting was the first political experience for those who attended, and we were sure that the job of explaining to them nominations, delegations, resolutions, would be impossibly complicated. It was tremendously interesting to watch and indicative, I think, of the innate political nature of all men. Within ten minutes they were completely at ease and had elected a chairman, secretary, and ten delegates to the district convention in Tippah. The delegates were teachers, housewives, packinghouse workers, a toy factory worker, in short, a genuine cross-section of the community . . .

Love,

Joel

August 6, 1964

From the floor of the State Convention of the Mississippi Freedom Democratic Party:

This is the most exciting, moving, and impressive thing I have ever had the pleasure of witnessing—let alone be a part of.

Miss Ella Baker presented a very stirring keynote address. She hit very hard upon the necessity for all the delegates to work and study very hard so they can prepare themselves for the new type of fight—a political fight. She also put great stress upon the fact that these people here today have braved extreme danger and now must redouble their efforts to get all their neighbors to join them in this struggle for Freedom.

Right after Miss Baker's speech, there was a march of all the delegates around the convention hall—singing Freedom Songs, waving American flags, banners and county signs. This was probably the most soul-felt march ever to occur in a political convention, I felt, as we marched with a mixture of sadness and joy—of humility and pride—of fear and courage, singing "Go Tell It on the Mountain," "Ain't Gonna Let Nobody Turn Me Round," and "This Little Light of Mine." You would just about have to be here to really feel and see what this means to the people who are here.

Attorney Joseph Rauh, a member of the Credentials Committee of the National Democratic Convention, who is going to present the legal case for the Mississippi Freedom Democratic Party at the National Convention, then addressed the group. Mr. Rauh is also Walter Reuther's attorney and his appearance indicated the support of Mr. Reuther who is, of course, one of the powers of the Democratic Party.

Mr. Rauh presented quite an optimistic picture concerning the chances of getting the FDP seated in Atlantic City, explaining that if the Credentials Committee does not want to seat us it will only take the support of eleven members of the 108-member Credentials Committee and the support of eight states to get the matter onto the floor of the convention where we will almost certainly win the fight. . . . Bob Moses [SNCC leader in Mississippi] didn't seem so confident. President Johnson is afraid he will lose the whole South if he seats the FDP. My own opinion is that we will not be seated, but will have won partial victory by exposing the terrible situation in Mississippi, and by forming some groundwork for progress in later years. . . .

The delegates then elected and ratified the district choices of delegates to the National Convention. There will be 44 delegates and 22 alternates going. . . .

Love,

Rita

Laurel, August 18 [1964]

I'm looking forward to the convention. I'm not sure what our chances for success are, but we seem to have the Mississippi delegation worried. They have a court injunction against the Mississippi Freedom Democratic Party and have been serving injunctions on all the local leaders to keep them from participating. It seems they've found an old law which would prohibit our using the word "Democratic" . . .

Love,

Diane

Source: Elizabeth Sutherland, ed., *Letters from Mississippi* (New York: McGraw Hill, 1965), 205–222. Reprinted by permission.

THE 1964 DEMOCRATIC NATIONAL CONVENTION

Democratic Party leaders feared that seating the Freedom Democratic Party would lead southern states to walk out as they had done in 1948 in anger over even the party's mild support of civil rights in its platform. A laboriously crafted compromise between the MFDP and the regulars satisfied no one. The regulars walked out of the convention planning to support the Republican nominee, Barry Goldwater, who had voted against the Civil Rights Act of 1964 passed that spring. (Most of the Al-

abama delegation joined them: Mississippi, Alabama, and three other southern states would cast their electoral votes for Goldwater in November.) The MFDP, offered two delegates at large, rejected the deal as well. Fannie Lou Hamer was among those who declined the compromise. Many believe that the disillusionment of the Freedom Party with the white Democratic and liberal establishment was a turning point in the civil rights movement, bringing large numbers of black activists to reject racial integration in favor of black separatism.

REPORT OF THE CREDENTIALS COMMITTEE

[1]

We recommend the seating as the delegates and alternates from Mississippi those members of the regular Democratic party of Mississippi who subscribe to the following assurance:

We, the undersigned members of the Mississippi delegation to the 1964 Democratic National Convention, hereby each formally assure the convention of our intention to support the convention's nominees in the forthcoming general election.

[2]

We recommend that the convention instruct the Democratic National Committee that it shall include in the call for the 1968 Democratic National Convention the following amended first paragraph:

It is the understanding that a state Democratic party, in selecting and certifying delegates to the Democratic National Convention, thereby undertakes to assure that voters in the state, regardless of race, color, creed or national origin, will have the opportunity to participate fully in party affairs, and to cast their election ballots for the Presidential and Vice-Presidential nominees selected by said convention, and for electors pledged formally and in good conscience to the election of these Presidential and Vice-Presidential nominees, under the Democratic party label and designation.

[3]

We recommend that the convention adopt the following resolution:

RESOLVED: That the chairman of the Democratic National Committee shall establish a special committee to aid the state Democratic parties in fully meeting the responsibilities and assurances required for inclusion in the call for the 1968 Democratic National convention, said committee to report to the Democratic National Committee concerning its efforts and findings and said report to be available to the 1968 convention and the committees thereof.

[4]

We recommend that the members of the delegation of the Freedom Democratic party, like the Democrats proposed, but not seated, as members of the Oregon, Puerto Rico and Virgin Islands delegations, be welcomed as honored guests of this convention.

[5]

Wholly apart from the question of the contest as to the delegates from Mississippi and in recognition of the unusual circumstances presented at the hearing, and without setting any precedent for the future, it is recommended that Dr. Aaron Henry, chairman, and the Rev. Edwin King, national committeeman designate, of the Freedom Democratic party, be accorded full delegate status, in a special category of delegates-at-large of this convention, to be seated as the chairman of the convention may direct.

Source: New York Times, August 26, 1964.

ASSESSING THE OUTCOME

A New York Times *editorial at the time regretted the decision of the Mississippi Freedom Democratic Party to refuse the Credentials Committee compromise.*

THE SOUTHERN DELEGATIONS

The compromise settlement of the conflict over seating the rival Mississippi delegations at the Democratic convention was a triumph for moral force and a credit to the party leaders who worked it out, despite its ill-considered rejection by both sides.

President Johnson and party officials originally intended to dismiss the integrated "Freedom Democrats" with a meaningless formula that amounted only to kind words and free tickets to the gallery. But the Freedom Democrats proved that a moral argument, if powerful enough and presented with dramatic force, can cut through the cynicism and frivolity that usually prevail in a convention atmosphere.

The compromise which awarded them two places as delegates at large reflected the widespread public resentment against the prolonged, brutal intimidation of Negro citizens in Mississippi. At the same time it recognized, as the convention rules required, that the white regulars could not legally be denied their seats, provided they were willing to affirm their loyalty to the national ticket. The subsequent action of these regulars, all but three of whom bolted the convention rather than promise support of the party's nominees, was characteristic in its arrogant disregard of any national consensus.

The Freedom Democrats, for their part, made a serious mistake in rejecting the compromise. Although it did not give them the even division of seats they deserved, it was still a substantial victory—far beyond any they had originally expected. It broke down the lily-white character of the delegation and, for the first time in a Democratic convention, provided recognition for Mississippi's long-silenced Negro citizens. The subsequent seizure by Negro demonstrators of the empty Mississippi seats during Tuesday night's session accomplished nothing. On the contrary, it dimmed the clear moral and symbolic triumph they had already achieved and provided new fuel for those who argue there is no "satisfying" the Negro militants. . . .

Some more affirmative developments are already clear. The day of the lily-white delegations from the South is over. The Democrats from the rest of the country have finally lost patience with the exclusion of Negroes from party affairs in the South and with the blatant trickery employed by the white supremacy faction. The inclusion of guarantees against racial discrimination in the call to the next Democratic convention and the increase in Negro enrollment helped by the Civil Rights Act signify the coming of a new order of equality in Southern politics.

Source: "The Southern Delegations," Editorial, *New York Times*, August 27, 1964.

Mrs. Hamer, not surprisingly, supported the Mississippi Freedom Democratic Party's decision to reject the Credentials Committee compromise.

"Is this America?"

Ruleville, August 30

This morning, Sunday morn, I was just in the middle of doing some washing when in marched Mrs. Hamer, sweat beading her face, dressed in old flat shoes and a short cotton dress gathered from the bodice so that it just flowed round her huge form, her hair plaited in half a dozen tiny braids standing out from her head. She embraced me the warm southern way, and launched into a high-powered, oft-times bellowing account of the Convention in Atlantic City.

She told how she had finished her speech by asking the question that was being asked all over the country: "Is this America?" She spoke of the effect of the exhibit of the car and the photographs of the three young men [killed in Mississippi], of the way in which the vigil on the boardwalk grew from 18 people to 3,000 and of how Negroes and whites alike came to say how much it meant to them. She insisted, and I'm sure she's right, that next year the FDP will be the regular party. She said how disillusioned she was to find hypocrisy all over America. She felt Johnson had really showed his hand against the FDP by preventing a floor fight. She declared that King, Roy Wilkins, Bayard Rustin, James Farmer, and Aaron Henry had been willing to sell out the FDP by their willingness to accept the compromise. However, when I urged the wisdom of not splitting ranks, she said that at the end all of these people had congratulated them on their sit-in. . . . She insisted that the FDP would have been prepared to split the votes with the regular Democrats, but that two votes at large was no deal.

On Friday night here at the mass meeting I realized that for southern Negroes, Mississippi Negroes especially, to see that crowd sitting down meant something that would have been completely lost if a compromise had been accepted that simply hushed everything up. One woman at the mass meeting said, "I looked at that Convention from the time it started. All the time til now I never seen no nigger in a convention, but they was there! Lots of them! Big ones and little ones, they was there!"

Source: Anonymous letter, from Elizabeth Sutherland, ed., *Letters from Mississippi* (New York: McGraw Hill, 1965), 221–222. Reprinted by permission.

A later assessment of this still controversial event comes from John Lewis, then with the Student Nonviolent Coordinating Committee, throughout his career a leading advocate of civil rights, and now a congressman from Georgia.

THE TURNING POINT OF THE CIVIL RIGHTS MOVEMENT

The atmosphere was electric. The optimism was unbounded. The sixty-eight men and women chosen that night to travel to Atlantic City represented much more than one state or one political party. They represented all of us, every American—black or white—who believed in the concept of interracial democracy. Those MFDP delegates truly carried the movement's hopes and dreams with them, and we didn't doubt that they would prevail. . . .

How could we not prevail? The law was on our side. Justice was on our side. The sentiments of the entire nation were with us. I couldn't see how those convention seats could be kept from us. . . .

The idea that Johnson was dictating everything here, from the number of delegates to who those delegates would be, was outrageous to me. But beyond that was the simple fact that too many people had worked too hard for too long to be told that they would now be treated as honorary guests and nothing more. That was too much, and that's what I told Andy [Andrew Young, who favored accepting the compromise].

"We've shed too much blood," I said. "We've come much too far to back down now." Anyone who had been in Mississippi that summer, I said, would feel the same way. . . .

As far as I'm concerned, this was the turning point of the civil rights movement. I'm absolutely convinced of that. Until then, despite every setback and disappointment and obstacle we had faced over the years, the belief still prevailed that the system would work, the system would listen, the system would respond. Now, for the first time, we had made our way to the very center of the system. We had played by the rules, done everything we were supposed to do, had played the game exactly as required, had arrived at the doorstep and found the door slammed in our face.

I'm convinced that had the decision to seat the MFDP delegates reached a floor vote, especially after Fannie Lou Hamer's testimony, the Mississippi regulars would have been ousted and replaced. There is no doubt in my mind. It was power politics that did in the MFDP, politics at its worst, really. And it was Lyndon Johnson, the consummate power politician, who taught us a painful lesson.

What's tragic is that Johnson didn't have to do what he did. He was so afraid that he would lose the rank-and-file South. Well, he *did* lose it. That November, in the presidential election, Barry Goldwater carried the states of Mississippi, Alabama, Louisiana, Georgia and South Carolina. But those were the *only* states he carried besides his home state of Arizona. Despite being swept in the South, Lyndon Johnson still won by one of the most monstrous landslides in presidential election history.

But he lost something even more critical than the presidency, and it was something the whole nation would lose as the decade began to turn dark.

He lost the faith of the people.

That loss of faith would spread through Lyndon Johnson's term in office, from civil rights and into the issue of Vietnam. That loss of faith in the President would eventually grow into a loss of faith in the federal government as a whole, and it would extend out of the 1960s, into the '70s and '80s, and on up to today.

That crisis of confidence, the spirit of cynicism and suspicion and mistrust that infects the attitude of many Americans toward their government today, began, I firmly believe, that week in Atlantic City. Something was set in motion that week that would never go away. It was a major letdown for hundreds and thousands of civil rights workers, both black and white, young and old people alike who had given everything they had to prove that you could work through the system. They felt cheated. They felt robbed.

It sent a lot of them outside the system. It turned many of them into radicals and revolutionaries. It fueled the very forces of protest and discontent that would eventually drive Lyndon Johnson out of office. It was a classic tragedy—a man unwittingly bringing about his own downfall by what he thought was the right decision.

The ramifications of not seating the MFDP were immeasurable. They permeated the political climate for years to come. The same questions that were asked by all of us that August are still echoing today.

Can you trust the government?

Can you trust your political leaders?

Can you trust the President?

Through Johnson, through Nixon and on through to today.

Are we getting the truth?

Are they lying to us?

Source: John Lewis with Michael D'Orso, *Walking with the Wind, A Memoir of the Movement* (New York: Simon and Schuster, 1998), 278, 280–283.

Chapter 13

VIETNAM: RESISTING THE WAR

Compelling immediate decisions of life and death, war is for both troops and the civilians at home an uncompromising test of beliefs and character. The Vietnam conflict presented some of the most difficult decisions that Americans have ever faced. Not since the war with Mexico in the 1840s had the United States been so deeply divided over who had passed war's tests and who had failed.

Like the Korean War, the Chinese revolution of 1949, and the bloody Indonesian uprising of 1965, the Vietnam War had an earlier phase in World War II, with a brutal Japanese occupation that destroyed everyday life for millions. Driven out of villages and towns, many ordinary people across Asia joined anti-fascist militias in the forests, hills, and jungles. Under communist leaders like Kim Il Sung in Korea and Mao Zedong in China, these partisan militias made important contributions to the defeat of fascism.

When the Second World War ended and the last Axis troops returned home, the Soviet Union and the Anglo-American alliance competed for power in Asia. To Moscow's advantage, the only remaining political forces in many of these countries were partisan militias led by communists. For the Anglo-American alliance, building postwar governments often amounted to returning to power unpopular colonial regimes or fascist collaborators. In Vietnam, this meant bringing back the French. Ho Chi Minh, the charismatic communist educated in France who had led Vietnam's anti-fascist partisans against the Japanese, refused to hand the country back to France. Thus began the French war in Indochina.

Badly weakened by the war, the French were no match for Ho's battle-hardened Vietminh. In 1954, they made their last stand at the remote Vietnamese outpost of Dienbienphu. Surrounded by the Vietminh, they called on the United States to save their colony. But the Republican President, Dwight Eisenhower, recognized the difficulties of persuading Americans to sacrifice their lives for another unpopular regime as they had in Korea. The United States decided against supporting the colonial regime and the French surrendered.

Peace accords signed in Geneva in 1954 temporarily divided the country but mandated for 1956 a democratic election across the whole nation. The United States government, realizing that no one could defeat Ho Chi Minh in a fair election, pursued much the same strategy followed in Korea at the end of World War II: it declared the anticommunist forces in the South to be the legitimate representatives of the whole country. In a fraudulent election in South Vietnam, the American puppet Ngo Dinh Diem received ninety-eight percent of the vote. The anticommunist government there began a clandestine guerrilla war against the North.

The Korea strategy failed dramatically this time. From the perspective of American policymakers, the world had become far more threatening in the intervening few years. The Soviet Union had grown stronger; revolutions were developing in Algeria, East Africa, and parts of Asia while the United States confronted a black civil rights movement and a Puerto Rican anticolonial movement within its own borders. Communists in South Vietnam whom Ho had encouraged to co-exist with the increasingly unpopular Diem regime organized the National Liberation Front that Americans would come to know as the Vietcong and began a guerrilla war in the South. President Kennedy sharply increased the number of American noncombatants in South Vietnam and lent that nation fighter bomber aircraft. Despite substantial aid to Diem, the United States was unable to stabilize the South. The commitment was soon to be greatly enlarged by Lyndon Johnson. Thus began our Vietnam war.

The United States increased the war effort and rained bombs and napalm on combatants and civilians in South Vietnam. Though the United States never declared war, over fifty-eight thousand American soldiers died there—and many more Vietnamese. The decision in 1967 of Muhammad Ali, the world heavyweight boxing champion and Olympic gold medalist, to give up boxing rather than fight the Vietnamese communists defined the dilemma of a generation confronted with its government's errors in Vietnam.

SETTING A NATIONAL DEBATE

Muhammad Ali, reviled first for his decision to join the Black Muslims and change his name, then for refusing to fight in Vietnam, later regained his world heavyweight title and the respect and affection of the entire world. In 1991 Muhammad Ali told his biographer, Thomas Hauser, about his decision not to serve in the army in 1967. It was not simply a choice dictated by his religion.

MUHAMMAD ALI, "I WANTED AMERICA TO BE AMERICA"

MUHAMMAD ALI: "I never thought of myself as great when I refused to go into the Army. All I did was stand up for what I believed. There were people who thought the war in Vietnam was right. And those people, if they went to war, acted just as brave as I did. There were people who tried to put me in jail. Some of them were hypocrites, but others did what they thought was proper, and I can't condemn them for following their conscience either. People say I made a sacrifice, risking jail and my whole career. But God told Abraham to kill his son and Abraham was willing to do it, so why shouldn't I follow what I believed? Standing up for my religion made me happy; it wasn't a sacrifice. When people got drafted and sent to Vietnam and didn't understand what the killing was about and came home with one leg and couldn't get jobs, that was a sacrifice. But I believed in what I was doing, so no matter what the government did to me, it wasn't a loss.

"Some people thought I was a hero. Some people said that what I did was wrong. But everything I did was according to my conscience. I wasn't trying to be a leader. I just wanted to be free. And I made a stand all people, not just black people, should have thought about making, because it wasn't just black people being drafted. The government has a system where the rich man's son went to college, and the poor man's son went to war. Then, after the rich man's son got out of college, he did other things to keep him out of the Army until he was too old to be drafted. So what I did was for me, but it was the kind of decision everyone has to make. Freedom means being able to follow your religion, but it also means carrying the responsibility to choose between right and wrong. So when the time came for me to make up my mind about going in the Army, I knew people were dying in Vietnam for nothing and I should live by what I thought was right. I wanted America to be America. And now the whole world knows that, so far as my own beliefs are concerned, I did what was right for me."

Source: Thomas Hauser, *Muhammad Ali: His Life and Times* (New York: Simon and Schuster, 1991), 171–172.

GOING OFF TO WAR

Most Americans who were called to serve in the Vietnam War went and fulfilled their duties faithfully. They all had their own story. Here are the accounts of four men.

PRIVATE FIRST CLASS REGINALD "MALIK" EDWARDS, AFRICAN-AMERICAN FROM LOUISIANA: THE UNITED STATES MARINE CORPS, DANANG, JUNE 1965–MARCH 1966

I grew up in Plaquemines Parish. My folks were poor, but I was never hungry. My stepfather worked with steel on buildings. My mother worked wherever she could. In the fields, pickin' beans. In the factories, the shrimp factories, oyster factories. And she was a housekeeper.

I was the first person in my family to finish high school. This was 1963. I knew I couldn't go to college because my folks couldn't afford it. I only weighed 117 pounds, and nobody's gonna hire me to work for them. So the only thing left to do was go into the service. I didn't want to go into the Army, 'cause everybody went into the Army. Plus the Army didn't seem like it did anything. The Navy I did not like 'cause of the uniforms. The Air Force, too. But the Marines was bad. The Marine Corps built men. Plus just before I went in, they had all these John Wayne movies on every night. Plus the Marines went to the Orient.

Everybody laughed at me. Little, skinny boy can't work in the field going in the Marine Corps. So I passed the test. My mother, she signed for me 'cause I was seventeen.

There was only two black guys in my platoon in boot camp. So I hung with the Mexicans, too, because in them days we never hang with white people. You didn't have white friends. White people was the aliens to me. This is '63. You don't have integration really in the South. You expected them to treat you bad. But somehow in the Marine Corps you hoping all that's gonna change. Of course, I found out this was not true, because the Marine Corps was the last service to integrate. And I had an Indian for a platoon commander who hated Indians. He used to call Indians blanket ass. And then we had a Southerner from Arkansas that liked to call you chocolate bunny and Brillo head. That kind of shit.

I went to jail in boot camp. What happened was I was afraid to jump this ditch on the obstacle course. Every time I would hit my shin. So a white lieutenant called me a nigger. And, of course, I jumped the ditch farther than I'd ever jumped before. Now I can't run. My leg is really messed up. I'm hoppin'. So it's pretty clear I can't do this. So I tell my drill instructor. "Man, I can't fucking go on." He said, "You said what?" I said it again. He said, "Get out." I said, "Fuck you." This to a drill instructor in 1963. I mean you just don't say that. I did seven days for disrespect. When I got out of the brig, they put me in a recon. The toughest unit.

We trained in guerrilla warfare for two years at Camp Pendleton. When I first got there, they was doing Cuban stuff. Cuba was the aggressor. It was easy to do Cuba because you had a lot of Mexicans. You could always let them be Castro. We even had Cuban targets. Targets you shoot at. So then they changed the silhouettes to Vietnamese. Everything to Vietnam. Getting people ready for the little gooks. And, of course, if there were any Hawaiians and Asian-Americans in the unit, they played the roles of aggressors in the war games. . . .

The only thing they told us about the Viet Cong was they were gooks. They were to be killed. Nobody sits around and gives you their historical and cultural background. They're the enemy. Kill, kill, kill. That's what we got in practice. Kill, kill, kill. I remember a survey they did in the mess hall where we had to say how we felt about the war. The thing was, get out of Vietnam or fight. What we were hearing was Vietnamese was killing Americans. I felt that if people were killing Americans, we should fight them. As a black person, there wasn't no problem fightin' the enemy. I knew Americans were prejudiced, were racist and all that, but, basically, I believed in America 'cause I was an American.

Source: Wallace Terry, *Bloods: An Oral History of the Vietnam War by Black Veterans* (New York: Random House, 1984), 6–8.

MANUEL "PEANUTS" MARIN, CHICANO FROM CALIFORNIA: NAVY SEABEES, AUGUST 1966–APRIL 1967

The reason I joined the navy was very simple, I was naive. I saw Pete Garcia with his navy uniform on. I thought he looked sharp. I wanted to wear one. When I was being processed in San Diego, they asked me why I joined the navy. I told them that I had gotten mad at my girlfriend. I'm not sure why I said that. It was partially true, but I guess I wanted to have a manly excuse. I didn't think of myself as a person who planned for the future. I couldn't actually come out and say that once I got of high school, I planned to be a communications technician for four years. Then I planned to get out and go to college. That was not on my mind, so I had to come out with something and that was the best answer at the time.

One of the reasons that went through my mind for joining the service was that I was once an illegal alien. I was brought over from Mexico at the age of one and being a permanent resident, I felt that it was a good trade for being allowed to live here (U.S.) and go to school. By serving this country, I felt it was a way of paying off. It still goes, regardless of what has happened in between, whether I'd disagree with the politics of being in the service or not. I'm still sincere about this.

When I was about to finish boot camp, they told me that the school for which I had signed up, storekeeper school, was full. So, they told me there were a few other things I could do. I could go on sea duty and eventually I could apply for a school, or I could choose another school that was open. I wanted to go to storekeeper's school because my friend was going. I'm an impatient person. There was no way I was going on a ship and hoped that eventually I was going to get into school. I wanted to get my training then. So, I signed up for electricans' mate school. I didn't know the slightest thing about being an electrician.

I went to electrician school and I couldn't handle it. I could do the manual part, but I couldn't handle the theory stuff. Some real nice people tried to help me pass the test, but I couldn't do it. That's when the guy in charge called me in and told me I wasn't doing very well on my test. He asked me if I wanted a couple of weeks to see if I could straighten out. I could see that I wasn't getting anywhere. All I was doing was butting my head against the wall. So, I told him to send me out. In my mind, it was almost as if my term of service was going to end quickly by getting rid of this and getting rid of that.

From there I was sent to Coronado, California and there they put me in the worst job possible, which was doing mess hall work. I was there for three months. It was hard work because we'd get up at four in the morning and work until seven or eight at night. After those three months, I was sent to a maintenance unit. That was a lot better because it was an eight to five job. That's when I got into the Seabees.

Most of the sailors that were in maintenance were Seabees and that's how I ended up in Viet Nam. One day we were in the cafeteria drinking coffee. When the chief came in and caught us when we weren't supposed to be there, and we all ran. That's when this one white guy had orders to go to Viet Nam and he didn't want to go because he was married. That guy was literally crying when he found out. I thought I was on the chief's hit list. So I thought that it was my out if I took that guy's place to go to Viet Nam. I told him to go and tell the chief that I would take his orders.

He ran into the chief's office. When he came back out he told me the chief said he didn't care what we did. Within a day or so I was getting all kinds of [shots] and getting ready to go.

One of the reasons I volunteered for Viet Nam, besides trying to get out of trouble, was my impatience. Doing mess hall duty was something I sure as hell didn't want to do for four years. Working in the maintenance crew was not something I wanted to do all the time either. I wanted to keep moving. By this time the war was gearing up and we'd hear all kinds of reports. So, that's where I wanted to be, where the war was. I didn't want to be washing dishes and other dumb stuff.

Before we were sent to Viet Nam we were sent to Camp Pendleton for three weeks of training. During the training the Marine trainers were, of course, anti-enemy, but they were also anti-Vietnamese. They would tell us that if we got into a certain type of situation, we shouldn't second guess. To wipe people out because if we didn't we would get killed. I didn't have any experience in those matters, but this Filipino guy named Dan didn't agree with that. He told me that the Japanese did the same thing during World War II and they killed a lot of children and families. I listened to him and my sentiments were with him because I could relate to the different information from what the trainers were telling us.

Before we left for Viet Nam, the first group of Seabees who had gone to Viet Nam had just gotten back. They were some of the first ones to experience combat, resulting in the deaths of Restituto Adenir and Donald Haskins. When we would talk to them, they gave us the run down on how they saw things over there. They would call the Vietnamese gooks. They told us of how some of the Vietnamese got mad when one of the guys had run over one of their kids and crushed his head. When they told us that, "The gooks were all mad," I could tell right away that there was some kind of insensitivity.

Source: Charley Trujillo, *Soldados: Chicanos in Vietnam* (San Jose, CA: Chusma House Publications, 1990), 41–44.

ROBERT E. HOLCOMB, AFRICAN-AMERICAN FROM NEW YORK CITY, ATTEMPTED TO ESCAPE THE DRAFT, BUT FAILED: ARMORER, PLEIKU AND AN KHE, FEBRUARY 1970–OCTOBER 1970

The FBI was on a rampage looking for me. Around the Fourth of July 1969. So I called the FBI, and told them I was out on the Long Island Expressway. And they came and picked me up and put me in manacles again. Then they took me to Whitehall Street, where everybody in New York City gets inducted.

One of the agents said, "Holcomb, this time we're gonna make sure you take the oath so in case this time you leave, you'll be a problem for the Army and not us. We don't wanna be bothered with you anymore."

They took me inside to say the oath, and I refused. So they took me outside.

The other agent said, "Listen, Bob, if you don't say the oath, we're gonna lock you up forever. You just won't be seen around anymore."

So I said, "All right." And we went back inside.

I raised my hands and said the oath.

I was sworn into the Army in manacles.

Then the agents took the manacles off, and they left. . . .

I had evaded the draft for more than a year, but my antiwar views were shaped long before, while I was a student at Tennessee State University.

After two semesters at Indiana University, I transferred to Tennessee State in Nashville to get farther away from home. I was rebelling from the middle-class values and way of life my parents, both schoolteachers, were grooming me in. I think my first protest came in a march for civil rights that Martin Luther King had organized back home in Gary when I was a junior in high school. I had printed a huge sign to carry in the march. From the time I could hold a pencil, I was always drawing something. The sign said, *"Nunc Es Tempes."* "Now is the time."

Tennessee State was a hotbed of social and political unrest in the mid-Sixties. Black awareness was on the rise. People like Nikki Giovanni, Kathleen Cleaver, and Rap Brown would be on campus and join our marches. We staged sit-ins at the governor's office and mansion, protesting poor living conditions for black people in the state, some of whom lacked food, decent shelter, and even real toilet facilities. We got into Che Guevara's theories on guerilla warfare, read Mao's little red book, and the revolutionary writings of Camus and Jean-Paul Sartre.

We thought the government was gonna begin to be more and more oppressive, especially to black and other minority people. So some of us even took our philosophy to the point that we felt we should arm ourselves and develop skills so that we could survive in the hillsides. We were essentially carrying the student movement into a revolutionary mold.

We wanted the war in Vietnam to cease and desist. We felt that it was an attack on minority people, minority people were being used to fight each other. Some of us would give safe haven to soldiers who went AWOL from Fort Campbell, Kentucky, because they did not want to go to Vietnam. They would hope to stay around the college campus scene until things just blew away. But they wouldn't blow away. You had to do something about it; otherwise, they'd be following you for the rest of your life.

I was arrested for violations of curfew after a riot. And for that and other infractions of school policies aimed at stopping protests, I was expelled. As tensions between the police and the black community continued to rise, I decided to leave Nashville. I just had the feeling that I was under surveillance and one day I'd be walking down the street and someone would roll down his window and I would be shot. The revolution I left behind petered out like it did everywhere else.

Free love came into the picture. Drugs came into the picture. There was always police repression. And there was Vietnam.

I decided to move to New York to continue my art study. Soon afterwards, I got a draft letter. At that point, I decided that I was gonna resist, because I didn't believe in the war. I had read tons of books about the war, including literature from Cuba and from China and from Hanoi itself, material that had filtered here through Canada and other sources. Wars are only fought over property, really. And the war in Vietnam was basically about economics. As I saw it, we were after a foothold in a small country in the Orient with rubber plantations, rice, timber, and possibly oil. And the people. A cheap source of labor, like you have in Hong Kong and Taiwan, making designer jeans and the insides of TV sets. That's what I understood the war to be about—a war that was not really for the many but for the few. I didn't have any problems fighting for capitalism, but I was not interested in fighting for a war in which I would not enjoy the rewards.

I considered the conscientious objector status, but I couldn't do that because I was not a religious fanatic. I decided that the best thing for me to do would be to leave the country. I was not interested in being locked into Canada. I was not interested in Cuba, because it had a very pure form of socialism and didn't permit the kinds of freedoms that I was accustomed to here. I did not consider myself an African. I was concerned with the better distribution of wealth and authority at home. I never really left the idea of capitalism and the idea of democratic government. I would have gone to a European or African country.

I went to the passport office in New York, and they told me that my application would be delayed because I didn't have a draft status that would permit them to issue me a passport. I filled the application out anyway, and I left. A few weeks later, an uncle who lives elsewhere in New York called to tell me that agents had come to his apartment looking for me because they knew that I applied for a passport.

I couldn't work because I couldn't file a social security number. I was basically hanging out, living with friends, and getting a little bit of money from my artwork or from house painting. My family did not support my ideas, so I really didn't have any support from them. They wanted me to straighten up, perform as I was trained to, forget my ideas about changing the government, and go into the Army. After a while, I was at the point I was no longer in a viable position to do anything constructive with my life, so I decided to turn myself in.

I was charged with draft evasion. The FBI offered me an option. I could work for them as a plant, an informant, or I could go to the service. For two weeks they kept me locked up in the Federal House of Detention hoping to sweat me into working for them. They wanted to plant me within various black or radical groups, like the Black Panthers, the Student Nonviolent Coordinating Committee, and the Symbionese Liberation Army. They said we could start off in New York, but there might be other cities involved. They would provide me with an apart-ment and with a subsistence allowance. For each person that I helped them capture on an outstanding warrant, they would pay me from $1,000 to $3,000. My questions to them were, Would I get concessions against the charge against me, how long would I have to do it, and would I be permitted to carry an arm to protect myself? They offered no promises of leniency or a time when I could get out. And no, I wouldn't be permitted to carry any kind of weapon. I said no deal. I did not want to fulfill that kind of role, especially unarmed.

Then I went before a federal district court judge and told him I'd prefer to go to war than go to jail or be an informant. He stamped my papers approved to go into the Army.

When they took me to the induction center on Whitehall the first time, the agent said, "You're not gonna go anywhere, are you?"

I said, "No."

He took the manacles off me and left me in the hands of the Army. The Army treated me just as they did any other recruit. They didn't know what my history was. I was free to roam around, so what I did was to roam around and roamed right out of the building.

I got in contact with the lady I was living with, Felice Mosley. I told her I was going into the war, and she got cold feet about waiting for me. We resolved some issues. We broke up. And, after two weeks to rest and recuperate with a friend, I told the FBI to pick me up.

After I finished basic training, they made me a security holdover for two months because they weren't sure whether I'd be subversive to the government in a war situation. I had to go over to the G2 every week to prove to them that I'd be a loyal trooper and fight for the red, white, and blue. Finally, they said, "Fine. We're gonna take you through a little more training in AIT school, and from there you'll more than likely go to Vietnam."

But an odd thing happened before I left Fort Gordon, Georgia. I was training some troops on how to fight with a bayonet. One of them came running down a path to stick the dummy with his bayonet. It was a guy I was in college with who had his ear severely damaged when he was beaten by the Nashville police. I thought to myself they must be taking all of us who were involved in any sort of black political struggle and putting us into the Army as soon as they could so we wouldn't be a problem anymore.

Source: Terry, *Bloods,* 206–210.

David E. Wilson and others who were members of pacifist faiths drew on the long-standing tradition of conscientious objection. Some of these men served in the military but refused to take up a weapon. Many conscientious objectors, assigned to medical and support staff, found it difficult to fit into the culture of the military.

198 TURNING POINTS: MAKING DECISIONS IN AMERICAN HISTORY

DAVID E. WILSON, CONSCIENTIOUS OBJECTOR: MEDICAL CORPS, VIETNAM, 1968–1969

I reported to the Overseas Replacement Center in Oakland, California. We were all locked up, nobody was allowed out of the compound. A couple of the guys literally tried to go over the wall. Apparently, these guys had a better idea than I did of what we were getting into. They were scared to death.

We left Travis Air Force Base in the middle of the night. From there we flew to a U.S. military terminal in Japan. We were allowed to get off and use the facilities, but nobody was allowed to go any further. There were armed guards, and they really kept an eye on us. There was no getting around them, they were there to keep us penned-up by the airplane, and they did. I felt like we were a bunch of cattle being herded into a slaughter pen.

Eventually, we landed in Bien Hoa. We no more than filed off the airplane when I saw all these guys standing by the side of the runway. They were going home. They were dirty and looked like they had been through hell backwards. They just kind of looked at us and shook their heads. I stood there and looked at these guys and I thought, "My God, these guys look like old men." And, they did. The oldest one in the group probably wasn't any older than twenty-five, but from the look on his face, I would have sworn that the guy was close to fifty.

We got on a bus that had all this wire mesh on the window. I'm thinking it's there because they don't want us to escape. So, I asked the driver what the hell was going on. He laughed; he said the mesh was there in case we got ambushed. It kept the grenades from coming into the bus. I thought, "O my God." That was my first realization that I was in some kind of danger. That feeling never left me; it started right on the first day and that underlying level of tension stayed there until the day I left. It got worse, but it started right there.

They took us into a supply room and started issuing guns. I told the guy that I was a conscientious objector and didn't want one. He said, "What the hell are they doing sending somebody like you into a unit like this?" He said, "You're crazy, you ought to have your head examined." He started to laugh and told me, "You'll be back in a week."

Then, our sergeant came in and tried to talk me into taking a weapon. I refused. He got a little nasty, standing there yelling at me and calling me an idiot. He used every line imaginable to try to tell me that the lives of my buddies depended on me carrying a weapon. He said, "What if you are alone with a wounded guy, and here comes Charlie trying to kill you. What are you going to do?" I told him, "I'll just have to deal with that when it happens. If it ever came to that, my instincts for self-preservation would probably take over, and I'd probably use the weapon." So, he said, "Well, why don't you just take it now?"

But, I was stubborn. The Army had given me a bunch of crap about being a CO, I hadn't knuckled under and I wasn't going to. I got more stubborn as time went on. It pissed me off, and I just decided the hell with these people. They can't make me do this; and legally, there was nothing they could do to force me to carry a weapon.

I did meet up with one other CO while I was there. He started going out on patrols and the next time I saw him, he was carrying an M-16. When I saw this I began to wonder if things were going to get that rotten for me.

I wound up going to a big base camp in Dong Tam. For the first few weeks in-country I worked with a bunch of other medics in an aid station. People were nice to me, nobody was antagonistic about the fact that I was a CO. But, people knew about it the minute I hit the front door. It seemed like no matter where I went, somebody knew. It was almost like they couldn't trust me, like I was some kind of a weirdo.

After a few weeks I got assigned to a platoon that served as the front line of defense for the base at Dong Tam. My heart was in my mouth when they flew me out there. I was there for about five minutes when this lieutenant came out and asked me where my weapon was. I told him I didn't carry a weapon. He goes, "What!?" I said, "I'm a conscientious objector." He said, "Well, what the hell are you doing out here?" I said, "I was sent out here." At that point, he dragged me into his tent.

The first thing he did was bring out his M-16. He said, "Here, hold this." So, I took it, I just stood there holding the thing, and he said to me, "Do you know how to fire that?" I said, "No." He just kind of shook his head. Then he said to me, "I think you ought to at least let me show you how this thing works." I said, "I don't want to know." He said, "Well, what if you need it?" I answered, "Why will I need it? I'm a medic." And he said, "Goddamnit, we need all the firepower in this unit that we can get. If we get pinned down out there somewhere, that gun that you are carrying, or not carrying, might be the difference between us getting nailed." Well, I didn't believe him. I said, "That's a bunch of shit, you got thirty guys out there armed to the teeth, what the hell difference is one more gun going to make?"

Source: Gerald Gioglio, *Days of Decision: An Oral History of Conscientious Objectors in the Military During the Vietnam War* (Trenton, NJ: The Broken Rifle Press, 1989), 116–118.

REFUSING TO FIGHT

Some Americans like Muhammad Ali refused to participate in the Vietnam War. Some went to prison, as Ali had done. Others left the United States and moved to Canada, perhaps encouraged by publications like the pamphlet reprinted here. In 1975 President Gerald Ford pardoned the young men who had refused to serve, and to Americans who had left the country he issued an appeal to return home.

"RED ROVER," ESCAPING TO CANADA,
TORONTO, FEBRUARY 8, 1970

Canada, the new Promised Land: for the growing legions of America's dis-possessed young men of conscience this high sounding epigraph has the ring of truth about it. How long now has the procession been struggling northward. It seems a decade since their exodus began. In fact perhaps it's only been half that much time, and yet it could have easily been a score of years. The clear-eyed es-capees are everywhere, scattered across vast Canada as if by a whirlwind. They come from all walks of life, all stations and situations. Some of the wealthy and influential upper class, some from the pain faced poor and a few long suffering swarthy ones are interwoven into the whole of the flesh fabric comprised mainly of omnipresent, common-and-durable-as-cotton middle class.

The reaction here in Canada seems generally to be favorable regarding her "draft-dodging" U.S. immigrants, as is evidenced in most Canadian mass media and, more important yet, official government policy. First and foremost is that lit-tle piece of paper: The Canadian Extradition Treaty. It's the golden key that opens the door to the "New Promised Land," and makes it the attractive citadel of safety and sanctuary that it is for war exiles. In this document there are listed 22 various crimes. Only if an American immigrant was accused or convicted of one or more of these offenses can he be forced to return to his country. Some of the crimes that warrant extradition from Canada in accord with the treaty between the two coun-tries are murder, piracy, arson, robbery, forgery, voluntary manslaughter, coun-terfeiting, embezzlement, fraud, perjury and rape. The treaty does not recognize refusal of induction or desertion from the U.S. military establishment as criminal. So that there could be no mistaking the government's position on this vital issue, the following statement was issued in the summer of 1967 (a time when Ameri-can Immigration was heavy) by none other than John Munro, secretary to the Minister of Immigration at that time.

> . . . compulsory military service in his own country has no bearing upon his admissibility to Canada either as an immigrant or as a visitor; nor is he subject to removal from Canada because of unfulfilled military obligations in his country of citizenship.

What more could a prospective immigrant ask for than official approval and a generally favorable press? There is more, and true to form one only need ask, knock or inquire to receive information, job prospects, shelter, special assistance, *et al.* Across the nation, from Nova Scotia to British Columbia, groups of sym-pathetic citizens have rallied to meet the pressing needs of young anti-war refugees. In Ontario alone there are ten anti-conscription groups or contacts avail-able. Below are the names, addresses, and phone numbers of the Ontario draft aid people. . . .

The last of the groups listed, the Toronto Anti-Draft Programme, is the largest and best equipped in Canada. During the early fall of last year they were handling as many as 50 visitors per day. Besides furnishing information to persons about immigration, they also provide special services to U.S. immigrants who have recently arrived. Medical aid, shelter and job counseling are among the services offered. Free of any charge, of course. When one takes into consideration that the money-addicts of the American Empire, Unlimited, have usually-mild-mannered Canada by the economical balls, it becomes clear that her stand, and the stand of her many citizens in aiding and comforting those who refuse to act as "Cops of the World" for the Empire, is indeed a gutsy and honorable one. Other faults aside, Canada is on terra firma when she stares down the bullying barrel of Yankee imperialism and shouts into it in such a fashion that the echo is heard 'round the world: No! No! No!!!!!!

Source: G. Louis Heath, "Escaping to Canada," *Mutiny Does Not Happen Lightly: The Literature of the American Resistance to the Vietnam War* (Metuchen, NJ: The Scarecrow Press, 1976), 495–497.

THE WAR AT HOME

A few women who opposed the war found that they could influence young GIs recently inducted into the military and still undecided about the many issues of the war. GI coffee houses, where soldiers and antiwar activists socialized, became the location of their efforts.

WENDY REISSNER, GI COFFEE HOUSE, NOVEMBER 8, 1968

MPs refused to allow the teams to distribute leaflets, but Friday night before the conference, we tried a new tactic. We decided simply to talk to the GIs without leafleting. Carloads of antiwar activists arrived on base and headed for the USO dance.

Our carload chose the snack bar as a base of operations. We filed in, ordered coffee, and spread out to cover as many tables of GIs as possible. Most of us started with, "I'm here to talk about the war in Vietnam." The GIs were friendly and quite eager to talk. After 20 minutes, almost every table was the scene of discussion and debate, and the time and place of the conference was being scribbled down on scraps of paper.

Four MPs marched up to the table where I was talking with three GIs and demanded my military ID card. On finding that I was not in the armed forces, they asked me to leave. All discussion stopped, and eyes were riveted as I walked across the room to leave.

After about 30 seconds, the soldiers I was talking to and others followed me out. As the others in our group were kicked out of the snack bar, more GIs came outside with them. They were indignant. Many offered to invite us in as their personal guests. As the crowd gathered, the MPs tried to disperse it. But each antiwar person went in a different direction with several soldiers and kept on talking about the antiwar movement for about an hour, while the MPs were frantically trying to keep up with all of us.

Source: Fred Halstead, *Out Now: A Participant's Account of the American Movement Against the Vietnam War* (New York: Monad Press), 435.

REVOLTS IN THE MILITARY

Particularly after the lengthy disengagement process called de-escalation began in 1968, opposition to the war spread within the military. Men on the Coral Sea *signed a petition demanding that their ship not be deployed to Vietnam. Underground newspapers appeared on military bases. "Fragging," the murder of officers by enlisted men, began to be extensively discussed, first in underground GI newspapers, then in national circulation media and in the halls of Congress. Even large numbers of officers began publicly to question the continuation of the war. Representative Paul McCloskey, a Democrat from California, used such evidence to argue that rapid withdrawal from Vietnam was necessary to preserve the future effectiveness of the American military.*

SAILORS PROTEST

In has become apparent that the majority of the Americans oppose the war in Vietnam. But the government has refused to be guided by public opinion. It has also become clear to many that the responsibility for ending the war will fall on those more directly involved: the military. The military man is given the task of carrying out the policy of the government without an effective means of influencing that policy.

Members of the U.S.S. *Coral Sea* have begun taking a part in ending the war by starting the Stop Our Ship movement (SOS). We began with a petition to Congress with the goal of stopping our ship from deploying to Vietnam.

On the original petition we gathered over 300 signatures in three days when it was ripped off by two chiefs who turned it over to the Executive Officer. This action alarmed many people. After requests to return the petition were ignored, another petition was distributed along with leaflets explaining the goals of the petition. This petition now has been signed by over 1,000 members of the crew.

Three sailors are now in the brig for their involvement with the SOS movement. Protests against the treatment of these three and similar harassment by the command have been ignored. A ship's regulation now prohibits the distribution of any literature not first censored by the Captain. The command is now attempting to rid itself of the ship's most active spokesmen by transfers, discharges, and brig time.

But the command can't muffle the noise of the discontent that this war has caused. At this time another attack carrier, the *Hancock,* has started a similar movement in protest of our involvement in Southeast Asia.

We are going to stop our ships. And we, the military men, are going to stop this war.

Source: Congressional Record, 92nd Congress, 1st Session, vol. 117, pt. 29: 38083.

HOW TO START A GI UNDERGROUND NEWSPAPER

Casual observers viewing the growth of the Armed Forces underground newspaper network since its birth a short sixteen months ago might very easily gain the misconception that such papers are printed at little or no risk to the persons involved. We wish it were so, but to date scores of GIs have been court-martialed, jailed, spirited off to Vietnam, or kicked out of the service altogether for working on them. Their crimes were often nothing more than a lack of experience or too much trust in the military establishment. We know better now; we've learned pretty much what works and what doesn't. In this leaflet we've compiled a brief guide for the potential GI underground newspaperman. It doesn't contain all the answers but should keep you out of jail long enough to learn the rest.

For starters you'll need to locate other GIs to work with you. So begin watching for guys who've had some college experience, draftees, or just anyone who seems to be the working type. Strike up conversations with them, sound them out, steer the topics to war protests, racial problems, or GI rights. If they sound pretty squared away then get them alone sometime and hit them with the paper idea; have a copy of one of the other papers with you and show them what you have in mind. If you've judged them reasonably well and sound like you know what you're doing, you shouldn't have any problems.

With several GIs together you can then start to produce the actual newspaper. Unless you're rich or something, this requires first locating free or very inexpensive office space, typewriters, a printing press of some sort and other essential items. Difficult? Not at all; many civilian organizations are more than willing to help. Check first at the student activities building of your nearest university; both there and off campus look for groups involved in the peace movement, draft counseling, civil rights, civil liberties, coffee houses, or minority group problems. Don't avoid the "radical" organizations in your search, as generally the more anti-military the group is, the more they'll do to help you. Also, don't be discouraged if you can't find anything near your base; it's not at all unusual to have to do your actual printing many miles from where you're stationed. In any case, just sound them out like you do GIs and you'll soon find what you're looking for.

Another essential is an off-base post office box. They're generally very inexpensive, easy to obtain, and most important of all, they're fairly safe from military snoopers. Having the box allows you to communicate with many organizations that you couldn't through your military address. Also, it will allow you to offer mail subscriptions to your paper which by far is the most painless means of distribution.

Along that line, whenever you mail anything (your paper included) to servicemen, use plain envelopes, first class postage, and make CERTAIN that nothing showing on the outside of the envelope gives the material away as being political in nature. Seriously, don't even put your full return address on the envelope if it sounds political or "subversive": peace signs, obscene words, anti-war slogans—for heaven's sake give us a break! Most of us receive our mail via lifers and that sort of thing just gets us into trouble.

The actual printing of your paper (How to run a mimeograph machine in three easy lessons, etc.) is something you're going to have to learn for yourselves. However, again there are several things to keep in mind. Keep your articles truthful. Keep your language reasonably clean. DON'T print your staff members' names on the paper. Borrow articles, ideas, and cartoons freely from the other GI underground papers but credit them to the originating paper.

Distribution is the part that really gets sticky. No other single area has caused more grief than this one. On-base distribution in particular is the rough one:

1) To legally distribute printed materials on a military base you must first obtain a written permit from the commanding officer.

2) No such permit has been granted in recent history without court action; so be prepared with attorneys before you make application.

3) Your application should be in the form of a letter to the commanding officer and should include ONLY a copy of what you intend to distribute, and the dates, times and places you intend to distribute it. The letter should be signed by a civilian (preferably an attorney) and should NOT contain the names of any GIs. If the C.O. asks for additional information (your staff members' names, your financial supporters' names, etc.), DON'T give it to him! At that point he's only trying to stall or trick you. He has NO right to any information other than what you first gave him; if he says that isn't enough, go to court.

4) Even if you obtain a permit, DO NOT let GIs attempt to hand out the papers openly. Use only civilian volunteers. GIs doing it WILL be black-listed whether they have a permit or not and probably will end up in jail on some petty charge. Use only civilians, make sure that they hand out only what, where, and when the permit specifies and you'll do OK. Do anything else and somebody's going to jail.

5) As an alternative to that route, the most commonly used method of on-base distribution is to simply forget the permit and hand out your papers secretly. As this method is clearly illegal, no one suggests that you use it—however, I will admit that my old paper distributed over twenty thousand copies altogether this

way and never had any problems. We smuggled them on base in small bundles and left them lying about when no one was watching: in the theater, on benches, in rest rooms, along the road, any place. By taking our time and being careful, none of us ever got caught. If your staff is composed entirely of GIs (as ours was) or you can't obtain a permit, do what you will.

Off-base distribution is much easier and may be accomplished by either civilians or out-of-uniform GIs. Suggested places to distribute are coffee houses, transportation centers (bus stations, etc.), entertainment centers, or any place else frequented by servicemen. But, again, the safest method of distribution is the secret, flop a copy down when no one's looking method.

Most of the rest of your operations you can play pretty much by ear or learn from the other GI papers. However, let me stress:

1) Never, never, never make public the names of your GI staff members.
2) Never "borrow" any government property for use in your paper.
3) Never print classified material.
4) If any of your staff use grass or drugs, tell them to keep their stuff away from your paper operations.
5) Keep well informed on Canadian immigration procedures.
6) Don't keep large quantities of material in your locker on base.
7) Don't be afraid to ask the other GI papers if you have a problem.

The GI newspaper underground is as young as it is exciting and productive. To date it has been expanding at a fantastic rate—if this is to continue we need new workers, more money, new papers. We need anything anyone cares to contribute. The personal risks involved in participating and not taming this military-industrial, war-producing racist animal known as the U.S. Armed Forces are even higher. We need your help. With the use of a little care and a lot of common sense yours' can be a valuable contribution in this struggle. So do it! All we have to lose is war. . . .

Source: Heath, "How to Start a GI Underground Paper," 438–441.

RICHARD BOYLE, A WAR CORRESPONDENT, DISCOVERS FRAGGING

After the disastrous battle of Hamburger Hill, GIs in the 101st Airborne put out an underground newspaper offering a $10,000 reward for the assassination of the officer who gave the order to attack. Hamburger Hill was a big story in the press, but the reward wasn't, nor were the fraggings that began to occur in increasing numbers in '69. Later the Army was to admit that there had been more than two hundred known fraggings in 1969. In 1970 there were 363 reported cases. Who knows how many more officers were shot by their own men in combat?

Although many of us in the Saigon press corps had heard rumors of frag-gings—attacks by enlisted men on officers with a fragmentation grenade, usually slipped under the floor of the officer's hootch—it wasn't being reported to the people back home.

Then President Lyndon Johnson, in response to the growing antiwar move-ment, once said, "You don't hear the boys in Vietnam protesting." Hawks con-sistently called for escalation "to support our boys." To be against the war, they claimed, is to stab GIs in the back. The Army brass was particularly worried about stories of GI unrest leaking out. They did everything they could to cover up, and until 1969 they were successful.

They covered up the story of the revolt in 1968 of black GIs at Long Binh Jail, the notorious Army prison outside Saigon. Fed up with abuse and beatings at the hands of the guards, black troops seized the prison, repelling successive at-tempts by hundreds of MPs backed up by armored cars to retake the prison. In the end, of course, the troops lost out.

The easiest way for the Army to cover up news of GI unrest was simply not to report it at the five o'clock follies. The Army's massive PR machine daily cranked out press releases about how the GIs supported the war, how high their morale was and how we were gloriously winning the hearts and minds of the Vietnamese people.

So the press simply never heard of the fraggings, of officers shot in the back by their own men, of near-revolts of whole units. Most of the newsmen, when they did go out in the field, spent their time in the officers' mess and in officers' clubs drinking with the brass. It seemed most newsmen didn't really like or un-derstand the grunts; they felt more comfortable with the lifers.

Besides, most of the grunts didn't trust the Saigon press corps. They knew the Army's Central Intelligence Division (CID) often sent agents onto bases dis-guised as newsmen to get information and evidence about fraggings or possible mutinies. El Cid, as the grunts called the spies, was everywhere.

But there was another, even greater, obstacle to uncovering stories of frag-gings. If a reporter wanted to go on base, he had to sign up for a military flight, giving the reason for his trip. If he told the truth and said he wanted to do a story about fraggings, the brass would try to block him every way they could—say he couldn't get to the base because of bad weather or, if they did let him go, send along a public information officer to follow him around and make sure no dam-aging information got out. If he lied about why he wanted to go, they would still make sure he saw and heard only what the PIO wanted.

The *Overseas Weekly* was the first paper to report on fraggings, probably be-cause most of our stories came from the GIs themselves. On stories the Army didn't want us to know about—and there were many—we usually had to sneak on base to get the story at all.

Source: Richard Boyle, *The Flower of the Dragon: The Breakdown of the U.S. Army in Vietnam* (San Francisco: Ramparts Press, 1972), 75–77.

EUGENE LINDEN,
ASSESSING THE FREQUENCY OF FRAGGING

Fragging is a macabre ritual of Vietnam in which American enlisted men attempt to murder their superiors. The word comes from the nickname for hand grenades, a weapon popular with enlisted men because the evidence is destroyed with the consummation of the crime. Fragging has ballooned into intra-Army guerrilla warfare, and in parts of Vietnam it stirs more fear among officers and NCOs than does the war with "Charlie.". . .

. . . Fraggings have occurred in every war in this century. The available statistics are too spotty and inconsistent to make any direct comparison; however, they do show a spectacular increase in the number of violent attacks by enlisted men on their superiors. In World War I, which involved over 4,700,000 American military, fewer than 370 cases of violence directed at superiors were brought to courts-martial. This low ratio was fairly constant through World War II and the Korean police action. It did not change significantly until Vietnam. Since January 1970 alone, a period during which roughly 700,000 Americans were in Vietnam, there have been 363 cases involving assault with explosive devices (fraggings using hand grenades, mines, and the like) and another 118 cases termed "possible assault with explosive devices." Forty-five men died in those attacks, and these figures are exclusive of fraggings by such other weapons as rifle or knife. Officers in the Judge Advocate General Corps have estimated that only about 10 per cent of fraggings end up in court.

Source: Eugene Linden, "Fragging and Other Withdrawal Symptoms," *Saturday Review,* January 8, 1972: 47.

OFFICERS' PETITION TO PRESIDENT NIXON,
FORT SHERMAN, CANAL ZONE, JULY 26, 1970

RICHARD M. NIXON.
President, United States of America.

DEAR PRESIDENT NIXON: We the undersigned are all officers in combat branches of the United States Army, and are all on orders to Vietnam. Currently we are at Ft. Sherman undergoing training at the Army's Jungle Warfare School in preparation for our duties as junior officers in Vietnam. First of all, we want to make it clear that we have accepted our orders, and that we are going to Vietnam; most of us will be there by the middle of August. Nevertheless, we have some serious reservations about the war and about the roles that we are being asked to play in it. We think that you as our commander-in-chief should be made fully aware of these reservations, because they are shared by a very large number of young men—officers and non-commissioned personnel—throughout the military services.

At this point in the Vietnam War, it is obvious that America is not willing to go all out to win the war. The country is reluctant to send over the large numbers of troops that the generals still say will be necessary to win. At the urging of your military advisors you ordered the attack on the Cambodian sanctuaries, but public opinion forced you to declare limits on the duration and the penetration of the invasion. The country has been shocked and outraged by the My Lai and Colonel Rheault incidents—incidents of mass killing and assassination which are and have always been characteristic of warfare. The American people do not want to pay the terrible prices of war—they don't want to see their own young men killed, and they don't want to face the brutal acts which these young men must perform on people of another country. In short, America has not been sufficiently convinced that the things we have been told that we are fighting for—i.e., democracy for the people of South Viet Nam, and protecting America from spreading communism—justify the methods necessary to obtain those ends.

We, too, find the continuation of the war difficult to justify, and we are being asked to lead others who are unconvinced into a war in which few of us really believe. This leaves us with nothing but survival—"kill or be killed"—as a motivation to perform our missions. But if this is the only thing we have to keep us going, then those who force us into this position—the military, the leadership of the country—are perceived by many soldiers to be almost as much our enemies as the Viet Cong and the NVA. There is a great amount of bitterness both towards the military and towards American building up within the military forces.

We find it hard to believe that you could not be aware of the extent of disaffection among the American troops; it is equally hard to believe that knowing about this disaffection you could hope to continue much longer to force young Americans to go to this war against their wills. As the war drags on, the troops will become increasingly opposed to the war and increasingly bitter about going. It seems very possible that if the war is allowed to continue much longer, young Americans in the military will simply refuse en masse to cooperate, thus causing a crisis similar to the current difficulties of the draft bureau. This day is coming quickly—you must have us out of Vietnam by then.

In your speeches and news conferences you often contrast the disaffection of the American student protesters with the devotion and patriotism of our soldiers in Vietnam. We want you to know that in many cases those "protesters and troublemakers" are our younger brothers and friends and girlfriends and wives. We share many common causes with them. Please get this country out of Vietnam before we, too, become completely disaffected.

The purpose of this letter is not to publicly embarrass you or the military—we are not sending copies to the press. We only want you as commander-in-chief to know that a large number of officers and soldiers in Vietnam and on their way to the war have serious misgivings about the war and their participation in it. To this date, officers have remained silent about their feelings, but we think it important that you be informed of the widespread dissatisfaction amongst us.

We sign this letter knowing that it will be seen by your military staff before you ever see it—if it gets to you at all. We also know of punitive action taken by the Army to officers who have written similar letters to you. Nevertheless, we must take chances to inform you of these feelings within the Army. Since you and the country seem to have decided that Vietnam is not worth the awful price of victory, we plead with you to get the country out of this half-hearted war at the extreme earliest moment.

Sincerely,

Source: Congressional Record, 92nd Congress, 1st Session, vol. 117, pt. 29: 38083.

REPRESENTATIVE PAUL MCCLOSKEY, "NO ONE WANTS TO BE KILLED IN THE LAST DAYS OF A WAR THE COUNTRY NO LONGER SUPPORTS," OCTOBER 28, 1971

Mr. MCCLOSKEY. Mr. Speaker, I place in the RECORD today a summary of evidence which indicates that the morale, combat performance and deterrent capabilities of our forces in Vietnam have deteriorated to a point where the national security is endangered.

The situation is clear. Many GI's in Vietnam are no longer willing to obey orders. To order an offensive operation today is to invite a wholesale mutiny. There is a growing danger of confrontation between American troops and their officers which could prove ugly and disastrous. There is likewise a growing danger of confrontation, if not combat, between the diminishing number of American troops and various groups of disaffected South Vietnamese.

This being the case, I suggest that the President has an obligation, as Commander in Chief, to preserve the remaining esprit de corps and professional competence of our Army by disengaging from Vietnam at the earliest practicable date.

If he fails to do so, the Congress must assume that responsibility. It behooves us to withdraw from Vietnam before the professional reputation of the Army as well as its deterrent capability in the future is damaged beyond repair.

For 2½ years now, we have admitted that we sought no military victory—that our people did not want to pay the cost of winning in Vietnam—that our young men understandably do not want to fight and die there—to kill people against whom we harbor no ill will, in a cause in which we do not believe.

With the publication of the Pentagon papers and a growing public realization of the enormity of the deceit practiced upon the American people—and even the Congress—in order to get us involved in Vietnam—keep us there—and justify our remaining there—it is no wonder that our servicemen rebel at being asked to stay behind to preserve the police state of the Thieu-Ky regime and to preserve the pride and prestige of a President who does not want to be the first American President to lose a war.

Is it not understandable that no one wants to be killed in the last days of a war the country no longer supports? This is not the first instance of deliberate refusal to obey orders. Newsweek reported last week that such refusals have become a common occurrence in Vietnam.

Fraggings today are commonplace in Vietnam.

Disaffection extends not only to the Army in Vietnam. A recent series of articles on our NATO forces in Europe has shown widespread discontent, drug use, breakdown of discipline, racial conflict—and most important, a breakdown in combat readiness.

I regret to suggest that this breakdown can be traced directly to the Commander in Chief's apparent failure to recognize that morale and a will to fight are as necessary ingredients of military power as missiles, guns, and tanks.

If the military establishment has fallen to the low ebb it has, then I think we must ask the Commander to change the policies which have caused the decay of a once proud service.

Source: Congressional Record, 92nd Congress, 1st Session, vol. 117, pt. 29: 38082.

Chapter 14

SOCIAL SECURITY: YOU DECIDE

In 1935, Frances Perkins, President Franklin D. Roosevelt's secretary of labor, described on national radio the recently passed Social Security Act as "using co-operation through government to overcome the social hazards against which the individual alone is inadequate." The Social Security Act, she said, was "deeply significant of the progress which the American people have made."

The Social Security Act disappointed many radicals because it did not go far enough to establish a cooperative and egalitarian fund insuring adequate security for individuals in need. It was a regressive tax: higher income workers paid a lower percentage of their total income into Social Security. It excluded farm workers, domestic servants, hospital and restaurant workers, and other job cate-gories that principally involved females or African Americans. And it drew no money from existing taxes and government revenues. Despite its limitations, Social Security dramatically changed the way Americans looked at their lives. Countless were ultimately rescued from an old age of poverty and dependence. Workers put money into Social Security with every pay check and planned to draw a pension from it when they were unable to work.

During the Reagan Administration it became popular to denigrate the ability of government to deliver effective services. Government came to be seen as a drag on the energy of competitive capitalist economies. Politicians, financiers, and political pundits embraced an economic philosophy of privatization known as neoliberalism. It drew on eighteenth- and nineteenth-century convictions that it is human nature for individuals to compete with their neighbors, and that if human beings are allowed to express this nature without being restrained by gov-ernment, economies will grow and prosper and everyone's lot will improve.

Although neoliberal experiments have brought increasing inequality in most of the world and forced workers in all countries to put in longer hours, in some countries neoliberal experiments have improved national economies. One of these countries is Chile.

In 1970 Chile elected a socialist president, Salvador Allende. When businesses and banks withdrew support for the economy and factory owners and storekeepers closed businesses in protest, the economy ground to a halt and the country descended into crisis. In 1973 a coup by General Augusto Pinochet backed by the American Central Intelligence Agency ended the socialist experiment and executed many leaders of opposition political parties, trade unions, and community groups. Thereupon Pinochet embarked on an experiment in radical neoliberalism. Using the formidable Chilean army to guarantee labor discipline, Pinochet brought to Santiago economists from the University of Chicago to guide the rebuilding of the Chilean economy. Confidence returned; foreign capital flowed into the country; and domestic capital invested vigorously in new enterprises. One Chilean neoliberal policy was the replacement of state retirement funds with a system of private accounts, known as *AFORES.* As the Chilean economy grew, money flowed into these accounts and the Chilean retirement system became for some years the envy of Latin America. Soon countries throughout the hemisphere began the difficult task of convincing their workforces to give up guaranteed state sector retirement funds for private retirement accounts at higher risk and higher yield.

In the United States, the Cato Institute, a conservative think tank that worked with Chilean privatizers, caught the attention of politicians, policymakers, and financial brokers. The economic boom of the 1990s, the investment of more and more pension funds in the stock market, fueled a meteoric rise in the Dow Jones industrial average. As ordinary Americans watched the growth of the stock market outpace the increase of their Social Security accounts, the argument of the Cato Institute and other conservatives had its effect. As a Democratic President and a heavily Republican Congress together discussed necessary actuarial adjustments in Social Security, the issue at the end of the twentieth century turned into a debate about the value of the program itself. Global financial instability, the uncertainty in the American stock market in 1998, and particularly the spectacular collapse of the Chilean economic miracle made privatizers less vocal than they had been in the middle of the decade, but the debate went on. Eventually, you and other voters will have to decide on the future of Social Security.

[ANOTHER NOTE ON THE USE OF THE INTERNET TO STUDY HISTORY]

Many of the documents in this chapter were taken from the internet. On general problems of taking historical material from this medium see the note in Chapter 10. Establishing the validity of the documents selected for this chapter is less of a problem than for those on the atomic bomb. These were all posted by the important people and institutions working to shape public opinion, speaking in their own names on their own web sites and taking responsibility for what they have said. It is as yet unclear how and whether the use of cyberspace will affect the way such decisions get made.

SOCIAL SECURITY ENACTMENT

The Social Security Act of 1935, although it did not cover all workers and provided quite modest benefits, was the basic legislation upon which the American social welfare system has been built. In addition to providing workers' pensions, it set up funds in each state to aid the unemployed, the disabled, the elderly poor, and unmarried women with dependent children.

THE SOCIAL SECURITY ACT, AUGUST 14, 1935

TITLE I—GRANTS TO STATES FOR OLD-AGE ASSISTANCE

APPROPRIATION

SECTION 1. For the purpose of enabling each State to furnish financial assistance, as far as practicable under the conditions in such State, to aged needy individuals, there is hereby authorized to be appropriated for the fiscal year ending June 30, 1936, the sum of $49,750,000, and there is hereby authorized to be appropriated for each fiscal year thereafter a sum sufficient to carry out the purposes of this title. The sums made available under this section shall be used for making payments to States which have submitted, and had approved by the Social Security Board established by Title VII, State plans for old-age assistance.

TITLE II—FEDERAL OLD-AGE BENEFITS

OLD-AGE BENEFIT PAYMENTS

SEC. 202. (a) Every qualified individual shall be entitled to receive, with respect to the period beginning on the date he attains the age of sixty-five, or on January 1, 1942, whichever is the later, and ending on the date of his death, an old-age benefit (payable as nearly as practicable in equal monthly installments) as follows:

(1) If the total wage determined by the Board to have been paid to him, with respect to employment after December 31, 1936, and before he attained the age of sixty-five, were not more than $3,000, the old-age benefit shall be at a monthly rate of one-half of 1 per centum of such wages;

(2) If such total wages were more than $3,000, the old-age benefit shall be at a monthly rate equal to the sum of the following:

(A) One-half of 1 per centum of $3,000; plus

(B) One-twelfth of 1 per centum of the amount by which such total wages exceeded $3,000 and did not exceed $45,000; plus

(C) One-twenty-fourth of 1 per centum of the amount by which such total wages exceeded $45,000.

(b) In no case shall the monthly rate computed under subsection (a) exceed $85. . . .

PAYMENTS UPON DEATH

SEC. 203. (a) If any individual dies before attaining the age of sixty-five, there shall be paid to his estate an amount equal to 3½ per centum of the total wages determined by the Board to have been paid to him, with respect to employment after December 31, 1936. . . .

PAYMENTS TO AGED INDIVIDUALS NOT QUALIFIED FOR BENEFITS

SEC. 204. (a) There shall be paid in a lump sum to any individual who, upon attaining the age of sixty-five, is not a qualified individual, an amount equal to 3½ per centum of the total wages determined by the Board to have been paid to him, with respect to employment after December 31, 1936, and before he attained the age of sixty-five. . . .

(b) The term "employment" means any service, of whatever nature, performed within the United States by an employee for his employer, except—

(1) Agricultural labor;

(2) Domestic service in a private home;

(3) Casual labor not in the course of the employer's trade or business;

(4) Service performed as an officer or member of the crew of a vessel documented under the laws of the United States or of any foreign country;

(5) Service performed in the employ of the United States Government or of an instrumentality of the United States;

(6) Service performed in the employ of a State, a political subdivision thereof, or an instrumentality of one or more States or political subdivisions;

(7) Service performed in the employ of a corporation, community chest, fund, or foundation, organized and operated exclusively for religious, charitable, scientific, literary, or educational purposes, or for the prevention of cruelty to children or animals, no part of the net earnings of which inures to the benefit of any private shareholder or individual. . . .

TITLE III—GRANTS TO STATES FOR
UNEMPLOYMENT COMPENSATION ADMINISTRATION

APPROPRIATION

SECTION 301. For the purpose of assisting the States in the administration of their unemployment compensation laws, there is hereby authorized to be appropriated, for the fiscal year ending June 30, 1936, the sum of $4,000,000, and for each fiscal year thereafter the sum of $49,000,000, to be used as hereinafter provided.

TITLE IV—GRANTS TO STATES FOR AID TO
DEPENDENT CHILDREN

APPROPRIATION

SECTION 401. For the purpose of enabling each State to furnish financial assistance, as far as practicable under the conditions in such State, to needy dependent children, there is hereby authorized to be appropriated for the fiscal year ending June 30, 1936, the sum of $24,750,000, and there is hereby authorized to be appropriated for each fiscal year thereafter a sum sufficient to carry out the purposes of this title. The sums made available under this section shall be used for making payments to States which have submitted, and had approved by the Board, State plans for aid to dependent children. . . .

TITLE V—GRANTS TO STATES FOR MATERNAL AND CHILD WELFARE

Part 1—Maternal and Child Health Services

APPROPRIATION

Section 501. For the purpose of enabling each State to extend and improve, as far as practicable under the conditions in such State, services for promoting the health of mothers and children, especially in rural areas and in areas suffering from severe economic distress, there is hereby authorized to be appropriated for each fiscal year, beginning with the fiscal year ending June 30, 1936, the sum of $3,800,000. The sums made available under this section shall be used for making payments to States which have submitted, and had approved by the Chief of the Children's Bureau, State plans for such services.

Part 2—Services for Crippled Children

APPROPRIATION

Sec. 511. For the purpose of enabling each State to extend and improve (especially in rural areas and in areas suffering from severe economic distress), as far as practicable under the conditions in such State, services for locating crippled children, and for providing medical, surgical, corrective, and other services and care, and facilities for diagnosis, hospitalization, and aftercare, for children who are crippled or who are suffering from conditions which lead to crippling, there is hereby authorized to be appropriated for each fiscal year, beginning with the fiscal year ending June 30, 1936, the sum of $2,850,000. The sums made available under this section shall be used for making payments to States which have submitted, and had approved by the Chief of the Children's Bureau, State plans for such services.

TITLE VI—PUBLIC HEALTH WORK

APPROPRIATION

Section 601. For the purpose of assisting States, counties, health districts, and other political subdivisions of the States in establishing and maintaining adequate public-health services, including the training of personnel for State and local health work, there is hereby authorized to be appropriated for each fiscal year, beginning with the fiscal year ending June 30, 1936, the sum of $8,000,000 to be used as hereinafter provided. . . .

TITLE VIII—TAXES WITH RESPECT TO EMPLOYMENT

INCOME TAX ON EMPLOYEES

SECTION 801. In addition to other taxes, there shall be levied, collected, and paid upon the income of every individual a tax equal to the following percentages of the wages (as defined in section 811) received by him after December 31, 1936, with respect to employment (as defined in section 811) after such date:

(1) With respect to employment during the calendar years 1937, 1938, and 1939, the rate shall be 1 per centum.

(2) With respect to employment during the calendar years 1940, 1941, and 1942, the rate shall be 1½ per centum.

(3) With respect to employment during the calendar years 1943, 1944, and 1945, the rate shall be 2 per centum.

(4) With respect to employment during the calendar years 1946, 1947, and 1948, the rate shall be 2½ per centum.

(5) With respect to employment after December 31, 1948, the rate shall be 3 per centum.

EXCISE TAX ON EMPLOYERS

SEC. 804. In addition to other taxes, every employer shall pay an excise tax, with respect to having individuals in his employ, equal to the following percentages of the wages (as defined in section 811) paid by him after December 31, 1936, with respect to employment (as defined in section 811) after such date:

(1) With respect to employment during the calendar years 1937, 1938, and 1939, the rate shall be 1 per centum.

(2) With respect to employment during the calendar years 1940, 1941, and 1942, the rate shall be 1½ per centum.

(3) With respect to employment during the calendar years 1943, 1944, and 1945, the rate shall be 2 per centum.

(4) With respect to employment during the calendar years 1946, 1947, and 1948, the rate shall be 2½ per centum.

(5) With respect to employment after December 31, 1948, the rate shall be 3 per centum. . . .

UNEMPLOYMENT TRUST FUND

SEC. 904. (a) There is hereby established in the Treasury of the United States a trust fund to be known as the "Unemployment Trust Fund" . . .

(b) It shall be the duty of the Secretary of the Treasury to invest such portion of the Fund as is not, in his judgment, required to meet current withdrawals. Such investment may be made only in interest bearing obligations of the United States or in obligations guaranteed as to both principle and interest by the United States. . . .

TITLE X—GRANTS TO STATES FOR AID TO THE BLIND

APPROPRIATION

SECTION 1001. For the purpose of enabling each State to furnish financial assistance, as far as practicable under the conditions in such State, to needy individuals who are blind, there is hereby authorized to be appropriated for the fiscal year ending June 30, 1936, the sum of $3,000,000, and there is hereby authorized to be appropriated for each fiscal year thereafter a sum sufficient to carry out the purposes of this title. The sums made available under this section shall be used for making payments to States which have submitted, and had approved by the Social Security Board, State plans for aid to the blind. . . .

Source: U.S., *Statutes at Large,* 49: 620.

SOCIAL SECURITY FACES THE TWENTY-FIRST CENTURY

Two important voices in the debate describe the problem and possible solutions. José Piñera, a Chilean fellow at the Cato Institute, has done a remarkable job of setting the terms of debate and has become the Johnny Appleseed of the Chilean system. President Bill Clinton has initiated a series of discussions about the future of Social Security, but he has not endorsed investing Social Security funds in the stock market.

JOSÉ PIÑERA, AN OPEN LETTER TO PRESIDENT CLINTON

Dear President Clinton:

In your state of the union address you called for an open debate on Social Security reform. I wish to respond to that call.

At Georgetown University recently, you publicly recognized that the U.S. Social Security system is going broke. You are right. Like the Titanic, it is heading toward disaster, while some keep insisting that there is no problem.

The truth is that the U.S. has only two options: to prolong the agony of the current system, or as you have said, "to experiment boldly." But so far only short-term solutions have been proposed. Some have suggested raising the payroll tax, but this would hurt job creation and increase the burden of a regressive tax on low-income workers. Others recommend increasing the retirement age, but that would especially burden blue-collar workers. These half-measures can only buy time. If the ship doesn't change course, sooner or later you're going to hit an iceberg—an aging population that cannot be supported by the workforce.

Another Way

There is another way. When I was labor and social security secretary of Chile in 1980, my country faced the same problem the U.S. now confronts. We decided to save our social security system by converting it from a pay-as-you-go model to individual retirement savings accounts. Workers now choose among competing private companies to invest the equivalent of what used to be their payroll taxes in a conservative portfolio of high rated bonds and equities. This allows workers to harness the powerful force of compound interest—reflecting the wealth-creating effect of the market—to ensure their security in retirement.

If empowering the common man—turning every worker into a shareholder—were the only benefit of such reform, that would be reason enough to convert to individual retirement accounts. But the Chilean example gives many more reasons. In the 17 years since Chile embarked on this course, complemented by other important market reforms, a flood of investment has benefited both individuals and the economy as a whole. As unemployment has fallen to its lowest in history, productivity has increased sharply, the savings rate has soared to around 25% of gross domestic product and economic growth has more than doubled to a 7% average during the last 13 years. If we keep up the present rhythm for another seven years, the size of the economy will have quadrupled in only 20 years.

This is a real economic and social revolution, allowing the country to improve education, health and the environment to a previously unthinkable level. This success has led seven other Latin American countries—Argentina, Bolivia, Colombia, El Salvador, Mexico, Peru and Uruguay—to emulate our example in the last five years, and several Central and Eastern European countries, including Russia, are actively considering similar reforms. . . .

Of course there are political challenges that inevitably lie in the path of any important reform—in particular, gaining public support and managing the transition. Let me share with you the lessons I learned from the Chilean experience.

- First and foremost, policy makers must emphasize the benefits to ordinary citizens. Transforming Social Security into an investment vehicle will boost the wealth of the U.S. economy, as many experts have calculated, but that won't capture the imagination of voters. The general public must understand that they will benefit from the ownership of wealth through the capital markets, giving them far more independence and freedom. This reform is about citizens' empowerment and not only about macroeconomic equilibrium.

- The public must understand that individual retirement accounts will help the poor. High-wage earners can always save for their own retirement. But medium- and lower-income workers don't have spare cash to save in separate individual retirement accounts; they suffer the most with negligible returns on their Social Security payments. They will gain the most from a system that allows them to invest their payroll taxes in real assets. Of course, there should still be a safety net provided from general tax revenues.

- Even though the reform is revolutionary, the execution must be conservative. Financial soundness and prudent regulations should be paramount in the design of the new system. Only when people understand that they will not lose their money will they appreciate the joys of, say, an average 6 percent real rate of return compounded over the course of their working lives.

- Make the reform optional. Give those who are already in the government system the option of staying in it or moving to the new system. Those who move should receive a recognition bond for their past contributions. In this way the new system is not compulsory.

- Make it absolutely clear that the elderly will not be harmed by the reform. On grounds of both fairness and prudence, I recommend guaranteeing the benefits of the elderly currently receiving Social Security and of those who decide to stay in the government system. That would be a move forward since those benefits are now subject to reduction by political whim.

- The country should be assured that the transition from the old system can be financed. True, the nation will have to foot the bill 'for current benefits while payroll tax revenues dwindle. But these expenses are "sunk costs"— they will have to be paid whether the system is reformed or not. When a worker moves out of the government system, payroll tax revenues will decline but so will future liabilities, because that worker will no longer be accumulating rights to further benefits. In the long run the burden on the system will be reduced. Budget surpluses present a historic opportunity to begin financing the transition.

- Take this message to the people. Political support will be forthcoming if people have good information. A Cato Institute web site already exists (www.socialsecurity.org) that allows one to calculate returns on the government program and comparable returns on equivalent savings invested in the market. Cynics can discount political calculations all they want— mathematical ones are more difficult to ignore.

In his recent testimony before the Senate Budget Committee, Federal Reserve Chairman Alan Greenspan stated that "the general broad principles, which are somewhat similar to the Chilean-type system, strike me as the way in which convergence of opinion is starting to move and a valuable first step in moving toward a solution." Policy makers must seize the day. The longer they wait, the more difficult change becomes. Every year the unfunded liability expands. Countries that phase out their tax-and-spend social systems and move toward investment-based schemes become more competitive, with a growing capital base, lower labor costs and, eventually, lower taxes.

Paradigm Shift
The global social security crisis is creating the opportunity for a fundamental paradigm shift regarding the role of government in modern societies. Thomas

Jefferson once predicted that "the ball of freedom, once set in motion, will roll around the world." Transforming Social Security in this way can be a massive blow against the economic drag of the welfare state that has characterized the 20th-century and stifled the creative spirit of mankind for too long. This would be true leadership and become your legacy for all time.

Source: http://www.cato.org/ (July 30, 1998).

REMARKS BY THE PRESIDENT ON SOCIAL SECURITY AT GEORGETOWN UNIVERSITY, FEBRUARY 9, 1998

THE PRESIDENT:
Social Security is a lot more than a line in the budget. It reflects some of our deepest values—the duties we owe to our parents, the duties we owe to each other when we're differently situated in life, the duties we owe to our children and our grandchildren. Indeed, it reflects our determination to move forward across the generations and across the income divides in our country, as one America.

Social Security has been there for America's parents in the 20th century, and I am determined that we will have that kind of security for the American people in the 21st century. . . .

In very specific terms, we've got a great opportunity because it is projected that we stay with the present budget plan, that taking account of the fact that we won't always have the greatest economic times as we've had now—there will be times when the economy will grow faster, times when it will grow slower, we may [have] recessions—but structurally, we have eliminated the deficit, so that over time we should have a balanced budget, and over time, most times we should be running a surplus now if we stay with the discipline we have now over the next couple of decades.

Now, if that's so, it is now estimated that with normal ups and downs in economic growth, over the next 10 years, after 30 years of deficits, that the United States will have a budge surplus in somewhere in the range of a trillion dollars in the aggregate over the next 10 years. I have said before we spend a penny of that on new programs or tax cuts, we should save Social Security first. I think it should be the driving principle of this year's work in the United States Congress—do not have a tax cut, do not have a spending program that deals with that surplus—save Social Security first.

That is our obligation to you and, frankly, to ourselves. And let me explain that. This fiscal crisis in Social Security affects every generation. We now know that the Social Security trust fund is fine for another few decades. But if it gets in trouble and we don't deal with it, then it not only affects the generation of the baby boomers and whether they'll have enough to live on when they retire, it raises the question of whether they will have enough to live on by unfairly burdening their children and, therefore, unfairly burdening their children's ability to raise their grandchildren. That would be unconscionable, especially since, if you move now, we can do less and have a bigger impact, especially since we now have the budget surplus.

Now, it's also known, however, that the changes that are underway today will place great stresses on the Social Security safety net. The baby boomers are getting grey. When my generation retires—and I'm the oldest of the baby boomers; I was born in 1946, I'm 51—and the generation is normally held to run for the 18 years after that, that's normally what people mean when they talk about the baby boomers—it will dramatically change the ratio of workers to earners, aggravated by increasing early retirements and other things, offset by gradual increase in the Social Security retirement age enacted back in 1983.

In 1960, there were 5.1 Americans working for every one person drawing Social Security. In 1997, there's still 3.3 people working for every one person drawing Social Security. In 2030, the year after the Social Security trust fund supposedly will go broke unless we change something, at present projected retirement rates—that is, the presently projected retirement age and same rates—there will be two people working for every one person drawing Social Security.

So what's the bottom line? You can see it. Today, we're actually taking in a lot more money from Social Security taxes enacted in 1983 than we're spending out. Because we've run deficits, none of that money has been saved for Social Security. Now, if you look at this little chart here, from 1999 forward we'll be able to save that money—or a lot of it, anyway. We'll be able to save a lot of it that will go into pure surplus in the budget. It can be invested. But other things will have to be done as well. That will not be enough.

And if nothing is done by 2029, there will be a deficit in the Social Security trust fund, which will either require—if you just wait until then—a huge increase in the payroll tax, or . . . a 25 percent cut in Social Security benefits. . . .

Now, again I say, if we act soon, less is more. If we can develop a consensus as a country to act soon we can take relatively modest steps in any number of directions to run this 2029 number well out into the future in ways that will keep Social Security's role in providing some retirement security to people without unfairly burdening your generation and your ability to raise your children to do that. And I can tell you, I have had countless talks with baby boomers of all income groups and I haven't found a single person in my generation who is not absolutely determined to fix this in a way that does not unfairly burden your generation. But we have to start now. . . .

I have asked the America Association of Retired Persons, the AARP, a leading voice for older Americans, and the Concord Coalition, a leading voice for fiscal discipline, to organize a series of four nonpartisan regional forums this year. The Vice President and I will participate. I hope the Republican and Democratic leadership will also participate. I was encouraged that Speaker Gingrich said the other day that he felt we should save the surplus until we had fixed the Social Security first.

The first forum, which will set out before the American people the full nature of the problem—essentially, what I'm doing with you today with a few more details—will be in Kansas City on April 7th. Then in subsequent ones we will hear from a variety of experts and average citizens across all ages. It is very important to me that this debate involve young people—very important, because you have a huge stake in it and you need to imagine where you will be and what kind of investment patterns you think are fair for you and how you think this is going to play out over the next 20, 30, 40 years. We want people of all ages involved in this. . . .

Acting today for the future is in some ways the oldest of American traditions. It's what Thomas Jefferson did when he purchased the Louisiana Territory and sent Lewis and Clark on their famous expedition. It's what Abraham Lincoln did when at the height of the Civil War, he and the Congress took the time to establish a system of land grant colleges, which revolutionized the future of America. It's what we Americans did when, in the depths of the Depression, when people were only concerned about the moment, and 25 percent of the American people were out of work, our Congress and our President still took the time to establish a Social Security system that could only take flower and have full impact long after they were gone.

Source: http://www.whitehouse.gov (July 30, 1998).

OPINIONS AND PROPOSALS

Many have joined this debate on an issue that will affect nearly everyone's life. Organized labor generally opposes privatization, as do liberal publications such as The Nation *and* Left Business Observer. *Many groups are working on reforms of the system to maintain its solvency: Senator Daniel Patrick Moynihan summarizes some of these plans. And some business publications such as* Fortune *have floated proposals simply to abolish Social Security and depend on private pensions. Eventually, perhaps soon, you will have to advise your representatives in Congress on how to reform the Social Security system.*

THE AMERICAN FEDERATION OF LABOR ON PRIVATIZATION OF SOCIAL SECURITY, AUGUST 23, 1996

Politicians bent on privatizing government services have turned their attention to Social Security, but workers and their unions will have none of it.

Calling Social Security "perhaps the federal government's most successful social policy achievement," the AFL-CIO Executive Council vowed to fight efforts to abandon the program for individual savings accounts.

The 61-year-old program currently provides some 43 million Americans with an average yearly benefit of $7,7000 under the old-age, survivors and disability social insurance programs that make up Social Security . . . with enough left over for a Trust Fund reserve of nearly $500 billion.

Periodic adjustments have been required to keep up the benefits funding . . . and Social Security currently is able to meet its obligations well into the next century. But rumblings over its longer-term viability have opened the door to the threat of privatization.

Several measures pending in Congress, including one by Sens. Alan Simpson (R-Wyo.) and Bob Kerrey (D-Neb.), would replace Social Security with individual, private savings accounts that would rely in some fashion on the stock market to generate retirement income.

"The AFL-CIO rejects all attempts to dismantle the Social Security system and to exaggerate the extent of its long-term financing problems," the council declared at its summer meeting in Chicago, assailing "the disinformation campaign currently being waged by Wall Street interests" seeking a share of privately run accounts functioning in place of Social Security.

The federation called on all unions to join with allied groups "in a coordinated campaign to educate Americans on the true value of Social Security and to discredit the false notion that private retirement accounts could match Social Security benefits."

The AFL-CIO pointed out that the Social Security system's benefit structure returns a higher share of low-paid workers' earnings in the form of benefits, but also pays higher benefits to higher contributors.

Social Security's costs "are less than 0.7 percent of annual benefits," the federation noted, "compared with administrative costs at private insurance companies that are, on average, 40 percent higher."

Unions were urged to include regular communication on Social Security in their publications, use educational material being developed by allied organizations and to encourage local leaders and activists to speak out publicly.

With $500 billion in the trust fund, Social Security is not in danger yet. In developing a prudent response to the trust fund's long-term financing needs, "the AFL-CIO will work to ensure that all Americans will be able to continue to rely upon Social Security."

Source: Colleen M. O'Neill, "Privatization Patter Roils Social Security Pot," *AFL-CIO News*, August 23, 1996.

SOCIAL (IN)SECURITY — *THE NATION,* EDITORIAL, JUNE 1, 1998

What precisely about the current Social Security "reform" debate makes it so hateful and repellent? Why—to quote Brookings economist Henry Aaron, normally a temperate establishment figure—are we headed toward "the My Lai of American social policy" if "partial privatization" reforms go through? . . .

Social Security isn't broke—and doesn't need the fixes Washington will propose.

A government advisory commission last year produced "exact" dates and dollars that gave apparent concreteness to the dimensions of the Social Security "crisis." Starting in 2029, it calculated, Social Security wont' have enough income to cover more than 75 percent of the benefits it must pay to aging baby boomers. But the specificity is illusory, all lever-pulling and smoke-blowing from the Wizard of Oz. The projections aren't economic (no even semi-sane economist does decades-long projections) but actuarial extrapolations based on assumptions that Social Security's own actuaries know are fictitious at best. Tweak them ever so slightly—lift real wages by a quarter- or half-percent per annum, or immigration by a little—and the same actuarial "crisis" disappears entirely. Federal law has mandated these projections for years, but—as the actuaries know well—they're redone every time they're revisited because the methodology is so poor. Until recently, apart from a handful of Washington technicians, nobody paid attention to them—knowing what they were worth. (Just a few weeks ago, we got an example of the slipperiness of these projections: Last year's economic growth moved Social Security's projected crisis date three years, to 2032.) . . .

But—just for a moment—let's pretend there is a crisis. What should we do?

Fairness, you might think, is the place to start. Most Americans pay more into Social Security than they pay in income tax. Yet polls show most Americans don't even know that contributions to Social Security are "capped" at $68,400 in individual's wages. By excluding wages above that line—those earned by the top 6 percent of U.S. households—and by excluding all nonwage income (dividends, interest, capital gains, rents, etc.) from Social Security taxation, guess what the effect is? It's enormously regressive.

Senators and representatives, who each make $136,673 a year, effectively pay at just half the rate of those earning below $68,400 yet receive the same maximum benefits as a middle-class worker at retirement—plus, of course, a hefty Congressional retirement package. Bill Gates likewise will get the same maximum benefits, but pays FICA only on his first ten minutes of income each year. Gates, of course, has $40 billion to tide him over; but 60 percent of U.S. workers retire without a private pension, and 66 percent of retirees count on Social Security for more than half their income.

At his first town meeting on Social Security in Kansas City, President Clinton—neatly forgetting that Medicare has no similar cap—took "lifting the cap" off the table. It must be put back on, at the center of the table. Social Security officials forthrightly admit that raising the cap alone would remove two-thirds of their projected actuarial crisis—something that somehow largely escaped the President's, and the press's, attention.

But what about putting some of Social Security's money into the stock market—doesn't everyone agree that over the long term markets outperform Social Security returns?

This is tricky but must be understood: First, there's an "apples and oranges" problem—Social Security provides disability benefits, survivor benefits and other features apart from just retirement income; factor these in, and the performance "advantage" of equity markets gets razor-thin at best. Second, Social Security benefits are already moderately progressive, meaning that the bottom 60 percent of retirees get more back than the affluent relative to their contributions.

Third, markets are subject to gravity—what goes up, comes down, in both long and short waves. Since the Little Crash of October 1987, U.S. markets have been on a nonstop charge; but if you'd gone into the same markets in 1970, you were worse off by 1980—not to mention where you'd be today if you'd bet on Japan in the mid-eighties or Southeast Asia's "sure thing" markets a couple of years ago. Forget hyper-collapse 1929-style for a moment; think instead about retiring to find that your income's eroding each year as you grow older. Will you do all right in the long term, as brokers and economists insist? Well, probably yes—but that gives a new and nasty twist to Keynes's caustic observation that "in the long run, we're all dead."

Fourth, market averages aren't the same as individual returns. Turn 120 million workers loose to bet the market (40 million of whom are marginally literate or numerate), and guess how many will beat the averages? The mutual fund industry's dirty little secret is that three-fourths of funds under-perform market indexes. Yet such funds have millions of naïve investors in them; in one recent survey, a majority of mutual fund investors couldn't even distinguish between a "load" and a "no-load" fund. . . .

There is a fifth issue, which connects Social Security privatization to what has so far been undiscussed in the debate. Right now, Americans are delighted that, for the first time in nearly thirty years, the federal budget's in balance. But it's in balance because each year the Treasury borrows $80 billion from the Social Security Trust Fund surplus, and "covers" the deficit in the rest of the federal budget. If a big piece of Social Security contributions go into private accounts, the trust fund surplus will disappear and the federal budget will plunge back into deficit—launching gleeful Republicans on another round of "cut, cut, cut." And which federal programs are likeliest to be cut by a Republican Congress? You fill in the blanks.

What we could—and should—be doing.

First, we should strengthen the existing Social Security system. Single and divorced women fare poorly under the existing system: As a group, they're twice as likely to be poor as the senior population as a whole. That should be fixed forthwith.

Second, we should help Americans acquire real wealth—but not at the expense of Social Security. Social Security is only one leg of the three-legged retirement stool. The other two legs are private pensions and personal savings.

Only 40 percent of workers today get private pensions (and, increasingly, those are risky defined-contribution, not defined-benefit, plans). With corporations earning record profits, now's the time to expand corporate responsibility for helping workers create real personal wealth. Mandate that all employees share in those profit-payouts to senior executives; vest workers early; make plans fully portable; let workers draw from them for a first-time home purchase, lifelong learning and major medical expenses.

On increasing personal savings, the issue grows politically more difficult— yet it is the core political and economic challenge of our time. The richest 1 percent of Americans have more wealth than the bottom 80 percent. The solution is simple: Most Americans should be earning more, and the richest should be paying more taxes. Period. The politics of getting there are hellish. . . .

Social Security is the difference between a decent life and poverty for half of all Americans over 65. More than 90 percent of us pay into it during our working lives, and more than 90 percent of us will count on its benefits when we retire.

Now count the cost of Washington economic "reforms" over the past twenty years—to a once-viable savings-and-loan system, to Mexican workers and peasants (who've paid for bailouts not once but twice), to the world's poor as they've worked off the global debt crisis. Think about the lives of Indonesian peasants, or Korean and Thai workers today—all set to pay for the "can't miss" marketization of Southeast Asia, just as Americans have so wonderfully benefited from downsizing, capital-gains reduction and globalization.

Now it's Social Security's turn to face the capital's ever-brilliant and ever-farsighted policy "reformers"—because a system that works doesn't meet the ideological test of a fully marketized humanity. Today Social Security, alone, barely guarantees an old age lived in dignity and some measure of peace for those who've worked their entire adult lives. Lose it to full or partial privatization, and we'll lose much more than our dignity.

Source: The Nation, June 1, 1998.

DOUG HENWOOD, THE MYTH OF SOCIAL SECURITY'S IMMINENT COLLAPSE

July/August 1995
Left Business Observer

By Doug Henwood

Thirty years ago, when Barry Goldwater proposed making Social Security voluntary, he was dismissed as a lunatic. Now, however, the radical transformation of Social Security—essentially its privatization—is the consensus among the political class and the pundits who serve them.

The strategy of the privatizers is proving quite successful. Sow doubts about the future solvency of the system. Chip away its near-universal political support by taxing benefits of "affluent" retirees, periodically lowering the definition of affluence. Encourage the "affluent" retirees of the future to provide for themselves, because of the system's wobbliness. And eventually turn the public pension system into welfare for the elderly poor—an easy target for cuts—while leaving the middle class and rich to fend for themselves. This isn't only happening in the U.S.; it's happening around the globe.

This might be dismissed as conspiracy theorizing—if you haven't been reading publications of international organizations like the World Bank, IMF and the Organization for Economic Cooperation and Development. (See, for example, the OECD's 1988 report, Reforming Public Pensions, which is full of advice on incremental reforms to "what was only a couple of decades ago considered as a central achievement of the welfare state [but which] is now being evaluated differently.") There, they've been quite explicit about what they're up to, because they're writing for an elite audience. But when journalists write for the masses, they have to be more careful.

Take, for example, a Time magazine cover story from March 20, 1995, headlined "The Case for Killing Social Security." The article opened by citing the cretinous Sen. Alan Simpson (R.-Wyoming), who "confronted" the Social Security Commissioner with "a poll showing that more people under the age of 35 believe in UFOs than in the prospect that Social Security will pay them benefits upon retirements." The article went on to recite the usual statistics about the system's imminent bankruptcy, as the boomers and then the Xers enter their golden years. The article concluded with a menu of options—privatize the whole system, cut benefits, or means-test them. A sidebar touted the virtues of Chile's system, the privatizers' favorite model, which was inaugerated by military dictator Augusto Pinochet.

Almost no one bothers to investigate the claim of Social Security's coming insolvency, which is based on projections in the annual report of the system's trustees. I did (Left Business Observer, 12/22/95), and discovered that the projections assume the economy will grow an average of 1.5 percent a year (after inflation) for the next 75 years—half the rate of the previous 75, and matched in only one decade this century, from 1910–20. Even the 1930s, the decade of the Great Depression, saw a faster growth rate.

What would happen if the economy grew at a peppier 2.2 percent rate? The trustees provide alternative projections based on that as well, and, gosh, the system remains solvent indefinitely. At 2.5 percent—still slower than the 75-year average—it runs a surplus. About the only other journalist to question the dire predictions for Social Security's future was Robert Kuttner, in his Business Week column (2/20/95). . . .

The Bank's report, Averting the Old Age Crisis, recommended a three-pillared system: (1) a mandatory system, financed out of taxes, to provide a minimal base pension; (2) a mandatory savings scheme, in which every worker is required to contribute a portion of his or her earnings to a kind of IRA, to be invested in the financial markets; and (3) a supplementary system of private savings, also to be invested in the financial markets. This is essentially the Chilean model that Time—and Wall Street, hungry for the boodle—adores so much.

What's wrong with this? First, the present system is mildly redistributive, with the rich slightly subsidizing the poor in retirement. A private system would end that transfer. And second, a private system would be no better equipped to handle the bulge of boomer retirees beginning around 2010 than the present system. Right now Social Security is financed by a wage base that grows roughly in line with the overall economy; why should the stock market do significantly better?

Most people think that money invested in the stock market finds its way into real investment in buildings and machines. In fact, almost none of it does; most firms finance real investment through their own profits. (Between 1901 and 1994, U.S. non-financial corporations financed less than 5 percent of their capital expenditures through the stock market.) The stock market is mainly an arena for the buying and selling of pre-existing shares and, through takeovers and spinoffs, of entire corporations. Investing in the stock market will no more create the wealth necessary to take care of elderly Boomers than Social Security taxes do.

In Chile, according to Joseph Collins and John Lear's excellent new book, Chile's Free-Market Miracle (Food First Books), the public system's minimum benefit was $1.25 a day in 1988. Less than a quarter of all workers make enough money to qualify them for more than this risible minimum public benefit. Tellingly, the army and national police kept their own generous public systems; while the new plan may have been good enough for the masses, it wasn't good enough for the forces in charge. Of course, Time was silent on all this. . . .

As for the stock market proposal, Abelson [Alan Abelson, columnist for *Barron's*, a financial magazine], who's been covering Wall Street for decades, commented: "If Congress and the President put aside their partisan differences—and any residual vestiges of prudence—and swiftly turn [the proposal] into law, there may be time enough for the Trust Fund to load up on stocks before the next secular bear market. In terms of expediting, the pauperization of geezers and completing the marvelous scheme to shrink benefits and save Social Security, the sheer brilliance of the concept cannot be gainsaid. (Did we neglect to mention that the saviors are all covered by retirement plans that are separate from Social Security?)" Shades of the Chilean police.

Source: Doug Henwood, "The Myth of Social Security's Imminent Collapse," *Left Business Observer,* July/August 1995.

SENATOR DANIEL PATRICK MOYNIHAN (DEMOCRAT-NY), "HOW TO PRESERVE THE SAFETY NET," APRIL 20, 1998

For some 20 years now, opinion polls have shown that a majority of non-retired adults do not believe they will get their Social Security when they retire. Partly this is a result of neglect by a Social Security Administration that has made little effort to stay in touch with Americans before retirement.

But there is also a more powerful influence at work: a serious ideological movement opposed to government social insurance as a threat to individual initiative and, indeed, liberty. There is now abroad a powerful set of distinguished academics and political activists who would turn the 60-year-old system of Social Security retirement, disability, and survivor's benefits over to a system that depends solely on personal savings invested in the market.

There are those who hold the belief—doctrinal in many ways—that the experience of stock market investors in a time of great economic growth can easily be applied to an entire population. Some adherents to this philosophy believe Social Security is a failed plan that perhaps should never have been put in place and should not be "transitioned" out, as the new term has it. They promise instead to make you a millionaire in the stock market.

I don't think that will happen.

That is not to say it should not, or could not, happen. Certainly we ought not preclude the possibility that it might. Which is why the legislation I introduced last month with Sen. Bob Kerrey of Nebraska includes optional personal retirement accounts into which can be deposited up to 2 percent of wages. We can thus respond to the argument of the privatizers without compromising the basic structure of the Social Security program.

The time to act is now, because we have a balanced federal budget for the first time in almost 30 years and because Social Security's problems become more difficult the longer we delay. If we continue to treat this program as the untouchable "third rail" of American politics, we could find one day in the not very distant future that the system has vanished. (The danger is real. Recall that those who for so many years prevented any change in the welfare system looked up one day to find that Title IV-A of the Social Security Act, Aid to Families with Dependent Children, had been repealed. Do not doubt that Social Security itself could be next.)

Under our bill, private accounts would complement Social Security, not replace it. Markets go up, but they also, frequently, go down. We believe the best approach to retirement savings in the 21st century is a three-tier system of the Social Security annuity, a private pension—which about half of Americans enjoy—and private savings.

The plan would return Social Security to a pay-as-you-go system. This makes possible an immediate payroll-tax cut of approximately $800 billion over the next 10 years, as payroll-tax rates would be cut from 12.4 to 10.4 percent. The bill would permit voluntary personal savings accounts, which workers could finance with the proceeds of this cut in the payroll tax.

The legislation includes a 1-percentage-point correction in cost-of-living adjustments for all indexed programs except Supplemental Security Income. We would also increase the retirement age to 68 by 2023 and to age 70 by 2073.

Finally, Social Security benefits would be taxed to the same extent private pensions are taxed. And Social Security coverage would be extended to newly hired employees in currently excluded state and local positions.

This package of changes ensures the long-run solvency of Social Security while reducing payroll taxes by almost $800 billion over the next decade and adding to the federal budget surplus. Beginning in 2025, payroll-tax rates would increase gradually to cover growing outlays and would rise only slightly above the current level in the year 2045.

Can this be done? It ought to be, but it won't be easy. It is time, then, for courage as well as policy analysis. Social Security, one of the great achievements of our government in this century, is ours to maintain. We can preserve it, and citizens ought not get to thinking otherwise.

Source: Daniel Patrick Moynihan, "How to Preserve the Safety Net," *U.S. News and World Report,* April 20, 1998.

DAVID R. HENDERSON,
"FIX SOCIAL SECURITY? WHY NOT ABOLISH IT?"

The movement to privatize the Social Security system has gained force in recent years, thanks to Steve Forbes (whose platform in the 1996 Republican primary proposed letting people opt out of Social Security so they could invest for their own retirement) and to President Clinton's advisory council on Social Security, which included a detailed plan for privatization as one of three proposals it made in January.

Conservatives and libertarians are this movement's strongest backers—which is ironic, because the effect of privatization would likely be huge tax increases that would expand government. Under privatization, those currently paying Social Security taxes would be allowed to save part of the taxes in their own personal retirement accounts. This would be popular, since many people, especially those in their 30s, are convinced that they can do better by investing themselves.

But here's the problem: Social Security is a pay-as-you-go system: Almost all of the taxes people pay in this year will be paid out to recipients this year. So if current working people are allowed to invest what otherwise would have been payroll taxes, there will be a shortfall of hundreds of billions of dollars a year for many years. Where is this money to come from?

Some privatization advocates, like Forbes, duck the question. But others, especially economists, have detailed how the transition would be handled, and in all these proposals taxes would increase dramatically. Take, for example, Boston University economist Laurence J. Kotlikoff's plan. Kotlikoff would end the portion of the current payroll tax that is used to fund old-age benefits. But he would force people to save this money in a personal retirement account invested only in government-approved assets that can be drawn on only in retirement. To finance the transition, Kotlikoff would impose a national sales tax at the rate of 10%, falling to about 2%, claims Kotlikoff—within 40 years. The proposal of the pro-privatization members of the President's commission hikes payroll taxes by 1.5 percentage points for 70 years and requires $1.2 trillion in new federal borrowing.

Privatization advocates worry that if nothing is done now, taxes will have to rise even more in the future. To maintain promised benefits the Social Security tax rate would have to rise over the next 50 years from its current level of 12.4% to as high as 23%, according to government actuarial estimates. But who really believes that the government could get away with a 23% tax rate for just one program?

The best way out of all these problems would be to do the politically impossible: abolish Social Security. The government, after all, is not our parent and shouldn't make our decisions for us. To end the program, Congress could decree that people under age 30 will never be able to collect benefits and at the same time cut their payroll taxes accordingly.

The next-best solution—and the one that would-be privatizers should support—is to draw a line in the sand and say, "No more tax increases." Then those who want to preserve the current system would be forced to compromise. The current schedule that would raise the age for receiving full Social Security benefits to 67 in 2027 could be accelerated—to 70 by 2015. Social Security benefits could be indexed to a realistic inflation index. And the formula that sets future benefits could be changed to keep real benefits constant rather than increasing them, as it does now. These changes alone would probably eliminate the funding crisis that is otherwise likely to begin around the year 2012.

We would still be left with a government-run shell game that gives us a lousy rate of return and imposes drastic penalties on those who work beyond age 65 or save too much. But at least we wouldn't be saddling future generations with tax rates guaranteed to produce lower economic growth and—ultimately—a lower standard of living.

Source: David R. Henderson, "Fix Social Security? Why Not Abolish It?" *Fortune Magazine*, September 8, 1997.